R|A 428 24 DUB

KU-019-360

Introduction

What is *Market Leader* and who is it for?

Market Leader is a multi-level business English course for business people and students of Business English. It has been developed in association with the *Financial Times*, one of the leading sources of business information in the world. It consists of 12 units based on topics of great interest to everyone involved in or studying international business.

This new Advanced level of *Market Leader* features authentic texts and listenings throughout, reflecting the latest trends in the business world. If you are in business, the course will greatly improve your ability to communicate in English in a wide range of business situations. If you are a student of business, the course will develop the communication skills you need to succeed in a professional environment and will broaden your knowledge of the business world. Everybody studying this course will become more fluent and confident in using the language of business in a variety of contexts and should further his or her career prospects.

The authors

Margaret O'Keeffe (*left*) has over 15 years' teaching experience and now teaches English in companies. She has taught at both the Pompeu Fabra University and La Salle University in Barcelona, Spain. She is the author of business English materials for the Universitat Oberta de Catalunya in Spain and is also an online tutor with the university. Her background is in the business world, working for both British Airways and British Telecom before becoming an English language teacher and CELTA teacher trainer.

Iwonna Dubicka (*right*) has over 15 years' experience as a Business English trainer, including teacher training and six years as Director of Studies of English at In Company Languages in Barcelona. She has also been an online tutor for the Universitat Oberta de Catalunya, Catalonia's open university. She is also the co-author of various English titles together with Margaret O'Keeffe, including *English For International Tourism* (Pre-Intermediate) published by Longman.

Iwonna Dubicka   Margaret O'Keeffe

PEARSON
Longman

www.longman.com

FINANCIAL
TIMES

Map of the book

What is in the units?

Listening and discussion

You are offered a variety of discussion questions as an introduction to the theme of each unit. You will hear authentic interviews with business people. You will develop listening skills, such as listening for key information, note-taking and summary writing. In this section, you will also extend your vocabulary by learning useful new words and phrases. A good business dictionary such as the *Longman Business English Dictionary* or a monolingual dictionary for advanced learners such as the *Longman Dictionary of Contemporary English* will also help you to increase your business vocabulary.

Reading and language

You will read authentic articles on a variety of contemporary topics from the *Financial Times* and other newspapers and books on business management. You will develop your reading skills. You will also be able to discuss and respond to the issues in the articles. There is a language review after each article and related exercises in the Grammar reference section for each unit. You will be able to revise language and structures which are common problem areas for advanced learners. You will become more accurate in your use of English at an advanced level.

Business skills

You will develop essential business communication skills, such as giving presentations, dealing with questions, taking an active part in meetings, negotiating, strategies for telephoning and teleconferences, English for networking, as well as using the language for a variety of business writing tasks. Each Business skills section contains a Useful language box which provides you with the language you need to carry out the realistic tasks in the Course Book.

Case study

The *Market Leader* case studies are linked to the business topics of each unit. They are based on business problems or situations and allow you to use the language and communication skills you have developed while working through each unit. They give you the opportunities to practise your speaking, listening, reading and writing skills in realistic contexts. Each case study ends with a follow-up writing task. A full writing syllabus is provided in the *Market Leader* Practice File.

Review units

The *Market Leader* Advanced Course Book also contains four review units which recycle and revise material covered in the preceding three Course Book units. Each review unit is designed so that it can be completed in two sessions or on a unit-by-unit basis.

www.market-leader.net

LONGMAN ON THE WEB

Longman.com offers classroom activities, teaching tips and online resources for teachers of all levels and students of all ages. Visit us for course-specific Companion Websites, our online catalogue of all Longman titles, and access to all local Longman websites, offices and contacts around the world.
*Join a global community of teachers and students at **Longman.com**.*

UNIT 1

Being international

> *Without knowing the force of words, it is impossible to know men.*
>
> Confucius, Chinese philosopher (c. 551–478 BC)

OVERVIEW ▼

- [ ] **Listening and discussion**
  Public speaking
- [ ] **Reading and language**
  International presentations
- [ ] **Business skills**
  Networking
  Writing: replying to a formal invitation
- [ ] **Case study**
  Working for Logistaid

Listening and discussion

A **Discuss these questions.**

1 Do you ever have to speak to an audience? How does/would it make you feel?

2 Have you ever heard a speaker who you felt was inspirational? What techniques did he/she use to engage the audience?

3 What, for you, makes a good presentation?

4 What might be some of the issues to bear in mind when giving a presentation to an international audience?

B 🎧 **1.1 Three business people talk about their experiences of giving presentations to international audiences. Listen and choose the best summary of each speaker's main point.**

a) Always organise the room so that the important guests are at the front.

b) Don't make assumptions based on the audience's reactions.

c) Be careful with the language you use when giving a presentation.

d) Be aware of and try to be sensitive to local customs.

e) Using jokes and humour is a good way to get the audience on your side.

f) Question-and-answer sessions are universally popular.

C 🎧 **1.1 Listen to each speaker again, take notes and answer these questions.**

1 What did Michael realise when he was talking to a group of executives in Geneva?

2 How does he describe his speaking style, and why does he want to change it?

3 What does he plan to do as part of his preparation for his next presentation?

4 What did Arianne find out when she was due to speak in Thailand?

5 How does she usually organise a room when she's giving a talk?

6 What did she do on this occasion?

7 In Japan, how might people in an audience show they are listening?

8 How might an audience show their approval in Germany and Austria?

D Complete these tips for giving presentations to international audiences using the words and expressions in the box. There is one item you don't need.

delivery	gestures	greet	handout	pace
	rephrase	row	script	visual aids

Be careful when you choose the colours for your .... ¹. For instance, yellow has negative connotations in many countries, including Mexico, Peru and Iran.

Using a .... ² can help with international audiences. It can keep you focused on precise language. It can also be used as a .... ³ for your listeners after you speak.

Adjust the .... ⁴ of your .... ⁵ to reflect what the audience is used to. North Americans prefer faster speech, whereas Europeans and Asians typically prefer more time to process information.

Take care, especially where language barriers may exist, to fully understand questions from your audience. Don't hesitate to .... ⁶ them to check your understanding.

Be sensitive to how different audiences react to .... ⁷. In some Asian cultures, for example, audiences find fast, sweeping arm movements distracting.

If you're going to .... ⁸ your listeners in their language, make sure you know how to speak it. And be sure your choice of language has your intended meaning.

E Discuss these questions.

1 How would you ideally set up a room for a small meeting / a seminar / a conference?

2 Which colours have positive and negative connotations for you?

3 Apart from speaking, how else can audiences show their reaction to a presentation?

4 What advice would you give an overseas speaker about to give a presentation in your country? Think about some of the following:

- seating arrangements
- length of speech
- body gestures
- audience reactions
- visual aids
- use of humour and personal anecdotes
- taboo subjects
- question-and-answer sessions.

Reading and language

slang expression or word used in informal conversation

jargon words and expressions used by a particular profession or group of people, and which are difficult for other people to understand

buzzword a word or phrase that suddenly everyone thinks is very important and uses all the time

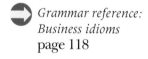

➡ *Grammar reference: Business idioms* page 118

A Look at the dictionary entries and say whether the examples indicated in *italics* in the text below are a) slang or b) buzzwords/jargon.

1 *Hey guys!* Anyone *fancy* a coffee?

2 This *cutting-edge* technology will *radically transform* the way we work.

3 Just 25 per cent of the company's *turnover* comes from the *home market*.

4 Could you *pop into* my office, I'd like to *bounce* some ideas *off* you?

5 The *cracker* somehow *hacked into* the bank's computer system during *downtime* by using a *backdoor*.

6 We aim to *empower* the customer to make informed choices.

B Read the magazine article about giving international presentations and answer these questions.

1 Why does the writer use the quote at the start of his article?

2 How could the speaker say this differently so that people could understand him?

3 What does *delivery* refer to in the second paragraph?

4 Find two examples where the writer helped other people with their presentations.

5 Where can you get help when preparing your talk?

6 What should you do when members of the audience ask you questions?

7 What examples of 'non-verbal messages' (paragraph 11) can you think of?

C Read the article again and find business idioms and expressions that mean the following.

1 it is potentially problematic and dangerous (paragraph 2)

2 an unsafe strategy (paragraph 3)

3 make possible or happen (paragraph 3)

4 most complete (paragraph 4)

5 not do things correctly (paragraph 4)

6 make as much use as possible of (paragraph 5)

7 explaining too much (paragraph 9)

8 don't understand (paragraph 11)

D Using the word given, complete the second sentence so that it has a similar meaning to the first. Use a maximum of five words.

1 His speeches have inspired thousands of people. (*proved*)
His speeches *..have proved an inspiration..* to thousands.

2 Can you explain this to us simply? (*give*)
Can you .... of this?

3 They've arranged the annual conference. (*made*)
They have .... the annual conference.

4 He has summarised his presentation in this handout. (*provided*)
He's .... his presentation in this handout.

5 You could hire an intercultural communication specialist to help you prepare your talk. (*someone*)
You could hire .... intercultural communication to help you prepare your talk.

6 We have to conclude the seminar now. (*bring*)
It's time .... a conclusion.

7 An international audience's non-verbal messages can be misinterpreted. (*open*)
An international audience's non-verbal messages can be ....

8 You can't assume anything with an international audience. (*any*)
You can't .... with an international audience.

INTERNATIONAL PRESENTATIONS

HOW NOT TO SOUND LIKE A FOOL

Author and coach Tom Leech describes how careful crafting of your message and style to appeal to international audiences can serve as a passport to success.

1 "We really appreciate the chance to talk to you folks from Japan. We have some new ideas we want to bounce off you that we think will really blow your minds."

2 Given today's high degree of business and governmental linkages, presenters often find themselves speaking to audiences from countries other than their own. Language and cultural differences make this a vastly different presentation situation from what speakers may be used to. The stakes can be high and the pitfalls many, so wise presenters will consider these differences in preparation and delivery.

3 When presenting internationally, the fundamental requirement is to recognize that business as usual is risky business. "They" are not the same as "we." We speak different languages, even if we both speak English. In addition to alternative meanings for the same words, we also act differently and view things from different perspectives. These issues set the stage for communication difficulties and potential misunderstandings.

4 The concept of presentations differs among cultures. In the United States, full-blown graphic presentations are a standard part of business. This style of presentation may not apply in countries where business proceeds in a less structured, slower manner and often on a one-to-one basis rather than in groups. Without knowing your audience, you can easily head down the wrong track.

Plan, Plan, Plan

5 The importance of careful planning cannot be overemphasized. Learn all you can about your listeners and how they do business. Use experts, such as the Department of Commerce and embassies that know the specific country well. Tap into advice from other local business people with relevant experience. Review the dos and don'ts guidance available in many publications. Organizations specializing in international meetings or managers of international hotel chains can provide valuable consulting and handle arrangements in other countries.

Pre-meeting Tune-Ups

6 Rehearse your presentation, preferably with listeners who are knowledgeable about the target country and culture. Adjust your speaking pace so participants can readily follow you. When necessary, rework your spoken message so it flows better. Simplify convoluted phrases that even English speakers can barely follow. In coaching an executive for whom English was a second language, we identified several phrases he kept stumbling over. We replaced these with words he could pronounce more easily.

7 Allow time to meet with interpreters, if they will be used. Especially review any technical terminology to help them stay with you.

On the Scene

8 You and your audience need to have presentation content that is understandable, accurate, and received positively. Use explanatory titles to increase comprehension. Tie your words closely to the visual aids. Lead your listeners through the aids, using a pointer to help them track you.

9 Summarize frequently and be aware of information overload. Whilst coaching a presenter heading for Japan, I immediately concluded that he was trying to cover too much, so we significantly reduced the amount of material. Reporting back later, he

Tom Leech, author and coach

said he quickly realized he still had too much information.

10 Watch your language. Avoid slang, colloquialisms, clichés, metaphors, and other expressions that mean nothing to the listeners. Limit acronyms and jargon, and then explain those you do use, checking for mutual understanding. Explain key concepts or data in several ways and allow ample soak-in time.

11 Listen intently to questions and comments. As appropriate, paraphrase them before responding to make sure that the question is understood correctly. Be patient if it takes a while for your audience to comprehend your message. Be aware that your audience's non-verbal messages may mean different things from what you think. Facial expression, eye contact, hand movements, touching, use of space, and timing are all ripe areas for misinterpretation and irritation. Be slow to make assumptions on the basis of non-verbal messages. Keep checking and be patient—they can't figure you out either.

▲ Adapted from *Executive Update Online*
http://www.gwsae.org

Business skills

Networking

A Look at the following tips on communicating and networking with people you don't know or don't know very well. Which of these tips are essential, desirable or best avoided in your culture? Discuss your answers.

1 Ask the person questions about themselves; don't just talk about yourself.

2 Show that you are really interested in the other person's answers.

3 Remember the person's name if you have met him/her before.

4 Arrange to meet again in the near future.

5 Allow the other person to finish his/her response without interrupting.

6 Compliment the person on their tie/bag/jewellery, etc.

7 Introduce him/her to someone you know.

8 Remember parts of previous conversations you have had with the person.

9 Give him/her your business card and ask for his/her card.

10 Make regular eye contact during the conversation, including with members of the opposite sex.

B Good networkers often have a couple of questions prepared. Look at these examples and decide which one(s) you would and wouldn't use. Give reasons for your choice. Add five of your own questions to ask a person you meet for the first time or don't know very well.

Useful language

Questions for networking

How much do you earn?

What do you like most about (living in … / your job / this event)?

What's your opinion on (this restaurant/event/place)?

Do you come here often?

What do you recommend I do/see (in your town/country/region)?

What's the weather like in your country/city/region at the moment?

What do you think of the new boss?

What's the political situation in your country/city/region at the moment?

C 🎧 1.2 Listen to the following conversation between some delegates at a conference on intercultural communication in business held in Brussels. Tick (✔) if you hear the speakers do any of the following.

	Melanie	Konrad
1 Ask for confirmation	☐	☐
2 Greet someone	☐	☐
3 Compliment someone	☐	☐
4 Accept a compliment	☐	☐
5 Agree with someone	☐	☐
6 Express interest	☐	☐
7 Refer to a previous conversation	☐	☐
8 Exchange business cards	☐	☐
9 Refer to future contact	☐	☐
10 Introduce someone to a useful contact	☐	☐

D Work in pairs. Introduce yourself to another participant at an international conference.

Student A: Turn to page 142.

Student B: Turn to page 149.

Useful language

Expressing / asking for an opinion
So, what did you think of the
talk/presentation /conference?
I thought the part about ... was really
interesting/useful/surprising.
I'm afraid it wasn't my sort of thing / was not exactly
what I was expecting.

Introductions
Could I introduce you to a colleague of mine?
I'm afraid I've run out of cards, but I can give you our
company website/e-mail/phone number.

Finding things in common
What about yourself? Have you lived here long /
worked for the company for long?
Really? That's a coincidence! So have/do/am I.

Invitations
Here's my business card. Please give me a call if
you're ever in ... (region /city).
Would you be interested in visiting our company /
having lunch / playing golf some time?
Thank you. That would be great / lovely / nice / very
interesting.

Finishing a conversation
It's been a pleasure talking to you.
Enjoy the conference / your stay / your meal.

Writing: replying to a formal invitation

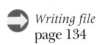
Writing file
page 134

E **You are the Branch Director of the Savings Bank of Girona in Edinburgh. You have recently been involved in a takeover of your company in which you had to overcome cultural differences regarding working practices. The Chamber of Commerce have asked you to give a talk. Reply to the invitation, including the following points:**

- Accept the invitation, thanking them politely
- Ask about conference details, e.g. the venue and how long the talk needs to be
- Say you'll send them a proposal for your talk

Although you may choose to reply by e-mail, you should use a formal writing style.

CASE STUDY

Working for Logistaid

Background

Logistaid is an NGO (non-governmental organisation) that provides emergency assistance in more than 80 countries. A group of logistics managers is undergoing a training programme in Amsterdam before being relocated to Indonesia with the organisation.

The logisticians are receiving training from the Centre for Intercultural Communication in Amsterdam. The programme includes how to adapt to their new environment and improve interaction in social and workplace settings.

Task 1

You are applying for the position of Logistics Manager with Logistaid. Look at the advert and make a note of any relevant skills and experience required. What kind of candidate do you think might be interested in this kind of work?

Logistaid

HOME   REGIONS   SO

Careers

Facility Locations

Sitemap

Logisticians

Logistaid is currently looking for trainee logisticians to work in various worldwide locations. Candidates will possess leadership skills, have a good command of English and another language, and be willing to work alongside local teams in a challenging intercultural context. Relevant experience in logistics is desirable but not essential. Training provided.

Logisticians are responsible for the technical and operational support of medical activities. Activities include:

- purchasing, transporting and distributing aid supplies
- maintaining vehicles, communications equipment, office and housing accommodation
- training and supervising local non-medical staff
- supervising and implementing repair and construction work
- related administrative activities
- liaising with local authorities and other organisations

Internet zone

Centre of Intercultural Communication

INTERNATIONAL RELOCATION PROGRAMMES

Organisations working internationally cite the following reasons for failure in a foreign country:

1 culture shock and adaptation challenges (including re-entry into the home culture)
2 difficulty in earning trust and establishing relationships
3 failure to understand local systems
4 language barriers and intercultural misunderstandings
5 differences in business practices and management styles

Task 2

Work in pairs. You are trainee logisticians for Logistaid and you are on your lunch break during the course. Read the intercultural communication programme and then talk to one of the other participants.

Student A: Turn to page 142.
Student B: Turn to page 149.

Task 3

Work in groups of three. You are networking with some of the course participants.

Student A: Turn to page 142.
Student B: Turn to page 149.
Student C: Turn to page 156.

Writing

You have been working in Jakarta, Indonesia, for three months. You have recently received this invitation to a dinner organised by the Regional Governor. It is a formal event at which local dignitaries, business people and representatives of organisations will be present. You have been strongly advised by your country manager to attend. Reply, accepting the invitation and mentioning you have a work colleague from the Amsterdam office who will be joining you in Jakarta next month, should they think it appropriate to send him/her an invitation.

 Writing file page 134

REGIONAL GOVERNOR OF JAKARTA

12th September

The Regional Governor is delighted to invite you as a representative of Logistaid to our annual International Relations Dinner that we are holding in honour of our foreign guests and in order to promote greater intercultural understanding between our countries.

The event will take place in the gardens of the Regional Governor's residence in Jakarta on October 14th at 6.00 p.m.

We would be grateful if you could reply in writing at your earliest convenience.

Yours sincerely,

Gus Siregar

Gus Siregar
Regional Governor of Jakarta

2 Training

> *The mediocre teacher tells. The good teacher explains.*
> *The superior teacher demonstrates. The great teacher inspires.*
> William Arthur Ward (American author and teacher, 1921–1997)

Listening and discussion

A **Discuss these questions.**

1 What kinds of courses have you been doing recently in your company or organisation?

2 Which of these learning styles do you prefer?

- self-study
- one-to-one
- face-to-face
- in a group
- online
- learning by doing

3 What kind of qualities do you think make a successful company trainer or teacher?

4 What do you understand by the training terms *coaching* and *mentoring*?

▲ Rosa Soler, training and development consultant

B 🎧 2.1 **Listen to the first part of the interview with Rosa Soler, a Spanish training and development consultant, and complete the information.**

1 Rosa helps companies with their training by .... a company's needs before deciding on the type of .... required.

2 The purposes of training activities like tower-building or .... are to assess skills such as teamwork, ... and .... communication.

3 'The in-tray' is an exercise used for assessing .... , during which the participants have to .... an agenda, but it is really designed to see how managers ....

4 Rosa runs various courses for her clients, which are often programmes involving .... and, less frequently, ...

C 🎧 2.2 **Listen to the second part of the interview and say whether these sentences about coaching and mentoring are true (T) or false (F).**

1 The aim of coaching programmes is to improve the business skills of employees.

2 Coaching-style programmes are specifically directed at training inexperienced managers.

3 Mentoring programmes are designed as long-term career plans for young high-flyers.

4 When a mentee is taking part in a complex mentoring programme, he/she is unable to follow additional courses.

5 The mentor is often a senior person in the organisation who must have an objective working relationship with the mentee.

6 The task of finding a suitable mentor is a challenging one, even for larger companies.

D Complete the table with the missing words related to company training. Sometimes there is more than one possibility for the noun/person.

Verb	Noun	
	Activity/process	Person
1 train	*training*	*trainer/trainee*
2 coach		
3 evaluate		
4		mentor/mentee
5 consult		
6	assessment	
7		appraiser/appraisee
8	instruction	
9	participation	

E Complete these sentences related to company training using a suitable word from the previous exercise in the correct form.

1 Our human resources department is running an intensive management .... programme next month.

2 We evaluate this course using a system of continuous .... , so all the tests, homework and classwork you do count towards your final grade.

3 Paolo is really good at .... managers in communication skills like chairing meetings and conflict resolution.

4 A lot of trainers could do with improving their skills in giving clearer ....

5 The team-building course we ran last year was very successful. We got some very positive feedback from the ....

6 Sarah has a lot of potential. It's a shame none of our senior staff have volunteered to act as her ....

7 We should get in a professional development consultant to .... the skills gaps of our staff.

8 Markus had been working for the company for over a year; performance .... from his line manager was well overdue.

F Discuss these questions.

1 Which courses are most/least popular at your place of work or institute?

2 What sort of training or coaching programmes do you think would be most beneficial for your company or organisation?

3 Would you be interested in participating in a mentoring programme, either as a mentee or mentor? Why (not)?

4 What kinds of courses are you considering doing in the near future?

A Discuss these questions.

1 Some online courses offer 'blended learning', where there is a mixture of face-to-face tuition and e-learning. Which style of learning do you prefer?

2 Would you consider doing an online MBA? Why (not)?

3 What do you think are the advantages of doing an MBA online?

B Read the article and make a note of the advantages associated with Universitas 21 Global.

Time to break out from campus

By Sumathi Bala

1 For associate professor Jeremy Williams, who has been teaching in tertiary institutes for more than two decades, making the crossover from a classroom to an e-learning environment was not a difficult choice. 'It was something that just happened one day, like a wake-up call, when I realised the way I was teaching the MBA courses was not authentic,' he says. 'Here I was waxing lyrical in a classroom on what happens in a business environment, but it doesn't really translate to what actually takes place in the marketplace.'

2 Mr Williams, who was an associate professor and MBA director at the Brisbane Graduate School of Business, accepted a post at Universitas 21 Global, the global online graduate business school. He became the institute's Director of Instruction and Assessment and associate professor of e-learning. 'To me, it was an opportunity to be at the start of something that would be big,' he says. 'E-learning is engaging, authentic and could be the way of learning in the future.'

3 Universitas 21 Global was launched in September 2000 with headquarters in Singapore as a S$90m joint venture between Universitas 21, Thomson Learning – a US-based educational publisher – and a global consortium of 16 universities. The online institute wants to tap into the vast potential demand for higher education, particularly in Asia. It also aims to break away from the elitist model of higher education by making tertiary education accessible to more people.

4 E-learning is seen as offering a less traditional model of learning, allowing instructors to act as facilitators or mentors. It also allows for greater expression, giving everyone in the virtual classroom space an equal voice. 'An online course is more democratic, everybody has a voice, where you don't have just your typical Anglo-Saxon who is loud and talks more,' says Mr Williams.

5 The Master of Business Administration degree conferred by the institute is globally recognised, as it bears the stamp of all 16 universities. By providing top-class business education online, Universitas 21 Global says that it is offering an alternative route for students in Asia, who cannot afford to pay for higher education or travel to the US, UK or Australia. To make its online MBA programme affordable, the institute charges varying tuition fees, depending on where the students come from.

6 Mukesh Aghi, chief executive officer at Universitas 21 Global, says: 'I think it's not fair to pay one price for education when the income level varies from country to country. Our pricing model takes into account the GDP of each country.' For instance, the institute charges US$20,000 for an American student following Universitas 21 Global's MBA programme, whereas a student in India would pay US$7,000 for the same course.

7 The reasonable cost structure, coupled with flexibility of both time and curriculum, offers a huge incentive for working professionals. Srinivas Lakshmikumar, business consultant with LogicaCMG, says that doing the MBA online was a natural choice, given his hectic travel schedule. 'Also, in countries like India, more and more people will have to start working early and fund their own education due to increasingly higher education costs,' says Mr Lakshmikumar. 'Not all can afford the traditional luxury of studying on full-time courses with support from parents.'

8 India is one of the key markets Universitas 21 Global is targeting to expand its business in Asia. 'Education is very much valued there,' explains Mr Aghi. 'Given the caste system, education becomes an equaliser.' Coupled with a large English-speaking population and an extensive use of the Internet, the online structure of the course makes it very attractive to prospective students and corporations.

9 China, on the other hand – where Universitas 21 Global introduced its online MBA course in April this year – could prove to be a challenge, says Mr Aghi. 'We're still in the process of getting approval from the ministry of education'. The online MBA programme will cost 70,000 renminbi (£4,600), about one-quarter of the cost of an MBA programme offered by universities in China.

10 However, Mr Aghi accepts that brand recognition is very important, especially when it comes to business education. The prestigious French business school, Insead, has a campus in Singapore, and the University of Chicago Graduate School of Business also offers an eMBA out of the city-state: Mr Aghi says building critical mass will not be easy. 'I agree brand recognition is very important in education. But at the end of the day, we're not competing with the bricks-and-mortar universities but complementing them. Our target group is someone who is probably married and is a working professional,' he says. 'We know we're the new kid on the block, that's our limitation. But I'm also confident we can become a recognised brand in five years.'

FINANCIAL TIMES

C Complete the following summary of the article.

Universitas 21 Global is an ....[1] MBA programme based in Singapore which is recognised by ....[2] and tertiary institutes worldwide. The course is seen to be more accessible, as the ....[3] vary according to the GDP of a student's country. The low cost and flexibility of online study make the course ideal for people who cannot afford to study at prestigious business schools ....[4].

The eMBA has also proven especially popular with Indian students, who often have to pay for their own ....[5]. China, however, may turn out to be a more difficult key ....[6] to break into. The chief executive officer at Universitas 21 Global admits it may take another five years for the course to become more widely ....[7], although he also points out that the eMBA has the advantage of attracting more ....[8] students.

D Find words and expressions from the article that have a similar meaning to the following.

1 higher education or at university level (paragraph 1)
2 a teacher in a university department (paragraph 2)
3 use or take from something (paragraph 3)
4 a university title officially given to someone (paragraph 5)
5 the minimum number of users, buyers, etc. necessary for a product to succeed (paragraph 10)
6 educational institutions that exist as buildings (paragraph 10)

E Identify the multiword verbs related to education in these sentences and decide on their correct meaning.

1 We predict 10 per cent of our students will drop out by the end of the course.

2 Last year, they broke away from the more traditional methods and started offering courses based on blended learning.

3 The university lecturer was excellent at teaching such a complex subject; he was especially good at breaking it down into manageable chunks.

4 One of India's oldest companies has signed an agreement with the institute and is putting its employees through the MBA programme this year.

5 We have been looking into the pros and cons of e-learning for many years.

6 She really fell behind with her studies last term when she was ill, but she's catching up with them now.

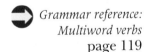 *Grammar reference: Multiword verbs* page 119

Write six sentences of your own using these verbs.

F Complete the extract with suitable multiword verbs from the box in the correct form.

bring in	get to	hype up	put on	set up	think ahead

The need for wider horizons

By Jeffrey E. Garten

It often appears to me that globalisation is a kind of fad at business schools. You have to be seen as addressing it, and there are many ways to .... it ....[1]: put the adjective *international* before a course in strategy or marketing; ....[2] a lot of students from outside your country; ....[3] some special programmes for foreign executives; conduct courses in other countries via the Internet. Often, it seems, there is more sizzle than steak.

I doubt that most faculties ....[4] the heart of what is necessary for their students eventually to be great global leaders. Too often, students are taught about the past rather than being given the wherewithal to ....[5]. But the big, fundamental questions need to be ....[6] the table and debated more vigorously in research and in classrooms.

FINANCIAL TIMES

Business skills

Telephone strategies: clarifying and confirming

A 🎧 2.3, 2.4 Listen to two telephone conversations about the staff induction day at Ashley Pharmaceuticals. What is the purpose of each call? Which conversation is more formal and why?

Useful language

Tips for successful communication
Be an active listener. When you don't know what someone meant, ask a clarifying question. When you think you understood, confirm it by repeating or rephrasing what was said.

Clarifying phrases and questions
Would you mind [repeating that / going over that again] for me?
Could I ask you to give me those details again?
Could you [explain/clarify] what you meant [by / when you said] ...?
And the date was ...?

Confirming phrases and questions
So that's nine o'clock on Thursday, then?
Let me [see if / make sure] I understood you correctly. You're saying ...
Is that [right/correct]?
Can I just check that?
[I'd like to / Let me just] confirm that ...

Correcting misunderstandings
No, [I meant to say that / what I meant was] ....
Not quite, it's ...
Well, actually, what I [said/meant] was that ...
Not exactly, I [said/meant] that ...

B 🎧 2.3 Listen to the first conversation again. What techniques does each speaker use to check or confirm the information they hear? Match each phrase (1–5) with a technique (a–c).

1 So, you didn't receive the programme we sent to you?

2 Can I just check that? Did you say nine o'clock?

3 And the room was ...?

4 So that's B2, thanks.

5 And it doesn't matter if I haven't got a copy of the programme?

a) Echoing/rephrasing what was said

b) Using questioning intonation to check information

c) Asking a direct question for checking/confirming

C 🎧 2.4 Listen to the second conversation again. Correct this room-booking planner and write Pierre's note to other receptionists about the room change for the staff induction day.

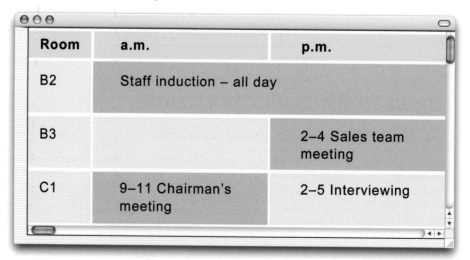

Room	a.m.	p.m.
B2	Staff induction – all day	
B3		2–4 Sales team meeting
C1	9–11 Chairman's meeting	2–5 Interviewing

Writing: e-mails

D Read the tips and the e-mails below. To what extent do the e-mails follow the advice?

Tips for writing effective e-mails

- Start with a strong subject line. Think of your subject line as the headline of an important news article. Make sure the subject line relates to the message content.
- Use the 'inverted pyramid' form of writing. Your most important statements should appear in the first paragraph. Follow up with supporting details.
- Limit sentence length and keep paragraphs short for easy reading. Put forward your recommendations or state the measures you will take to resolve a problem, for instance.

- Use sub-topic headings within your e-mail message, especially if the message is lengthy. Refer to the sub-topics in your first paragraph. This will provide a helpful guide for your reader.
- Ask for an action. For example, let your recipient know what you need in order to complete a task.
- Avoid misinterpretation of dates by spelling out the month, for example 24 Jun 05 or Jun 24 05
- Proofread your e-mail and use the spell check.
- Reread your message one last time before you send it. Think about how you would react if you were on the receiving end of your message.

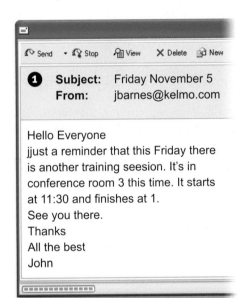

1 Subject: Friday November 5
From: jbarnes@kelmo.com

Hello Everyone
jjust a reminder that this Friday there is another training seesion. It's in conference room 3 this time. It starts at 11:30 and finishes at 1.
See you there.
Thanks
All the best
John

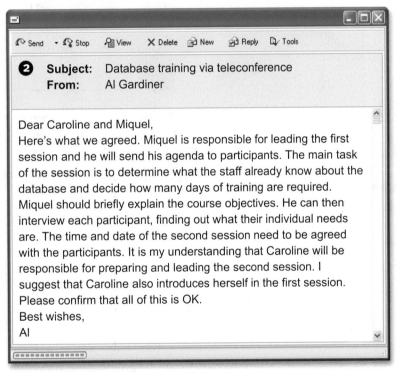

2 Subject: Database training via teleconference
From: Al Gardiner

Dear Caroline and Miquel,
Here's what we agreed. Miquel is responsible for leading the first session and he will send his agenda to participants. The main task of the session is to determine what the staff already know about the database and decide how many days of training are required. Miquel should briefly explain the course objectives. He can then interview each participant, finding out what their individual needs are. The time and date of the second session need to be agreed with the participants. It is my understanding that Caroline will be responsible for preparing and leading the second session. I suggest that Caroline also introduces herself in the first session. Please confirm that all of this is OK.
Best wishes,
Al

E Read the e-mails again. Which is the more formal? Identify examples of formal and informal language in the e-mails.

Writing file page 135

F Write a formal and a less formal e-mail. Use some of the expressions in the e-mails above to help you.

1 You work for a small company where everyone is on first-name terms. You've heard about a staff development day and you might like to attend, but you don't have any details about the event to help you decide. Write to Pat Fischer, the Human Resources Manager, asking for more information.

2 You are a manager with a team of ten staff. You would like to organise interviews for the annual staff appraisals. Write a message that you can send to all your staff about this topic and ask them to reply giving you three options for dates and times they can do.

Training at SmileCo

Smile

Background

SmileCo is a leading confectioner in the fast-moving consumer goods (FMCG) market, with many famous brands in its portfolio. The company has recently acquired a rival confectionery company, Reedley, and now has a merged field sales team of over 200 in the UK, including ten regional managers.

The company relies heavily on receiving timely market information from its sales force. Key to SmileCo's success is up-to-date information on the company and competitor product range, merchandising, promotional activity, customer base and rival sales-force activity. Analysing quality market information is crucial to decision-making and planning in an increasingly competitive market.

Listening 🎧 2.5
The new Director of Sales for the recently merged SmileCo, Harry O'Riordan, is in a meeting with the Human Resources Manager, Gabriella Henderson, and the IT Manager, Kamal Satinder. Listen and answer these questions.

1 What problems do they identify with the sales team's current information-gathering system?

2 What solutions are discussed?

3 What training needs do they initially identify?

EVERLY

CONSULTANTS

Expert training for your sales team

This workshop sets out to show how your sales team can maximise the impact of their face-to-face contact with customers. With any field-based sales force, the time spent with customers is relatively limited, and we know that you have to make the most of it. We offer a drama-based approach that responds to your business needs.

We design sessions for clients which include professional actors role-playing examples of sales encounters with different customer types. This will help your team to think differently and to realise that one sales pitch doesn't fit all.

Testimonials

'Formal training can be boring. Not this session – it was interactive, effective and lots of fun.'

'Our investment with them has paid off because our sales team has become better able to achieve their ever-moving goals.'

Task 1

Telephone strategies

SmileCo's IT Manager, Kamal Satinder, calls Geraldine Parker at Pollack Learning Alliance to tell her about the proposed new information-gathering system for the sales team and to ask her company to handle the training programme. Work in pairs.

Student A: Turn to page 143.
Student B: Turn to page 150.

Task 2

Clarifying and confirming a training proposal

Geraldine Parker from Pollack Learning Alliance and Kamal Satinder, IT Manager at SmileCo meet to discuss the training proposal further. Work in pairs.

Student A: Turn to page 143.
Student B: Turn to page 150.

Task 3

Devising a training programme

You are the Director of Sales for SmileCo. Devise a training programme for your sales team.
- What are your priorities?
- Should the training be done by an internal team or external training companies? What are the pros and cons of these options?
- Is it better to choose short intensive courses or extensive courses?
- Should you implement a new data-collection system or offer more training with the current system?
- You have a limited training budget. How will you decide which of your sales staff need customer awareness training? How could the rest of the staff benefit from this training?
- What can you do to accelerate the integration process between the two newly merged sales forces and develop a unified team spirit?

Writing

You are Kamal Satinder, IT Manager at SmileCo. Write an e-mail to the Director of Sales outlining the training programme for the new data-collection system.

 Writing file page 135

Partnerships

*❝A friendship founded on business is a good deal
better than a business founded on friendship.❞*

John Rockefeller, American oil magnate (1839–1937)

Listening and discussion

A **Discuss this question.**

In which areas does the private sector operate or help to fund public services in
your country? Here are some examples:

- hospitals and health care
- schools and education services
- housing and urban planning
- utilities (i.e. water, gas, telephone, electricity)
- infrastructure projects (e.g. roads) and transport
- army, courts, prisons, police and security services

B 🎧 3.1 **Listen to the first part of a radio programme about public private
partnerships in the UK. Complete the notes with between one and four words
in each gap.**

Traditionally, public private partnerships in the UK are related to
. . . . [1], such as . . . . [2] and . . . . [3] services in hospitals.

The Private Finance Initiative (PFI) is different from earlier partnerships.
It is now the main way that the UK government finances . . . . [4].
PFI allows the government to build new . . . . [5] projects without
. . . . [6].

A wide spectrum of projects are funded using PFI, for example new
. . . . [7] and waste-disposal systems. PFI projects now tend to be
much bigger than they were . . . . [8] ago.

C 🎧 **3.2 Listen to the second part of the discussion and complete the summary of the arguments for and against PFI projects.**

Arguments in favour of PFI	Criticisms of PFI projects
1 The government can commission public services it couldn't otherwise afford.	1
2	2
3	3
4	

D **Complete these sentences using the correct form of the words given in brackets.**

1 ..Privatisation.. (*private*) is the full transfer of publicly owned assets into the private sector through a sale on the stock market.

2 Critics argue that .... (*compete*) .... (*tender*) for public services emphasises cost-cutting over quality of service.

3 The .... (*run*) and .... (*maintain*) of this public hospital have been .... (*source*) to a private company for the next five years.

4 Government .... (*spend*) on transport, roads and railways has declined in the past 30 years, and many services have now been .... (*private*). Nonetheless, the private .... (*own*) of rail services is proving to be controversial in the UK.

E **Discuss your views on public private partnerships.**

1 What are some of the advantages and disadvantages of private sector involvement in public services? Think about the following issues:
   - value for money
   - accountability
   - public interest
   - employment rights
   - risks

2 How does private-sector involvement in public services in your country compare to the PFI model in the UK?

3 Do you think there are any 'core' public services that the private sector should not fund, sponsor or operate? Why (not)?

4 Do you think the notion of publicly funded services will disappear in the future?

Reading and language

A Discuss these questions.

1 Which public services especially need to be improved in your country?

2 What factors do you think could affect the success or failure of public private partnership projects?

Infrastructure: Experience of the 1990s has put people off

By Sarah Murray

1 The failure of inefficient and under-funded governments to provide citizens in the developing world with essential services such as water, power and sanitation provides a compelling argument for private sector involvement in these activities. However, it is difficult to persuade companies to participate when pricing remains too low to repay investments, and when lenders are reluctant to back projects in places where political risk is high.

2 Private money flooded into infrastructure projects in the 1990s, particularly power projects in Asia and Latin America, which was a target for multinationals that invested widely as former state monopolies were privatised. But as problems emerged – both in the region and in companies' home markets – many withdrew, and today Latin American countries are embracing the privatisation of energy resources with less enthusiasm. Even if investors could be tempted back into power or water distribution projects in emerging markets, the higher tariffs associated with private systems are often politically unacceptable.

3 'The private sector not only has to improve operations and collection, but also has to increase the level of investment and correct for historical under-investment,' says Francisco Toureilles, director for infrastructure at the International Finance Corporation (IFC).

4 In the case of water, passions run high, with many arguing that access to water is an essential human right that should not have to be paid for. However, Michael Klein, vice-president for private sector development at the World Bank and IFC, points out that many are paying for it already. Those without access to water, he says, are often forced to buy from vendors, paying ten times or more than people connected to modern water systems. 'The idea that you can't raise prices because it's not affordable is, in many cases, just plain wrong,' he says.

5 But even if the argument for a private-sector role in infrastructure development has been won, the question is how to persuade business to participate, particularly since the experience of the 1990s has made companies and lenders more risk averse. 'Companies got badly burned in Latin America,' says Dan Bond, who co-chairs the Experts Group on Developing Country Infrastructure Finance. 'They invested heavily before the regulatory regimes were worked out, so they were building the foundations on shifting sand.'

6 Another difficulty is that infrastructure projects generate local currency revenue, while the long-term financing is in dollars or euros. A sudden devaluation, such as the 1999 Brazilian currency crisis, means that what seemed a promising enterprise can no longer service its debt. 'We're trying to figure out how to get projects' sponsors interested again, and one of the key things we see is some type of risk sharing between the public and private sector,' says Mr Bond. 'Because the private sector is certainly not going to step back in and take the kind of risks it did in the 1990s.'

7 Besides financing difficulties, recouping investments remains a challenge. The World Bank estimates that power prices cover an average of about 60 per cent of the costs, while water prices cover just 30 per cent. 'So whether it's public or private, if nobody pays for this stuff, it doesn't get built,' says Mr Klein. 'The private sector can't recoup the investment, and the public systems don't get expanded and become decrepit.'

8 The participation of multilateral institutions is seen as one answer. The IFC hopes to foster public-private partnerships by providing upfront financing, advising governments on how to structure contracts and establishing transparent processes, thus creating conditions it believes can attract investors.

9 Mr Klein believes other opportunities lie between big government and donor-funded projects and primitive systems such as collecting water from bore holes or using wood as fuel. Local entrepreneurs, he says, can provide services that, while more expensive than modern systems, are an improvement on what is available. Here, government legislation is the obstacle. In Africa, national electricity companies supply power to little more than 10 per cent of the population, and yet most African countries forbid the building of intermediate electricity systems.

10 In the few places in the world where this is permitted – as in Yemen and Cambodia – hundreds of small companies have bought generators and established wires connecting neighbourhoods or villages. 'Prices are higher than for national systems, but there are no modern systems, so people prefer this to nothing,' says Mr Klein. 'This isn't a perfect world. But it's second best in a world where the best is far away.'

FINANCIAL TIMES

B Read the text quickly and match the two parts of the sentence summaries. Order the sentences in the way they appear in the text.

1 Governments in developing countries have failed to

2 Private companies are now more wary of investing in

3 Michael Klein would disagree that

4 Developing countries tend not to

5 The International Finance Corporation is trying to

6 Michael Klein suggests local entrepreneurs

a) provide more costly services rather than no services at all.

b) increase the participation of institutions and attract investors.

c) charging higher prices for essential services is politically unacceptable.

d) use the same currencies for financing projects and generating revenue.

e) infrastructure projects in Latin America than in the 1990s.

f) provide basic services such as water, power and sanitation.

C Choose the meaning of the words in italics, according to the text.

1 *back* a project (paragraph 1)
   a) provide political support for
   b) provide finance for

2 *got badly burned* (paragraph 5)
   a) lost a lot of money
   b) lost property in fires

3 *get* projects' *sponsors interested* (paragraph 6)
   a) encourage sponsors
   b) create interesting sponsors

4 *recoup the investment* (paragraph 7)
   a) get returns on money invested
   b) ask for their money back

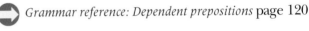 *Grammar reference: Dependent prepositions* page 120

D Look at this example of the passive from paragraph 4 of the article, then complete the following sentences using the verbs in brackets in the passive.

... water is an essential human right that should not have *to be paid for.*

1 Despite improving the image of the public sector, a major change still .... *(need to / make)* from the top down.

2 A think tank .... *(set up)* in the coming year in order to advise the government on how to spend public money more wisely.

3 More companies .... *(have to / persuade)* to invest in our educational project for African countries.

4 The relationship between public and private sectors .... *(should not / build)* on only mutual benefits. Any resulting projects must be to the public good.

5 The water company .... *(forbid)* to continue with the project after it has emerged a number of directors have exchanged money under the table.

6 As soon as the contract .... *(sign)*, several scandals erupted. A politician had had financial links with the project and .... *(force)* to resign.

E Rewrite these sentences using *get* or *have* where possible and putting the verbs in the correct form and position.

1 The Prime Minister want / pass the new legislation / by next month
   The Prime Minister wants to get/have the new legislation passed by next month.

2 The TV company still try / approve the joint venture / by the government

3 The Polish minister hope / build a highway / in two years

4 Many still believe the only way to / bring business in line / is through the establishment of global rules, such as are being discussed in Geneva

5 PPPs are types of contracts whereby the public sector / build or manage some kind of service / by the private sector

6 PPPs have often failed because governments / not involve the public / in projects.

Grammar reference: Passive page 121

Business skills

Negotiating: being vague and being precise

A Look at the extract from the book *Leigh Steinberg Has a Game Plan* on the left and discuss these questions.
- When was the last time you negotiated? What was the outcome?
- To what extent do you agree with the six rules for 'winning with integrity'?
- Do you know of any other rules or tips for successful negotiating? What are they?

LEIGH STEINBERG WINS WITH INTEGRITY

Steinberg follows 12 rules for winning with integrity. Six of the best are:
- Learn everything you can about the other party.
- Make sure the other party believes that you have options.
- Set the stage for cooperation, not conflict.
- Never show fear or anger in the face of intimidation.
- Be the best listener you can.
- Plan ahead for what you are willing to give up.

B Match these negotiating expressions (1–8) to the correct function (a–h).
1 Given/Seeing (that) you can't deliver any sooner, we'd like a 5% discount.
2 What would you say to a 4% discount and a free sample?
3 Supposing we/you were to make that three free samples.
4 I think we could work/go with that.
5 We're looking at an initial order of 100 bikes.
6 Would you be willing to come down a bit in price?
7 Somewhere in the region of $400.
8 Are you saying that you have those items, in that colour, in stock?

a) Describing your needs
b) Making a suggestion
c) Introducing a condition
d) Requesting a concession
e) Hypothesising or 'sounding out' the other party
f) Reaching agreement
g) Asking for precise information
h) Being vague

LET ME GET THIS STRAIGHT. ARE YOU SUGGESTING YOU'D LIKE TO BE RE-LOCATED?

C 🎧 3.3 Listen to the following extract from a negotiation. What is being negotiated, and what is the outcome?

D 🎧 3.3 Listen again and say whether the speakers are (a) being vague, (b) being precise or (c) asking for precise information. Note down some of the expressions used.

Speaker	Vague	Precise	Asking for precise information	Expressions used
Kathy				
Giovanni				

E Role-plays. Negotiate the following situations. Take notes on what is agreed.
Student A: Turn to page 143.
Student B: Turn to page 150.

When you have finished negotiating, review what happened. Could you have reached a more satisfactory outcome if you had done something differently? Did the other party make any mistakes?

Report writing: layout and structure

F What is the logical order of these headings for a feasibility or recommendation report? What other sections might be included in this type of report?

- recommendations
- conclusion
- executive summary
- introduction
- findings

G Complete these tips with the words in the box.

| draft re-edit errors headings layout plan register |

Report writing tips

Read a similar report first; write a . . . .[1] or outline and then write your first draft.

Edit for style and . . . .[2], e.g. formal language, passive or active forms.

Proofread for typical . . . .[3], e.g. subject-verb agreement, prepositions and punctuation.

Organise . . . .[4] and structure with appropriate title and . . . .[5].

R. . . . .[6] and rewrite if necessary.

Take a break or ask someone to read it before you rewrite your final . . . .[7].

H Complete the report on concepts for negotiating on page 159 with these sentences (one of them is not used).

A After each negotiation session, review what happened.

B The end result may be agreement, agreement to continue later, or end the negotiation.

C BATNA stands for your Best Alternative To Negotiated Agreement.

D This report on negotiating aims to outline the main characteristics of a typical sales or business negotiation.

E An example would be agreements between suppliers and customers who intend to do repeat business.

F Both sides should share goals and be willing to trade to attain their objectives: a 'win-win' situation.

G Negotiation is conferring with another person or group to arrive at a settlement of some conflict.

H Define your own goals, your opponent's goals and the conflict.

I In business, negotiation is an important management skill.

I Write a brief report on one of the negotiations you role-played in Exercise E.

Writing file pages 138–139

3 Konopnicka Airport takes off

Background

Konopnicka Airport is one of the regional airports operated by the Polish Airports Agency (PAA). Last year, more than 5.5 million passengers passed through the passenger terminal, and a significant growth of freight volume and passenger traffic is forecast for the period to 2020. Passenger traffic has already grown at rates exceeding forecasts and is expected to increase to around 9.4m in four years' time. Capacity of the passenger terminal has been set at 12 million passengers yearly.

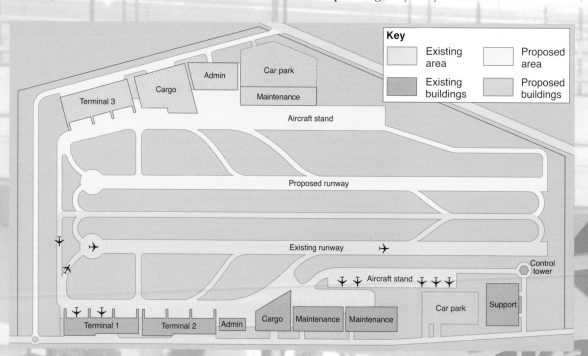

Konopnicka Airport is well suited for further development as an international hub airport and enjoys a geographic advantage, along with other Central European airports, that may relieve the air traffic congestion in many Western European countries. In order to adapt Konopnicka Airport to the increasing freight and passenger traffic, the PAA and the Ministry of Infrastructure have taken the decision to add a second runway and construct a new world-class passenger terminal, a cargo terminal and a catering base.

Listening 🎧3.4

Listen to Jozef Pulaski, Director General of PAA, talking to Karen Armstrong, Chief Financial Officer for the British Airports Enterprise, and Stefan Znaniecki, a consultant in public-private partnerships in the UK. They are discussing ways to finance new infrastructure projects. Complete Jozef's notes from the meeting.

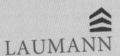

Laumann wins contract for Polish airport

Laumann, the German construction firm, has won an open international tender competition for the expansion of Konopnicka Airport in Poland.

The proposal submitted by Laumann will be financed by Weber-Merkel Bank in Frankfurt. Construction work is due to start early next year.

Laumann is one of the world's largest international construction companies, with more than 80% of the corporation's turnover coming from projects developed outside Germany.

PAA can maintain control of public-private venture by

.... 1

.... 2

Options for financing the project

1) State Treasury: cannot provide the finance needed in time for expansion project.

2) Commercial banks: Interest?

.... 3

3) 4

4) Most likely option is

.... 5

Choosing a contractor

Put the Konopnicka Airport expansion project

.... 6?

Ask potential contractor to

.... 7

Negotiate risk allocation, e.g.

.... 8

Task

Negotiating a PPP

Work in pairs.

Student A: Turn to page 144.
Student B: Turn to page 151.

Writing

Write an executive summary of the negotiated PPP agreement.

 Writing file pages 138–139

1 Being international

Vocabulary
business idioms

Complete these sentences using a suitable idiom from the box in the correct form.

> get back on track   get someone's input on something   go over   keep track of
> kick around   kick off   run out of   stick to the point

1 I'm afraid I .... handouts. If you give me your e-mail, I'll send you a copy.
2 The round-table discussion at the conference went off topic for a while, but then everyone ....
3 I'm sorry, I wasn't listening. Do you mind .... the main points again?
4 Our boss never .... in meetings. She's always going off on a tangent and telling us her views on the world.
5 I know *we* like it, but could we .... our customers' .... on the new slogan?
6 As you can see from the agenda, we've got a lot to get through today. I suggest Rachel .... with the first item.
7 First of all, I'd like you to brainstorm and .... some ideas on intercultural communication, and then we'll look at what the experts say.
8 When our British and American colleagues attend meetings, it's hard to .... what they're saying. They use so many colloquial expressions.

Business skills
networking

Match the expressions (a–h) to the functions (1–8).

1 Introducing yourself
2 Introducing others
3 Expressing an opinion
4 Asking for an opinion
5 Finding things in common
6 Inviting someone
7 Accepting an invitation
8 Finishing a conversation

a) So, what did you think about the speaker's views?
b) Would you be interested in a further meeting?
c) That'll be great! When did you have in mind?
d) I'd like you to meet my manager, Alex Prades.
e) I'm not sure if I completely agreed with her.
f) Well, it's been great talking to you.
g) That's amazing! We were both born in Rome!
h) Please call me Leszek. Here, take one of my cards.

Presentations

Choose the correct alternative to complete each quote on speaking in public. What's your opinion of these views on public speaking?

1 Only the prepared speaker
2 All the great speakers
3 Once you get people laughing, they're listening
4 It is delivery
5 Most speakers
6 There is nothing in the world like

a) were bad speakers at first.
b) a persuasive speech to fuddle the mental apparatus.
c) speak ten minutes too long.
d) that makes the orator's success.
e) deserves to be confident.
f) and you can tell them almost anything.

Writing
formal correspondence

You are giving a presentation on business culture in your country. Write a formal letter confirming your attendance at the conference and include the main points of your talk. Think about the following and add some of your own ideas:

- local customs and traditions
- entertaining foreign visitors
- taboo subjects when socialising/networking

2 Training

Reading

Read this article and complete it with words or phrases related to training and development taken from the box. Two of them are not used.

> business schools   coaching   develop   developing partnerships
> have been running   three-year programmes   the school   trained
> training for executives   will be offered

HEC MONTRÉAL WINS AFRICAN ASSIGNMENT

By Linda Anderson

HEC Montréal is celebrating after beating off competition from top global ....[1] to provide programmes for the African Development Bank.

The school will run four ....[2] in English and French for the bank. The project will be one of the largest ....[3] has ever done in terms of ....[4] and managers in a global perspective.

The four projects ....[5] in Montreal, Tunis and Cairo and will consist of executive, management, leadership or new ....[6] programmes.

The African Development Bank has adopted a new strategic plan and has identified strategic planning, corporate governance, project management and creating and ....[7] as areas where it wishes its staff to ....[8].

FINANCIAL TIMES

Business skills

telephoning

Match the two halves of the telephoning expressions. Identify whether they are confirming, clarifying or correcting information.

1 Would you mind
2 Could you explain what you meant
3 I just want to
4 So, the courses are going to
5 I'm sorry, I don't think
6 Well actually, what I meant

a) to say was the course starts after the New Year.
b) going over the training objectives again?
c) run over the New Year holiday then?
d) I've made myself clear.
e) check the exact course dates with you.
f) when you said full attendance is required?

Writing

e-mails

Look at this informal e-mail. In most of the lines (1–11) there is an extra word that doesn't fit. Write the extra word or put a tick (✔) if the line is correct.

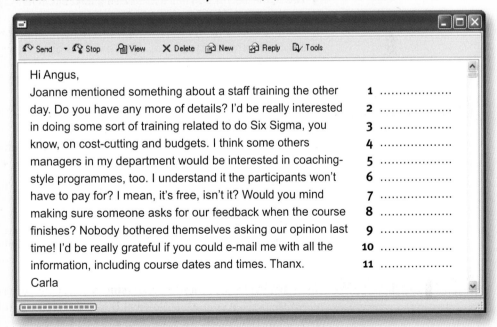

Hi Angus,
Joanne mentioned something about a staff training the other   1 ....
day. Do you have any more of details? I'd be really interested   2 ....
in doing some sort of training related to do Six Sigma, you   3 ....
know, on cost-cutting and budgets. I think some others   4 ....
managers in my department would be interested in coaching-   5 ....
style programmes, too. I understand it the participants won't   6 ....
have to pay for? I mean, it's free, isn't it? Would you mind   7 ....
making sure someone asks for our feedback when the course   8 ....
finishes? Nobody bothered themselves asking our opinion last   9 ....
time! I'd be really grateful if you could e-mail me with all the   10 ....
information, including course dates and times. Thanx.   11 ....
Carla

Writing

Rewrite the previous e-mail in a formal style to the HR manager.

Vocabulary

word-building

Complete these sentences using the word in brackets in its correct form.

1 (mentor) .... a young executive requires a great deal of skill and in-depth knowledge about the company.
2 The university (lecture) .... was a man in his fifties who really enjoyed teaching young people about business management.
3 Human resources departments have difficulties (assess) .... the true success of staff training and development programmes.
4 I'm due for my first (appraise) .... with my line manager tomorrow. It's making me a bit nervous.
5 Could you give me a hand? I've got the (instruct) .... leaflet, but I don't understand a thing!
6 Gerry isn't an ordinary teacher; he calls himself a training and development (consult) ....
7 The course leader knew he had to change the activity, as all the participants were looking bored and (motivate) ....
8 The young (train) .... were very keen to get started in their new work placements.

3 Partnerships

Vocabulary

word partnerships

Match 1–8 with a–h to make suitable word partnerships and then complete the opinions on public private partnerships below using the collocations. Discuss your views on these comments.

1 change	5 poor	a) sector	e) of services
2 private	6 lack	b) from perfect	f) planning
3 far	7 reputation	c) of money	g) life better
4 make	8 delivery	d) for	h) their ways

1 PPPs combine the best the public and .... offers, while limiting the shortcomings of either the 'privatisation' approach or the exclusive public sector ....
2 There are a lot of reasons for delays in infrastructure, but the most important are .... , very .... , inadequate laws and frequent personnel changes at the ministry.
3 The public sector still has a .... being a bit set in its ways, and having staff who are never going to .... , but this is simply not the case.
4 Many believe that while .... , only private enterprise has the energy, the finance and the inventiveness to .... for the world's poor.

Grammar

dependent prepositions

Complete these extracts from newspaper articles using a suitable verb from the box in the correct form. One is not used.

admit apply decline depend encourage expect hope invest need try

China recently released regulations allowing foreign companies to ....[1] in television-programme-production joint ventures. Shandong TV-net ....[2] to comment on the timing of its IPO (Initial Public Offering), saying it was still ....[3] for government approval.

Civil servants in the UK are now ....[4] to broaden their development through working in other departments or sectors. The Department of Trade and Industry now ....[5] all its senior civil servants to spend at least a week every year working in an outside organisation.

The Polish transport minister ....[6] to see a highway connecting Warsaw with Germany within four years. Currently, traffic is squeezed on a narrow road filled with cars toying with death as they ....[7] to pass transport trucks. President of Basell Orlen Polyolefins in central Poland says, 'Poland really ....[8] to speed up its road construction. We ....[9] on bulk traffic to transport our goods.'

Negotiating
being vague or precise

A government official (A) is talking to a middle manager from the construction company, Roberts & Walters Construction (B). Complete the dialogue with the correct negotiating expressions from the box. Identify whether they are vague (V) or precise (P).

> But you signed a contract
> I'm afraid it's looking unlikely
> look at the refinancing of this project
> look into the possibilities very carefully
> otherwise we have no alternative but
> see what can be done
> that will involve taking on extra labour
> the project suffered serious delays when
> whatever it takes
> your company would be responsible for any delays

A: Are you saying you won't have the offices built until January of next year?

B: Well, to be realistic, ...[1].

A: ....[2] saying completion is due for November of this year!

B: That's true, but you're also aware that ....[3] we discovered archaeological remains as we were excavating.

A: I know, I know. But our agreement on risk allocation was that ....[4] in the building schedule. Can't you speed things up? The new owners are moving into our old government offices at the end of the year.

B: The thing is, ...[5] or overtime, which is going to be expensive, and the remaining budget doesn't allow for that. I really think we need to call an urgent meeting with all parties involved to ....[6].

A: Yes, yes, ...[7]. But, this building has to be ready by the end of December, ...[8] to start fining your company for every day that the project overruns.

B: OK, I'll talk to the on-site manager again and ....[9]. And the emergency meeting?

A: Mmm, we'll certainly ....[10].

Writing
report layout and structure

Imagine you are the manager in the previous exercise and you are working on a construction project for new government offices. Write a progress report to your boss explaining recent developments and include your recommendations for completing the project on time. In your report, use at least two examples of the passive and two examples of the structure *to get* or *have something done*.

Examples:

Construction work must be completed by the end of December.
We need to get/have the refinancing of the project approved in order to finish on time.

Energy

❝ There is no wave without wind. ❞
Chinese proverb

Listening and discussion

A **Discuss these questions.**

1 Which sources of energy are generally considered to be environmentally friendly? Why (not)?

2 What ways are there of saving energy in a) the home? b) a large company?

B 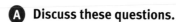 **4.1 Listen to Anthony Fitzgerald talk about current trends and developments in the industry and choose the most accurate endings for these summary sentences.**

1 It is thought that there is a limited supply of ...

   a) fossil fuels and natural gas will not be available in 200 years' time.

   b) oil and gas, and neither will be available 50 years from now.

2 According to Anthony Fitzgerald, the sector is ...

   a) not doing so well due to increased levels of competition nowadays.

   b) doing well, despite there being more competition than there used to be.

3 One effect of deregulation in the industry has meant that gas companies ...

   a) are now not obliged to purchase from any one source.

   b) can now purchase from only one source.

4 Following the new regulations, the more established companies have had to ...

   a) put their activities into one package.

   b) divide their activities into separate areas of business.

5 Two significant issues in the gas sector are diversification of sources and

   a) security of supply.

   b) dependence on supply from the Middle East.

▲ Anthony Fitzgerald, gas industry expert

C 🎧 **4.1 Listen again and correct the eight errors in this summary of the interview.**

Natural gas is far less environmentally friendly than other fossil fuels like oil and coal, but it is also being replaced by newer sources of energy, as it will probably run out in 50 years' time.

The gas sector is unlikely to continue doing well for some time to come, and the opening up of markets, together with deregulation, has created more competition in the industry.

Changes in how the sector is regulated mean that gas suppliers can now sell from anywhere. New regulations have also forced some companies to bundle their activities, dividing their companies into separate areas of business.

Apart from competition, other factors that have affected the sector include a fall in the use of natural gas, as well as attracting a wider customer base. This has led to mergers between gas and oil companies, as seen in Germany, and the creation of energy giants.

Other concerns in the gas sector include security of supply and diversification: the Middle East relies heavily on certain countries and regions for its gas supply, so countries like Spain now import gas from a variety of countries.

D **Discuss these questions.**

1 Which energy sources are becoming increasingly more costly? Why do you think this is?

2 What do you think will be the implications in the business world in the case of an energy shortage?

3 What are the main energy companies in your region or country?

4 A number of energy companies have merged recently. What are the benefits of this for a) the companies? b) their customers?

E **Complete these article extracts with an appropriate word or phrase from the box.**

> energy consumption   energy efficiency   energy watchdog
> fossil fuel   global warming   greenhouse gas emissions
> renewable energy   wind power

India's population of about 1 billion represents about 16 per cent of the world's population, but accounts for less than 2 per cent of its energy consumption. Nevertheless, the growth in ....[1] in India is expected to result in a more than doubling of ....[2] over the next 25 years, according to the International Energy Agency (IEA), the ....[3] for the developed world.

Germany introduced a package of measures in its National Climate Protection Programme in 2000. These include voluntary reduction agreements, minimum tariffs for electricity from ....[4] and legislation to encourage ....[5]. As a result of these and earlier policies, Germany has become the world leader in ....[6] installations. The benefits are counterbalanced, however, by the burden on taxpayers and consumers.

Nuclear energy offers the hope of producing power on a large scale without burning ....[7]. That would solve what many regard as the biggest threat the planet faces: ....[8], caused by a dramatic rise in the level of carbon dioxide since industrialisation.

How 'green' is your car?

Cars will carry colour-coded labels warning potential buyers of their impact on climate change, under measures to be launched by the UK government this week. The stickers are based on a car's emissions of carbon dioxide, the gas that scientists have identified as the principal cause of man-made climate change. Four-wheel drives will suffer the ignominy of having to display red stickers, while small, fuel-efficient models will sport labels in shades of green.

▲ Adapted from
The Observer

A Read the news extract and discuss these questions.

1 Why are petrol-guzzling four-wheel drives popular with consumers?

2 Do you think the British government's labelling initiative will prove effective?

3 What initiatives is the government taking in your country? What else could they do?

4 What alternatives are there to petrol-driven cars?

B Read the article *A dream of a hydrogen economy*. Identify the four main challenges involved in switching to hydrogen as a source of energy. How would you describe the tone of the article?

C Read the article again and choose the correct definitions for these words and phrases according to the context.

1 revving up (paragraph 1)
   a) making a car engine go much faster
   b) becoming more active

2 fleets (paragraph 2)
   a) groups of cars owned or controlled by one company
   b) able to run or move very quickly

3 a long shot (paragraph 2)
   a) an attempt in sport to throw, kick or hit the ball
   b) worth trying, even though it's unlikely to succeed

4 waste (paragraph 3)
   a) things such as money or skills that should be used effectively, but are not
   b) unwanted materials or substances that are left after a particular process

5 have yet to yield (paragraph 4)
   a) still have not produced
   b) have not provided profit from an investment yet

6 takes up roughly (paragraph 5)
   a) fills a particular amount of time or space approximately
   b) accepts a suggestion, offer or idea in an aggressive way

7 match (paragraph 5)
   a) be equal to something in value, size or quality
   b) be suitable for a particular person, thing or situation

8 rugged enough to withstand (paragraph 6)
   a) not likely to break easily and strong enough to remain unharmed by heat, cold, pressure, etc.
   b) be capable of defending yourself successfully against people who attack, criticise or oppose you

9 *they* (last sentence of paragraph 9) refers to:
   a) the Department of Energy
   b) gas hybrids

10 *that* (beginning of paragraph 10) refers to:
   a) the fact that gas hybrids can't solve the problem
   b) the fact that a substitute is needed for gasoline

A dream of a hydrogen economy

by Robert F. Service

1 Switching from fossil fuels to hydrogen could dramatically reduce urban air pollution, lower dependence on oil and reduce the build-up of greenhouse gases that threaten to trigger severe climate change. With those perceived benefits in view, the US, the European Union, Japan and other countries have sunk billions of government dollars into hydrogen initiatives aimed at revving up the technology and propelling it to market.

2 Car and energy companies are pumping billions more into building demonstration fleets and hydrogen fuelling stations. The only problem is that the bet on the hydrogen economy is at best a long shot. Recent reports from the US National Academy of Sciences and the American Physical Society conclude that researchers face huge challenges. The transition to a hydrogen economy, if it comes at all, will not happen soon.

3 Top of the list of difficulties is finding a simple and economical way to produce hydrogen. Today, by far the cheapest way to produce hydrogen is by using steam and catalysts to break down natural gas into H_2 and CO_2. But 15 per cent of the energy in natural gas is lost as waste heat during the reforming process. The upshot, according to Pete Devlin, who runs a hydrogen production programme at the US Department of Energy, is that it costs $5 to produce the amount of hydrogen that releases as much energy as a gallon of gasoline.

4 In addition to stripping hydrogen from fossil fuels, DOE and other funding agencies are backing innovative research ideas to produce hydrogen with algae, use sunlight and catalysts to split water molecules directly and siphon hydrogen from agricultural waste and other types of 'biomass'. Years of research in all these areas, however, have yet to yield decisive progress.

5 If producing hydrogen cheaply has researchers scratching their heads, storing enough of it on board a car has them utterly confused. Because hydrogen is the lightest element, far less of it can fit into a given volume than other fuels. At room temperature and pressure, hydrogen takes up roughly 3,000 times as much space as gasoline containing the same amount of energy. That means storing a useful amount in a fuel tank requires compressing it, liquefying it or using some other form of advanced storage system. Unfortunately, pressurised gas tanks are bulky, taking up to four times the volume of a conventional fuel tank to match the driving distance of a gasoline engine.

6 Another area in need of progress is the fuel cells that convert hydrogen to electricity. Fuel cells have been used to power spacecraft, but their high cost and other drawbacks have kept them out of everyday applications such as cars. Various technical challenges – such as making them rugged enough to withstand the shocks of driving and ensuring the safety of cars loaded with flammable hydrogen gas – are also likely to make hydrogen cars costlier to engineer and slower to win public acceptance.

7 Hydrogen fuel-cell cars also face an obstacle from outside: the infrastructure they need to refuel. If hydrogen is generated in centralised plants, it will have to be trucked or piped to its final destination. But because of hydrogen's low density, transporting the gas over long distances is too inefficient and expensive to be realistic – at least with current technology.

8 It will need a massive new hydrogen infrastructure to deliver the goods. For a hydrogen economy to catch on, the fuel must be available in 30 to 50 per cent of filling stations when mass-market hydrogen cars become available, says Bernard Bulkin, the former chief scientist at BP. Energy and car companies are unlikely to spend such sums unless they know mass-produced hydrogen vehicles are on the way. 'We face a chicken-and-egg problem that will be difficult to overcome,' says Michael Ramage, a former executive vice-president of ExxonMobil Research and Engineering, who chaired the NAS hydrogen report.

9 Because many of these problems require fundamental breakthroughs, many US researchers question their country's early heavy emphasis on expensive demonstration projects of fuel-cell cars, fuelling stations and other technologies. In response to the litany of concerns over making the transition to a hydrogen economy, Jo Ann Milliken, who heads hydrogen-storage research for DOE, points out that DOE and other funding agencies are not promoting hydrogen to the exclusion of other energy research. She says the inescapable truth is that 'we need a substitute for gasoline: gas hybrids are going to improve fuel economy, but they can't solve the problem'.

10 Yet, if that is the case, many energy experts argue, governments should be spending far more money to lower the technical and economic barriers to all types of alternative energy – hydrogen included – and bring it to reality sooner.

FINANCIAL TIMES

D **Discuss these questions.**

1 The final paragraph of the article mentions types of alternative energy. How many alternative sources of energy are you aware of?

2 What are some of the advantages, disadvantages and technological drawbacks of these alternatives?

3 Which sources of energy do you predict we will rely on in the future?

 Grammar reference: Discourse devices page 122

Business skills

Problem-solving

A 🎧 4.2 Listen to two conversations. What problem is discussed in each?

B 🎧 4.2 Listen again. Complete the sentences with the expressions used.

Conversation 1

I ....¹ that the staff turnover in our Rotterdam branch is consistently higher than in other branches.

It ....² that it's just a coincidence.

............³, they have a lot of work there are the moment.

It's too early ....⁴.

Maybe it ....⁵ take a trip over there and talk to him.

Conversation 2

It ....⁶ we've sold out of air-con units already.

I think we ....⁷ our order for next year.

The ....⁸ is the storage space.

Look, ...⁹. We don't need to make a decision right away.

C Look at the phrases in Exercise B. Which phrases and expressions are used to ...

a) introduce a problem?
b) suggest the cause of a problem?
c) propose a solution?
d) avoid making a decision?

D Match the two parts of the sentences to form useful expressions for discussing solutions to problems.

1 If we were
2 I suggest we
3 There is potential
4 We might as
5 I'd say it all
6 They could consider
7 A more in-depth study would come
8 It could work, provided

a) well think about a new heating system.
b) comes down to local conditions.
c) reducing the electricity bill.
d brainstorm some ideas.
e) we invest in R&D.
f) for increasing sales in our overseas markets
g) to place an early order, we could sell more
h) up with some solutions.

E 🎧 4.2 Role-play. Listen to the problems outlined in Exercise A again.

Student A: Turn to page 144.
Student B: Turn to page 150.

Proposal writing

F Look at the expressions in the Useful language box. Which are more often spoken? Which are more formal written linkers? Which can be both?

> ### Useful language
>
> **Linking expressions**
>
> **Adding extra information**
> in addition to, too, also, as well as, what's more, moreover, with regard to, with reference to, furthermore
>
> **Contrasting information**
> however, nevertheless, despite, in spite of, although, yet, (even) though, but
>
> **Introducing the result of previous information**
> as a result, so, consequently, as a consequence, given, due to, thereby, therefore, because of
> **Giving the reason for something**
> as, since, because, that's why, for this reason
>
> **Expressing a sequence of events**
> firstly/secondly/etc., in the first/second/etc. place, then, after that, finally, the final point/step/issue

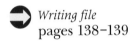
Writing file
pages 138–139

G Your company is relocating to new offices next year. Your managing director has asked you to investigate the problem of a lack of transport links to the new location and to propose a solution. Look at these informal notes and write a three-paragraph introduction to your report. Give your report a title. Use a maximum of 200 words and look at the panel below for tips on writing style.

Points for intro.

Background – move to the new business park on the outskirts in Jan. – city-centre offices expensive, company needs more room to grow, and it'll bring the offices and warehouse together in one place.

Problem – admin staff complain about how they're going to get there. I've checked with transport companies – they're not rerouting or planning new services soon because the park's new.

Proposal – morning/lunchtime/evening mini-bus to and from Kings Square because the bus, underground and train networks are good there. Cost about 53,000 euros a year. Benefits – cheap, quick service that'll keep staff happy.

> **Writing style**
> - Write with the reader in mind.
> - Keep your language simple.
> - Avoid slang, jargon and clichés.
> - Use gender-neutral language.
> - Use short sentences and paragraphs rather than complicated constructions.
> - Choose your words with care. A misused word can lose you credibility.
> - Choose a formal or semi-formal writing style, depending on your audience.

Energy saving at Supersun

Background

Supersun is a chain of 30 supermarkets in California. Tight profit margins and strong competition mean that the company has had to become increasingly creative with marketing strategies to retain customers and increase their customer base.

The company is now considering another, simpler method to improve the bottom line. Energy is the supermarket industry's biggest operating cost next to shelf stock, and Supersun could significantly reduce costs by improving energy performance.

Ever increasing energy bills and the government's 'clean air' legislation are also forcing the retail sector to find ways to reduce energy consumption and CO_2 emissions.

CERG CALIFORNIA ENERGY RESOURCE GROUP

The Financial Power of CERG®
for the Supermarket Industry

Make energy performance your competitive advantage

With profit margins below 2% and energy costs as high as $50 or more per square metre, supermarkets can make significant financial gains by focusing on energy performance.

For the average supermarket chain, a 10% reduction in annual energy costs …

▶ boosts profit margins by 9%

▶ increases earnings per share by nearly 10%

▶ is equivalent to a $400 increase in sales per square metre.

Listening 🎧 4.3

Listen to part of a meeting between Supersun's Store Managers and the company Finance Director, Jo Hopper. Make a list of action points for the new Energy Project Team to work on.

Task 1

You are members of the Energy Project Team. You have been asked to investigate some energy saving ideas. Read your information and report back to your team.

Student A: Turn to page 145.
Student B: Turn to page 151.

Retailers hit by a second gas and electricity price hike

CalPower today followed in the footsteps of other energy companies by announcing a significant gas and electricity price rise. Gas customers will pay an average 11.8% more, while electricity customers will see an average 8.8% increase. Today's price rise is CalPower's second rise this year, bringing their total increase up to nearly 17%. The company is blaming a rise on wholesale prices for its latest round of increases.

Typical energy consumption in supermarkets

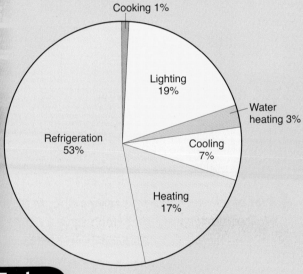

Store Managers' Monthly Meeting Agenda

1 Minutes of the previous meeting
2 Collection of data on energy costs
3 Report CO_2 emissions targets
4 Set up Energy Project Team

Task 2

You are members of the Energy Project Team. Devise an energy strategy for your company. Consider the following points:

- Brainstorm some ideas for encouraging the staff involved in the energy-efficiency campaign.
- What options would you prefer for reducing CO_2 emissions?
- What renewable energy sources could you consider to reduce your dependence on electricity?
- Decide some short-term and long-term measures to save energy and suggest a schedule for implementation, e.g. phase out refrigeration units.
- Several energy-saving innovations may decrease operating costs over the medium to long term. However, many of these measures will clearly increase capital costs. What arguments could convince management of the benefits of this investment?

Carbon dioxide per square metre from energy use

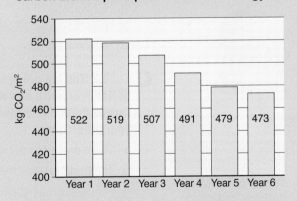

Writing

Write a report outlining your proposals for improving your company's energy efficiency and profit margins.

 Writing file pages 138–139

Employment trends

> *A lot of fellows nowadays have a B.A., M.D., or Ph.D. Unfortunately, they don't have a J.O.B.*
>
> Fats Domino, US musician, singer and songwriter

Listening and discussion

A 🎧 **5.1** Listen and decide which work pattern each person is talking about. What are the advantages and disadvantages of each? There are two items that you don't need.

a) Seasonal work
b) Teleworking
c) Casual labour
d) Migrant worker
e) Self-employment
f) Shift work
g) Fixed-term/Temporary contract
h) Part-time work

▲ Sean McGuinness, Business Studies Lecturer

B 🎧 **5.2** You are going to listen to Sean McGuinness, Business Studies Lecturer at Hammersmith and West London College, talking about the future of work. Do you think the following statements will be true or false? Listen and check your predictions.

1 There are fewer permanent contracts in the UK than there were a decade ago.

2 The trend is away from self-employment and temporary jobs in the UK.

3 People are now staying in their jobs longer.

4 There is increasing flexibility in employment contracts.

C 🎧 5.3 **Listen to the next part of the interview with Sean McGuinness. Put the topics in the order he mentions them.**

a) Occupations that are experiencing growth
b) Development of job enlargement
c) Proportion of people using the Internet and e-mail at work
d) Recommendations for government employment policy
e) Description of the 'hour-glass' economy

D 🎧 5.3 **Listen again and make notes for each of the five sections in Exercise C.**

E **Complete the sentences with these words and phrases from the interview.**

bargaining power	employment tenure	job stability
middle-management	minimum-wage	mobile workforce
service sector	skilled manual	

1 Jobs in the . . . . , such as catering and cleaning, are traditionally very low paid.

2 The average length of . . . . has, surprisingly, increased in the last decade in the UK.

3 Some experts predict that the expansion of the European Union will produce a more . . . . , with people moving around more for work.

4 With the economic downturn and new flexible contracts, there is less . . . . than there was a generation ago.

5 Will the phenomenon of job enlargement produce a reduction in . . . . positions?

6 Employees with fewer skills have always had less . . . . when it comes to negotiating pay and conditions.

7 Fewer . . . . workers, like plumbers and electricians, are being trained these days.

8 The government has recently introduced new . . . . legislation in an attempt to protect salaries.

F **Discuss these questions.**

• Do you share Sean McGuinness's views about the need for employment legislation? What are the arguments for and against regulating work?

• What are the employment trends in your region/country in terms of a) length of working week b) overtime c) holidays and d) unemployment?

• Do you think there is an acceptable work-life balance in your country or is there a corporate 'work-all-hours' culture?

• Do you think there is likely to be a reduction in the working week in the foreseeable future?

Reading and language

A Look at these factors that affect job satisfaction. Number them in order of importance in your view (1 = very important, 2 = quite important, 3 = not important). What other factors might you consider? Discuss your answers.

- flexible working hours
- friendly work atmosphere
- interesting work
- location
- perks, e.g. company car
- job security
- good pay
- promotion opportunities
- getting on well with the boss
- recognition for work

B What do you think are the main benefits and problems of managing a call centre in India? Read the first two paragraphs of the article on page 45 and check your answers.

C Read the whole article and choose the correct option to complete these sentences.

1 Despite significant growth in the sector, a high turnover of staff in India's call centres has led to ...
   a) loss of contracts.
   b) criticism of its work culture.
   c) closure of many call centres.

2 Young workers recruited by a call centre in India ...
   a) often leave the job to work in another centre that pays better.
   b) often leave, even if they don't have another job to go to.
   c) both (a) and (b).

3 As a result of some unfair tactics by competitive call centres, some multinationals are now ...
   a) increasing employee count at a faster rate.
   b) opening call centres in more remote places.
   c) retaining workers with attractive work facilities.

4 Allowing more mature employees to work from home or part-time is another way of ...
   a) telecommuting from home.
   b) attracting more experienced employees.
   c) dealing with the problem of staff turnover.

5 Despite high attrition rates, call centres in India are expected to ...
   a) continue to grow.
   b) do worse than those in the West.
   c) both (a) and (b).

 Grammar reference: Cohesive devices page 123

D Discuss these questions.

- Do you think that your job will be 'a job for life'? Why (not)?
- Which work sectors are currently experiencing a high turnover of staff in your country? Why do you think that is?
- In what other ways can a company make an unpopular job more attractive in order to retain employees?

 Grammar reference: Using inversion for emphasis page 124

India: Call centres ring the changes

by Edward Luce

1 India's call centres have a lot to answer for, according to the traditionalists. Not only has the booming sector helped spawn a brash new generation of profligate consumers, they say, but its revolving-door work culture is also undermining virtues such as loyalty, hierarchy, patience and discipline. Such anxieties might appear futile in view of the fact the sector has almost quadrupled its headcount in the past three years to more than 350,000 employees and looks set to continue expanding at 50 per cent a year.

2 Such concerns are also becoming the chief headache of Indian call-centre managers. Attrition rates, particularly in the larger hubs of Bangalore, Delhi and Mumbai, have jumped to more than 50 per cent a year in the past 18 months. This is still comfortably below the worst rates in western centres, where it could exceed 100 per cent. It is now posing serious challenges to India's increasingly stretched human resource managers. 'Until very recently, India had a culture where you took a job for life and never dreamed of leaving it unless you had a firm counter-offer,' says Noni Chawla, a management consultant and head-hunter in Delhi. 'But these young call-centre workers think nothing of taking a job, doing four weeks of training and leaving without anything else in the bag.'

3 There is an economic logic to such restlessness, however. In spite of India's unmatchable supply of English-speaking graduates – roughly 2.5m a year graduate in India, most of them with some level of English – the industry's rate of expansion has meant that demand has often outstripped supply. This is particularly true of the more established centres. 'I would advise companies that are setting up in India to avoid Bangalore in particular,' says Paul Davies, managing director of Onshore Offshore, a UK-based consultancy. 'There is a circuit where new companies come in and poach employees at higher salaries.'

4 One solution has been for companies to choose more isolated locations – as HSBC has recently done, when it opened a call centre on the coast of Andhra Pradesh. India has more than 50 towns with a population of 500,000 or more. Nevertheless, the strategy has its risks. One multinational that recently opened a centre in the Rajasthan capital of Jaipur has found it hard to boost its employee count at the pace it would wish. 'India has a lot of English speakers, but investors should not overestimate the number that are ready to work,' said Raju Bhatnagar, president of ICICI OneSource, an Indian third-party call centre, with 4,200 employees in Bangalore and Mumbai. 'It is probably better to face problems of attrition than of shortage of supply.'

5 Another remedy, which has taken on increasingly bizarre forms, is to make the workplace more attractive. Some companies have introduced salsa classes. Others have moved to multi-cuisine canteens. Almost all have on-site recreational facilities, such as football tables and cafés, albeit with limited success. 'You can only really attract people with such gimmicks,' says Mr Chawla. 'Retaining them is a different matter.'

6 More seriously, companies are also becoming more alert to dealing with employee trauma, particularly for those who work on the telephone, for example abusive calls. 'All calls are recorded, so we sit everyone around and replay it and ask everybody to suggest where it could have been better handled,' says Mr Bhatnagar. 'It helps the employee realise that it was nothing personal. In fact, only about 1 per cent of calls are abusive and training can do much to help.' 'The typical Indian response to anger is to fall silent, which only makes the Western customer worse,'

says Mr Davies. 'But they learn very quickly.'

7 Another solution – still in its infancy – is to hire part-time older employees, including housewives, and to allow them to telecommute from home. About 80 per cent of India's call-centre employees are aged between 20 and 25 and do not consider the industry to be a long-term career.

8 Another option, which one company is considering, is to open a call centre on campus and allow students to drop in and out and work part-time. 'The more flexible we can be, the more likely the employees are to stick around,' said a human-resources manager in Delhi.

9 Ultimately, though, there is not much companies can do to surmount the two core problems: that very few people like to sleep during the day and work at night (the permanent 'jet-lag syndrome') and that, in spite of some of the more glamorous-sounding outgrowths, most work in call centres is repetitive and is likely to remain so.

10 At the same time, there is little to suggest the problem of an inherently footloose workforce will pose a mortal threat to India's continued expansion. 'Call-centre attrition is a universal problem,' says Mr Bhatnagar. 'It has got worse in India, but not nearly to the extent you would see in the West.

FINANCIAL TIMES

Business skills

Resolving conflict

A Do you agree or disagree with the following statements? Discuss your answers.

- Conflict isn't necessarily a bad thing.
- It's best to keep things rational when there's a conflict rather than show your emotions.
- The most common kind of workplace conflict is between colleagues of the same grade.

B Look at this checklist of techniques used to deal with conflict. Which do you most often use? Which get the best/worst results? What other techniques have you used or seen used?

Conflict resolution techniques	Often	Sometimes	Hardly ever
Avoid the person or issue			
Change the subject			
Get an 'independent' mediator			
Admit you are wrong, even if you think you're not			
Turn the tension into a joke			
Work towards a mutually acceptable solution			
Apologise and give in			
Try to understand the other person's perspective			
Identify exactly what you agree or disagree on			
Complain until you get what you want			

C Read this description of communication problems. Do you consider yourself to be a good listener? How do you show other people you're listening to them?

According to Roger Fisher and William Ury in their book *Getting to Yes*, there are three major problems in communication: Firstly, people may not be talking to each other. Frequently each side has given up on the other and is no longer attempting any serious communication. Secondly, people don't pay enough attention to what other people say. Then there are misunderstandings which are compounded when people speak different languages.

The solution they propose is to listen actively; acknowledge what is being said and question your assumptions. Understanding is not agreeing, but unless you can show that you grasp how the other person sees things, you may be unable to explain your point of view to them. You therefore maximise the chance of having a constructive dialogue.

D 🎧 5.4 Listen to a conversation between two work colleagues. What techniques does Terry use to show he's listening actively to Yolanda? How would you resolve their situation?

Useful language

Active listening, paraphrasing and checking understanding
Let me see if I follow you. You're saying that ...
From your point of view, the situation looks like this ...
Do I understand correctly that what you're saying is ...?
OK, let me make sure I understand you. You say that ... Have I got that right?
I'm sorry, I missed that. Could you please repeat it?
I'm not sure I follow/understand you. Could you say that again?
Please go on.
I appreciate how you feel.
I can see why you feel that way.
Yes, you have a point when you say ... and here's how it looks from my angle ...

E Role-play. Read your information and try to resolve the conflicts with your partner.

Student A: Turn to page 145.
Student B: Turn to page 152.

F 🎧 5.5 How would you answer these questions? Listen to Rob Giardina. Does he mention the same points as you?

1 Why are there sometimes problems and misunderstandings when people write e-mails to each other?

2 What can you do to avoid these misunderstandings?

3 What can you do to solve the problem when there's obviously a conflict?

▲ Rob Giardina, international communications consultant

Writing: e-mails

G You're very busy at work at the moment and haven't had time to finish the monthly sales report. Read this e-mail from your manager and write a reply.

| Send | ▾ Stop | View | ✕ Delete | New | Reply | Tools |

From   Lynne Atkins
To   Yolanda Fowler
Subject Monthly sales

Where's that report?
Lynne

Writing file page 135

CASE STUDY

Delaney: call-centre absenteeism

Background

Delaney is a Dublin-based call centre working for a major car-hire company. Delaney employs 240 full-time and part-time agents. Most agents are women in their mid- to late 20s, many of them fluent in Spanish, French or German. The car-hire company has centralised most of its European operations to this call centre.

In common with many call centres, Delaney has high levels of staff turnover. The average length of service is only three years. This means high costs in terms of recruiting, selecting and training a call-centre agent. Added to that cost is the fact that new agents are not as productive as experienced agents. There is also concern about the competitiveness of the Irish call-centre industry.

Report

Read the report. What possible reasons could there be for the high levels of absenteeism and staff turnover in the company?

Report on Absenteeism
Executive Summary

The Human Resources Department monitored absenteeism over a 12-month period.

The findings show that there are high levels of absenteeism in the company. The average is seven days taken in sickness per agent each year.

The most common causes are reported as headaches and migraine, colds and flu, back problems and stress.

This level of absence may be causing delays in answering calls and is placing extra work and stress on colleagues.

In addition, there is the cost of finding replacement staff to cover the absence and the uncertainty that absence can cause in future planning.

Ultimately, callers and our clients may become dissatisfied with the level of customer service. The imperative therefore is for the company to find ways to reduce absenteeism and to deal with it when it occurs.

The consultant's report

Delaney recently hired a consultant to run a series of stress-management workshops. In her final assessment report, the consultant has highlighted a number of sources of conflict in the company. Read her report.

Task 1

Team Manager Mira Biswas and Tricia Monroe, one of her agents, meet to discuss Tricia's sickness absence. Work in pairs.

Student A: Turn to page 146.
Student B: Turn to page 152.

Stress Management Workshops at Delaney Call Centre

Final Assessment Report

As part of the training, staff were given a job satisfaction questionnaire to complete anonymously. A summary of the points are as follows:

- Staff report high levels of boredom and stress. Morale is generally low and many complain about an unfriendly workplace environment.
- Agents and team leaders alike mentioned the pressure of workload. Here is some representative feedback.

  'There are strict performance targets, and we lose the bonus if we don't meet them every month, plus we get a rude e-mail from the team leader.'
  'It's sometimes impossible to meet the targets. We only have five minutes to deal with each caller, but if there's a complicated booking or the customer can't decide what he wants, then you're stuck. The team leader just doesn't appreciate this.'
  'It makes me feel bad that I'm being unhelpful to callers, rushing them through the bookings, and I think they get angry and resentful sometimes for that reason.'
  'I'm desperate for a break sometimes after dealing with a difficult customer, but there's nowhere to go to chill out, and you'd be in trouble anyway for leaving your work station.'
  'I'm under pressure from my team manager to make sure my staff are meeting the targets. There's absolutely no flexibility, no room for manoeuvre or individual decision-making.'

- The majority of agents mentioned they are unhappy about call monitoring. They are hostile and feel suspicious about why calls are recorded. These comments typified their concerns:

  'I feel like I'm being spied on, that the team leader doesn't trust me to do my job.'
  'I have to watch every word I say.'
  'If a caller is rude, I don't feel supported by management.'

Task 2

Work in groups. You are the management team at Delaney. Prioritise the issues to deal with. Discuss and decide how best to resolve the issues.

- Decide company policy to manage and reduce absenteeism rates.
- Define good practice for use of call recording and monitoring.
- Review staff performance targets and the bonus scheme.
- Decide company internal e-mail policy.
- Devise a strategy to reduce staff attrition rates.

Writing

Some employees have complained that e-mails sent through the company e-mail system cause a threatening work environment. Write an e-mail to all staff stating the company's e-mail policy. Consider these points.

- Monitoring of staff e-mails
- Personal use of e-mail
- Prohibited content
- Dos and don'ts in the use of the company's e-mail system
- Training to ensure staff understand the importance of e-mail etiquette

 Writing file page 135

Business ethics

> *A business that makes nothing but money is a poor kind of business.*
>
> Henry Ford, US industrialist (1863–1947)

Listening and discussion

A **Discuss these questions.**

1 To what extent do you think competitive labour and production costs can affect a company's employees?

2 Name some companies that have had bad press over one of the following issues:

- employment practices
- product pricing
- environmental concerns
- financial irregularities

Was anything done to rectify the problems as a result?

▲ Miguel Morán,
International Dean,
EAE business school,
Barcelona, Spain

B ∩ **6.1** **Miguel Morán is talking about business ethics and social responsibility. Read the summaries, then listen to the first part of the interview and choose the more accurate one.**

1 Miguel Morán says that corporate responsibility or citizenship is largely to do with the action taken by companies in relation to the local environment and is a kind of compensation paid back to society. He says many companies only pay lip service to these issues. However, if a company is involved in unethical practices, it will be found out by its shareholders in the long run. He adds it's also difficult for multinationals to ensure workers in developing countries have decent wages due to local labour laws. Finally, he says it is up to governments to ensure that companies respect not only labour laws but also the human dignity of their employees.

2 Miguel Morán says that corporate responsibility is largely to do with how companies manage their business in order to present a positive image to society. Miguel believes that to be seen to be ethical is at least a step in the right direction towards social responsibility. He adds it's also difficult for multinationals to ensure workers have decent wages due to competitive local labour costs. Finally, he says it is the responsibility of multinationals to ensure that they respect the human dignity of their employees.

C Express your opinion on these statements by marking each one with one of the following symbols. Then compare and discuss your answers.

A+ = agree strongly   D = disagree in most cases
A   = agree in most cases   D+ = disagree strongly

1 Multinationals don't employ child labour any more.
2 Companies that employ children before the age of 14 should also pay for their education.
3 Banning child labour in some countries may create extreme poverty.
4 The Western world shouldn't force its codes of conduct on other countries.
5 Ultimately, social responsibility is up to the state and not business people.
6 Very few international companies have unethical practices.

D ∩ 6.2 Listen to the second part of the interview with Miguel Morán and compare your answers in Exercise C with his views. Use the following letters to record Miguel's views.

T = True   F = False   NS = Not stated

After listening, did any of your opinions change?

E ∩ 6.2 Listen to the second part of the interview again and complete these extracts with exactly five words for each gap.

1 What do they do? .... , and they just get them to do simple tasks.
2 The bottom line is that these children .... , who are living not only in poverty, but often in extreme poverty.
3 Companies must be responsible ethically and socially, but it's .... Western companies that child labour exists.
4 I think it's a mix. But our Western markets are .... and higher and higher wages.
5 But I think it is very positive that we are at this point where many companies are .... they are acting ethically or not.
6 New governments in Europe are .... done in the past.
7 Let's be honest. There are an awful lot of well-known companies that .... ethical but are producing unethically.
8 At the end of the day, it all comes down to ....

F Complete these views on CSR (Corporate Social Responsibility) with a suitable expression from the box.

> the bottom line   If I had to   the time has come for   Let's be
> two sides of the same coin   pay lip service to   face it

1 .... define CSR, I would say: the pursuit of profit is not enough; that companies need principles and that stakeholders want to see those principles in action.
2 .... honest, a decade ago few companies with social and environmental programme were unwilling to speak out for fear of being called hypocrites.
3 Let's .... , ethics and responsibility are ....
4 I don't think companies can just .... CSR and ignore what's happening around them without contributing to society.
5 I think .... companies to adopt and embrace CSR because .... is they know it's more likely to create wealth and shareholder value.

Reading and language

A Discuss these questions.

1 In contrast to Henry Ford, the economics guru Milton Friedman believes that 'the one and only social responsibility of business is to make profits.' What is your opinion?

2 In what ways, if any, do you think that a company is responsible to the following groups: shareholders, employees, suppliers, customers and the wider community? Can you think of any other groups?

B Read the first part of the article quickly. How would you summarise the writer's opinion? What do you think the word *waffle* means in the headline?

BUSINESS LIFE:Corporate responsibility without the waffle

By Alison Maitland

1 Passion, commitment, engagement, trust: it sounds like the start of a beautiful friendship. But when chief executives rely on these words to persuade a sceptical world of their company's responsible approach to society, they risk being a turn-off.

2 Almost every corporate responsibility report today kicks off with a message from the CEO or chairman. It presents an ideal opportunity to explain in concrete terms what being 'responsible' means for your business. It is a chance to show shareholders and other stakeholders that you understand the social or environmental risks facing your industry and that you are tackling them at board level.

3 These are issues that big investors will want to know even more about in the coming year – how companies are handling potential threats to long-term shareholder value, such as climate change, the explosion in obesity or human-rights lawsuits. New regulations, such as the forthcoming operating and financial review in the UK, will reinforce the need for a broad approach to risk management.

4 Yet some chief executives' messages are curiously cut off from these developments. Indeed, it can be hard to work out precisely what risks a company faces among the warm, fuzzy generalisations that still populate the language of corporate social responsibility.

5 Take the following from 'A word with Franck Riboud', chairman and chief executive of Danone, best known for dairy products such as yoghurt. 'Danone Way is a response to a real need – which is to preserve and pass on a culture based on our dual commitment to business success and social progress,' he says.

6 Or this from the foreword to Toshiba's latest corporate social responsibility report by Tadashi Okamura, president and CEO: 'For almost 130 years, Toshiba has been a force for social progress ... Along the way, we have earned the trust of society, and it is this trust that is our true reason for being. It is our motivation and our inspiration.'

7 John Elkington, co-director of SustainAbility, an international consultancy that tracks trends in non-financial reporting, says few forewords feel as if they have been written by the CEO as opposed to the public relations department. 'You rarely get a sense from the foreword about whether the CEO or chairman has read the report, or what they have found interesting and surprising.'

C Look at the article again. Find the words and expressions which have a similar meaning to the following.

1 provoking a negative reaction (paragraph 1)

2 people or organisations directly or indirectly affected by the activities of a company (paragraph 2)

3 trying to deal with difficult problems (paragraph 2)

4 problems taken to a court, by an individual or an organisation, for a legal decision (paragraph 3)

5 unconnected with (paragraph 4)

6 understand something by thinking about it (paragraph 4)

7 not clear, difficult to understand (paragraph 4)

8 promise to do something or behave in a certain way (paragraph 5)

9 short introduction (to a book or report) (paragraph 6)

10 records or studies the development of something over time (paragraph 7)

D Read the second part of the article below. Identify the four points the author believes CEOs should address and examples of good company practice.

8   To be effective, what should your introduction 11 cover? First, specific examples of the challenges the company faces and how you are tackling them.

9   Arun Sarin, chief executive of Vodafone, talks about potential abuse of human rights and labour standards in the group's vast £23bn supply chain and how it is starting to manage these risks through a code of ethical purchasing.

10   But his opening lines risk leaving readers disoriented. 12 'We already have a clear compass,' he states. 'One of our four values is "passion for the world around us" and one of our six strategic goals is to "be a responsible business".' He leaves us guessing what the other values and goals are.

11   The second thing is evidence of transparency. Bob Eckert, chairman and CEO of Mattel, refers to the global manufacturing principles that the toy manufacturer put in place in 1997. 'We've welcomed independent, third-party auditing of our adherence to these principles and we've posted the results for public viewing on our corporate website (www.mattel.com),' he writes.

12   Third, a recognition of the importance of governance. In his letter, Mr Eckert says that corporate responsibility at Mattel will 14 from now on be overseen by the board's nominations and corporate governance committee, which is renamed the governance and social responsibility committee.

13   Novo Nordisk, the Danish drugs group, links good governance directly to the way companies face up to society's changing expectations. 'It is continuous hard work,' write Lars Rebien Sorensen, president and CEO, and Mads Ovlisen, 15 chairman. Last year they strengthened their risk-management system, continued their work on board self-evaluation and developed a new share-based incentive programme for executives.

14   Fourth, credibility. In Gap's first social responsibility report this year, Paul Pressler, president and CEO, begins by telling readers that, when he decided to join the company in 2002, his teenage daughter asked him: 'Doesn't Gap use sweatshops?' Much of the rest of his message is about what the company is doing to improve conditions in the garment industry and how difficult this is. It is both personal and believable.

15   It is high time for plain speaking across the board. The foreword to next year's corporate responsibility report will mark you out either as a leader who has contemplated the risks ahead or as a CEO who has jumped on to the bandwagon without really knowing why.

FINANCIAL TIMES

E Discuss the following questions.

1 Governments in the US and the EU are considering legislation to stop food companies advertising junk food to children. How far should the food industry be held responsible for people's health problems?

2 If you were the CEO of one of the companies mentioned in the article, what would you see as the risks ahead for your company, and what would be its social responsibility?

F Look at these extracts from various CSR reports. Match the correct expression (a–h) with the multiword verbs in italics.

a) gradually stopped using
b) done, as expected or promised
c) do the same thing
d) avoid doing anything about

e) can be included in or classified as
f) ensure we do what we've promised
g) formally established
h) explain in a clear way

1 We think it is vital that we *set out* what we expect of our suppliers.

2 The company's policy is not to *shy away from* difficult issues.

3 We hope this initiative will motivate others in the industry to *follow suit*.

4 The company is taking action in this area and has already *phased out* a number of suspect chemicals.

5 This will enable our stakeholders to *hold us to account*.

6 Our strategy *falls into* three categories.

7 Their work is *carried out* in accordance with safety standards.

8 The Social Responsibility team was *set up* in 2003.

 Grammar reference: Multiword verbs page 125

Business skills

Ethical problem-solving

Useful language

Proposing solutions
In this situation, I'd ...
In this case, I'd ...
What I'd do/say is ...
If it were the case that ...

Looking at problems from different angles
Having said that, ...
On the other hand, ...
At the same time, ...
There are a lot of issues at play here.
You could argue that ...

Giving reasons for opinions
on the grounds that ...
for the reason that ...
Seeing/given that ...

Playing for time
That's a difficult/tricky/
interesting one.
Let me see, ...
It (really) depends on ...

A Work in pairs. Look at these ethical work problems and discuss how you would respond to the three situations. Use some of the expressions for problem-solving in your answers.

Situation 1: An accounting dilemma
You work in accounts. Whilst checking the company accounts one day, you discover that your financial director has been claiming irregular expenses. Expenses include opera tickets, two digital cameras and a laptop computer which you think he bought for his daughter. Some of the expenses have already been paid to him, but not all. What would you do?

Situation 2: A generous present
One of your suppliers sends you an unexpected present of a case of 12 bottles of expensive wine. The following week, they call you to ask if you have received the wine and whether the company is going to renew their contract for the next year. You tell them the decision has not been made yet, and they intimate that if you renewed their contract, they would give you more presents, including a weekend away for two. You have already drunk three of the bottles during family meals. What would you do?

Situation 3: Choosing tenders
Your company is going to build new offices in Algeria, and you are responsible for examining tenders for all the contractors interested in building the new office. The two best tenders are of equal merit, and you were intending to recommend them both and let the Board of Directors decide. This morning, over coffee with your managing director, he mentions that he is very good friends with one of the two contractors on the shortlist and would be very disappointed if they did not win the contract. What would you do?

B 🎧 6.3 Listen to some people talking about the situations and compare your answers with their response. Did you come to the same conclusion as the speakers?

C 🎧 6.3 Listen again to the three speakers and complete these extracts with between four and six words.

Speaker 1

1 .... speak to him to confirm or reject my suspicions.

2 .... go to someone higher up in the organisation.

Speaker 2

3 .... respond to this kind of blackmail when I got the call.

4 .... that, if .... that the decision was made in their favour, and I kept on receiving presents, I'd reject them .... it's unethical.

Speaker 3

5 You know, you .... your job may be on the line, you might have debts, a mortgage to pay ...

6 If the two offers were *exactly* equal in merit, ... in choosing the director's friend.

Managing meetings

D 🎧 **6.4 Look at the tips for managing meetings and writing up action points. Listen to an extract from a problem-solving meeting discussing procedures for employing staff. What was on the agenda? Do you think the meeting was managed well and effective? Why (not)?**

Tips for effective meetings and action points: PARTAKE

PARTicipants: choosing the right ones is the key to the success of any meeting. Make sure all participants can contribute and choose good decision-makers and problem-solvers. Try to keep the number of participants to a maximum of 12.

Agenda: check all meeting aims have been addressed; will you need a future meeting?

Key points and actions: summarise the who/what/when. Minutes should be short and concise and issued within 24 hours.

End by allocating ten minutes to review how you performed as a team: what were the positive/negative points, e.g. time-wasting, misunderstandings or conflicts?

E **Discuss these questions.**

1 What kind of meetings do you normally attend?

2 How many participants are there? Who are they?

3 In what language(s) are the meetings held?

4 Who chairs or leads the meetings, if anyone?

5 How is it made clear who is responsible for each action point?

6 Do you enjoy participating in meetings? Why (not)?

7 How do you decide which meetings to attend?

F **How do you think meetings in your company or organisation could be more effective? Hold a meeting to discuss the agenda on page 160. Make sure one person leads or chairs the meeting, but all participants need to take notes.**

Writing: action minutes

G **Using your notes from the previous meeting, write up a summary of the action points or minutes for what was decided.**

 Writing file page 136

Stitch Wear clothing

Background

Stitch Wear is a popular US-based company, manufacturing casual wear and sports clothing, with branches in the US and Europe and factories primarily in Pakistan and Indonesia.

It has recently received bad publicity due to working conditions in the manufacturing countries, namely in the Punjab province of Pakistan, where the provincial government has now outlawed child labour. A British newspaper broke the story on Stitch Wear employing children under 14 in its Asian factories. The Worldwide Labour Association (WLA) then followed up with an extensive campaign, inciting the public to boycott Stitch Wear's products.

The board of directors has recognised the need to rethink the company's policy on corporate responsibility. They have given the PR department the task of devising a strategy, including high-profile corporate sponsorship of community projects. Stitch Wear now needs to boost company sales, remain competitive in the clothing industry and present a more positive ethical image to the public.

Stitch Wear
sales for last three quarters

	Billion dollars
First quarter	5.1
Second quarter	5.0
Third quarter	4.9

main competitor
sales for last three quarters

	Billion dollars
First quarter	4.9
Second quarter	5.0
Third quarter	5.1

The media

Look at the newspaper article. How will the scandal affect Stitch Wear?

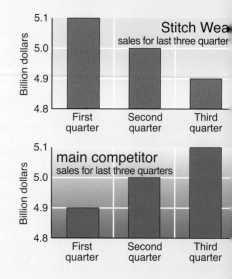

Manchester Daily

Have we been stitched up?

Stitch Wear, the US-based clothing company specialising in casual wear and sports clothing, is due for a clean-up as news hits the street that Stitch Wear may be 'stitching up' its customers.

This paper has found evidence supporting claims by the Worldwide Labour Association (WLA) that the company has been using children under 14 years of age in sweatshops across the globe, from Pakistan to Peru.

Spokesperson for ILA, Tania Yong said, 'The provincial government of the Punjab province in Pakistan outlawed child labor two years ago, but we know for a fact that Stitch Wear are still employing children as young as ten.'

The WLA are raising awareness with their publicity campaign 'Who stitched us up?' They're asking consumers to check the ethics of companies. Tania Yong explains: 'What may seem a great bargain in the store is probably the product of a small pair of hands, often undernourished and, more often than not, without the basic right to the kind of education that children in the West simply take for granted.'

Listening 🎧 6.5

Listen to an ethics consultant talking to the Head of PR (Public Relations) at Stitch Wear about Corporate Social Responsibility projects by competitors in the industry. Note down any suggestions that are made and whether the response from the Head of PR or the consultant is favourable or not.

Suggestions for CSR improvement	Response
1 Consultant: be careful with language in the CSR report; has to sound real and sincere.	Head of PR agrees.
2	
3	
4	
5	

CSR meeting agenda

1 Proposal for a CSR report, assuring that no children under 14 will be employed by the company or its suppliers; Stitch Wear is committed to its social and environmental responsibilities.

2 Visit overseas manufacturers more frequently to ensure point number one is enforced.

3 Set up a series of educational, technical training and/or health programs for child employees (14–16).

4 Purchasing department: consider a sustainable supply chain, including a supplier-screening policy.

5 Suggestions for new slogan and marketing campaign to endorse Stitch's CSR philosophy.

6 Sponsorship of local projects involving children/young teenagers.

7 Creation of a new team under the supervision of a Corporate Responsibility Officer.

8 Any other suggestions

Task

The Head of PR has called a meeting with the other departmental heads to discuss how the company can improve its CSR profile. You need to decide on how to deal with the current crisis and present the solutions to the board of directors. Not all the proposals need be accepted. Your initial concern is to improve the company's public image, but any proposals will need to be viable and attractive to financial stakeholders. Work in groups of four.

Student A: Turn to page 146.
Student B: Turn to page 152.
Student C: Turn to page 156.
Student D: Turn to page 158.

Look at the agenda for the meeting and make any preparatory notes regarding how these issues will directly affect your department.

Writing

Write up the action points from the meeting that directly affect your department. Bear in mind these proposals will initially be presented to the board of directors, but will also need to be acceptable to financial stakeholders as much as the media.

➲ *Writing file* page 136

Stitch Wear

4 Energy

Linking ideas

A Match the three parts of the sentences.

1 The homes are designed to use solar panels		
2 He talks about protecting the environment	yet	we'll have to find other fuels.
	as	you can never find a parking space.
3 The hydrogen economy is still a dream	as well as	his car's a real petrol guzzler.
	so	a sudden surge in demand.
4 I always take the bus to work	due to	the years spent on scientific research.
5 There was a power cut	despite	electricity for heating.
6 The world's oil supplies will soon run out		

B Which of these linkers could be used to replace the linking expressions in the previous exercise?

in spite of   in addition to   because of   since   because
therefore   as a result of   even though

C Which linkers from Exercises A and B do the following?

a) add extra information
b) contrast information
c) introduce the result of previous information
d) give the reason for something

Vocabulary

A Put the collocations from the box in the correct sentences.

carbon-dioxide emissions   energy consumption   energy-efficient
environmentally friendly   fossil fuels   four-wheel drive   global warming
greenhouse gases   renewable energy   wind power

1 Oil and coal are examples of ....
2 .... and solar panels are examples of sustainable or ....
3 Carbon dioxide and methane are examples of ....
4 Their new .... guzzles about a litre of petrol every kilometre.
5 .... is the general increase in the Earth's temperature caused by ....
6 During the next 25 years, ... is projected to grow at the fastest rate in China.
7 These cleaning products are .... because they're biodegradable.
8 They've installed new .... light bulbs in the offices to cut electricity bills.

B The case study on page 40 looks at energy costs in Supersun supermarkets. The Energy Management Team put this information on the staff noticeboards. Complete the notice using the correct form of the word in brackets.

Good results in our first year

Since the implementation of our new energy-efficiency programme, we have seen a five-per-cent ......[1] (*reduce*) in our energy bills. Our ......[2] (*invest*) in renewable energies, including solar panels in our new Highwood store, has also allowed us to cut CO_2 emissions in line with recent government ......[3] (*legal*).

We would like to congratulate all of you for making this programme a success. There is no doubt that this ......[4] (*improve*) in our energy ......[5] (*perform*) gives us a ......[6] (*compete*) advantage in the retail food industry. That's good news for our customers, for our business and for all of us.

Writing

A You are a member of the Energy Management Team where you work or study. Write a short report (250 words) outlining your proposal for improving energy efficiency.

B You are the manager of a gym. You have had several complaints from members recently that the facilities are very full during the peak lunchtime and evening periods, so much so that they can't always get access to the training machines or certain gym classes. Also, they complain they have to queue for showers, and the water is often cold. Discuss the problems and suggest some possible solutions.

You have been asked by your regional manager to write a report on your proposed solutions to the problems at the gym before you implement any changes. Write an introduction of 200–250 words to your report. Include the following points:

- Give some background: how long the gym has been open, the facilities, how many members there are and when the peak periods are.
- Explain the problems
- Summarise your proposals

5 Employment trends

Vocabulary

Choose the phrase from the box to describe each work pattern. There are two extra options you don't need.

Casual labour   Fixed-term/Temporary contract   Full-time
Migrant worker   Part-time   Seasonal work   Self-employment
Shift work   Teleworking   Unemployed

1 We're looking for someone to work mornings only.
2 The hotel needs 50 more staff for the summer months.
3 The job plays havoc with your sleep patterns. This week I'm on nights.
4 The position is for four months to cover maternity leave.
5 It saves me commuting time, but I miss the company being at home.
6 She's between jobs at the moment, but she's got a few interviews lined up.
7 It wasn't hard to get a resident's permit when we first came here, and there was plenty of work.
8 Being your own boss is more stressful, but more rewarding too.

Cohesive devices

Read this article and replace the underlined sections with one of the expressions in the box to improve the style.

in this respect   its   its   them   their   this   this knowledge

By the year 2050, for the first time in history, there will be more people in the world over the age of 60 than under the age of 15. The fact that there will be more older people[1] has profound implications for employers and should provide an incentive for companies to fight age discrimination and accommodate older workers, creating challenging careers to persuade older workers[2] to stay in their jobs longer. The best employers are already thinking about their policies and practices towards age, but the vast majority are not. Often cited as an example of an employer with good age policies[3] is B&Q. Because of the nature of B&Q's[4] business, the British DIY retailer B&Q has found that having older workers on the company's[5] staff has enhanced sales and customer loyalty.

Older employees often have a basic knowledge of DIY, and customers, who tend to associate older people with a basic knowledge of DIY[6], feel comfortable asking older people's[7] advice.

Inversion for emphasis

A customer writes an e-mail to complain to Delaney, the call centre in the case study on page 48. There are six errors in the word order. Find them and correct them.

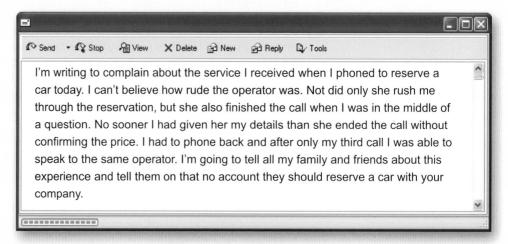

I'm writing to complain about the service I received when I phoned to reserve a car today. I can't believe how rude the operator was. Not did only she rush me through the reservation, but she also finished the call when I was in the middle of a question. No sooner I had given her my details than she ended the call without confirming the price. I had to phone back and after only my third call I was able to speak to the same operator. I'm going to tell all my family and friends about this experience and tell them on that no account they should reserve a car with your company.

Writing e-mails

Write a reply to the Delaney customer's e-mail.

Communication skills

Match the expressions which have a similar meaning.
1 Sorry, I missed that. Could you go over it again?
2 Let me see if I follow you. You're saying that you're overworked.
3 Please go on.
4 From your point of view, they aren't being very co-operative.
5 I appreciate how you feel.
6 Yes, you have a point when you say that. Here's how it looks to me.

a) As you see it, they are not helping very much.
b) I'd like to hear more.
c) If I understand you correctly, you feel you have too much to do.
d) That's a fair comment. This is how it strikes me.
e) I can see why you feel that way.
f) Would you mind repeating that? I didn't quite catch it.

6 Business ethics

Reading

Read this short article about business ethics. In most of the lines (1–12), there is one extra word that does not fit. Some of the lines, however, are correct. If the line is correct, put a tick (✔) in the space next to that line. If there is an extra word in the line, write that word in the space.

Child labour and oil spills grabbed the headlines when corporate

responsibility first came to prominence in the mid-1990s. Now I think   1 ....

the time has come out for tax avoidance to be put on the agenda. It all   2 ....

comes down for to paying what you owe, where you owe it. In many   3 ....

cases, multinationals are simply not paying taxes even though they pay the   4 ....

lip service to transparency. Let's face at it, that gives them an unfair   5 ....

advantage over national companies. I think it is crystal clear that the   6 ....

use of tax havens is irresponsible, even if that it is entirely legal. The bottom 7 ....

line is there this is not an argument about legality; it is an argument about   8 ....

responsibility. I put this view to the CEO of Harper Chemicals. He said   9 ....

"I must say you there is no black-and-white answer. I don't think you   10 ....

can not necessarily write down precisely what is morally right and wrong.   11 ....

Our general policy is that we want to respect the laws of countries in which   12 ....

we operate."

Vocabulary

Look at these words related to Corporate Social Responsibility. Complete the table.

Adjective	Noun
............[1]	passion
committed	............[2]
trusting/trustworthy	............[3]
............[4]	persuasion
sceptical	............[5]
............[6]	risk
............[7]	environment
threatening	............[8]
developed/developing	............[9]
............[10]	success
............[11]	progress
inspired/inspiring/inspirational	............[12]

Reading

Harper is an international chemical company. Read the company CEO's report on corporate responsibility and use the correct multiword verbs from the box to replace the underlined expressions.

| carried out   falls into   follow suit   hold us to account |
| phase out   set out   set up   shy away from |

Our director of corporate citizenship was appointed five years ago. Her first task was to <u>formally establish</u>[1] a team that would co-ordinate our efforts. Our aim is complete transparency, allowing our stakeholders to <u>ensure we do what we've promised</u>[2]. We are not going to <u>avoid doing anything about</u>[3] difficult issues. It is our policy to <u>explain in a clear way</u>[4] what we are doing to be a more responsible company. Our approach <u>can be classified as</u>[5] two phases: firstly, to identify the products which are harmful to the environment, and secondly to <u>gradually stop using</u>[6] these chemicals. All our work is <u>done, as expected,</u>[7] in accordance with safety standards. We hope this initiative will motivate others in the industry to <u>do the same thing</u>[8].

Writing

You work for the PR department of Stitch Wear (see the case study on page 56). You receive this e-mail from a young customer. Write to the customer explaining what your company is doing about the scandal.

I read the recent news story about Stitch Wear using children in Asia to make your clothes. I don't think ten-year-olds should be making shirts for us, and my friends and family feel the same way. We're all going to boycott your stuff until you stop exploiting kids.

Maxine Powell

Finance and banking

Money is better than poverty, if only for financial reasons.
Woody Allen, film director and actor

OVERVIEW ▼

☐ **Listening and discussion**
Changes in international banking

☐ **Reading and language**
Marconi repays £669m of debt; US Airways vows to rise again

☐ **Business skills**
Giving presentations
Describing financial performance
Writing: introduction to a presentation

☐ **Case study**
Cost-cutting at Erstaunliche Autos

Listening and discussion

A Discuss these questions.

1 Which are the most popular banks or savings banks in your country? Why do you think they are successful?

2 How do you prefer to bank? What are the advantages/disadvantages of Internet banking compared with visiting your local branch?

3 In what ways is your banking different from the way you or your company carried out financial transactions five or ten years ago?

B Complete the sentences with the words and phrases from the box in the correct form.

| ATM   bond   capital   corporate restructuring   letter of credit   trade |

1 'I'm sorry, sir, we don't accept credit cards here.'
'Oh, do you mind telling me where the nearest .... is?'

2 We usually deal with .... in our export department. It's the best way to ensure our customers pay the right amount for the goods within a specified period.

3 Bribery and corruption at the company prompted some .... of the board of directors and resignation of the CEO.

4 Charlotte didn't have a lot of savings, but she'd inherited some old .... and gas shares from her grandmother which had accumulated interest over the years.

5 They started .... securities in the hope they would make some quick profits.

6 A market where debt or equity securities are traded with a view to raising long-term finance is referred to as a '............' market.

▲ Joan Rosàs, Director of International Business Development, la Caixa savings bank, Barcelona, Spain

La Caixa is Spain's largest savings bank. The country's 46 savings banks are private foundations that cannot be bought or sold. They do not issue equity and therefore have no shareholders.

C 🎧 **7.1 Listen to an interview with Joan Rosàs, who talks about recent changes in international banking. Say whether these sentences are true or false.**

1 Factors affecting international banking have been new technologies, globalisation, regulatory frameworks and an increase in the use of more complex banking services.

2 Thanks to new regulations, the way banks and businesses can move money around the world has changed significantly.

3 Joan Rosàs says that e-mails and electronic direct debit are examples of how technology has improved international business.

4 Cheque truncation is an example of how IT systems have improved international banking transactions.

5 According to Joan Rosàs, all companies now have direct access to capital markets.

6 Bond issues, mergers and acquisitions and corporate restructuring are all examples of fairly basic business banking services.

D 🎧 **7.2 Listen to the second part of the interview with Joan Rosàs and complete these notes on future developments in international banking.**

> **Banks and financial institutions**
>
> Large, ... [1] banks will remain, but we'll see an increase in .... [2] banks. .... [3] banks will continue to .... [4] because they are business-orientated and tend to focus on .... [5].
>
> **Products and services**
>
> We'll see an increase in new products or services like .... [6] services, which consist of a package including .... [7] accounts, ... [8], renting, pension funds, ... [9] finance, all under one label.
>
> **New delivery channels**
>
> 'Clicks and .... [10]' banking is where you combine both the .... [11] network with .... [12] banking. '............ [13]' banking uses the Internet only.
>
> WAP services use .... [14] for all banking transactions. .... [15] banking means you can bank from home using the .... [16].

E **Discuss these questions.**

1 How are the trends described in the interview affecting business in your country?

2 What new delivery channels have you used for carrying out your banking transactions (e.g. Internet, WAP services, digital TV banking)?

3 What other changes do you think will take place in the way we carry out banking and financial transactions in the future?

BUSINESS RECOVERY

There was a time, not so long ago, when a company that failed was placed in the hands of a receiver, who wound it up, paid off the taxman and the banks, and distributed the remaining handful of coins among other creditors.

Today, closing down a business in trouble is increasingly seen as the last resort. Creditors have learnt that it is better to hire temporary executives, organise a voluntary debt restructuring, or even stand aside as the business trades on with court-approved protection.

FINANCIAL TIMES

Ⓐ Discuss these questions.

1 Which of these factors can potentially cause a company financial problems? Can you think of any other internal or external factors?

- poor budgetary and cashflow control
- increases in energy and other costs
- large acquisitions
- high leverage (amount of borrowing)
- executive salaries

2 Read the extract on the left about business recovery. What are the arguments for and against turning around a business in trouble?

Ⓑ Work in pairs.

Student A: Read the article about Marconi.
Student B: Read about US Airways.

Answer these questions and tell your partner about your article.

1 What factors appear to have caused the company's financial problems?
2 What has the company done and what is it doing now to solve its financial crisis?
3 Does the company seem likely to go bankrupt? Why (not)?

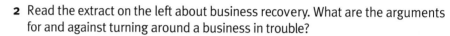

Marconi repays £669m of debt

Mark Tran

1 Struggling telecoms equipment maker Marconi today took a giant step towards recovery as it announced the early repayment of £669.5m of debt following its restructuring last year. The money was paid well ahead of the 2008 deadline set by creditors, and will save Marconi £55.8m in annual interest charges. 'The early paydown of all of our restructuring debt is an excellent achievement,' Mike Parton, the Marconi chief executive, said. 'We have emerged with a strong balance sheet, and can now fully focus our efforts on growing our business.'

2 Today's repayments follow better-than-anticipated returns from the sale of businesses and improved trading performance at the company. Following an increase in confidence among telecoms customers, Marconi announced its first quarterly profits for three years in May. Last month, the improved trading performance enabled three directors, including Mr Parton, to raise almost £9m from cashing in stock options granted after they met performance targets, including those for debt reduction.

3 Marconi staved off collapse in May last year thanks to a restructuring in which banks and bondholders agreed to write off most of the company's debt in return for control. Shareholders saw their holdings virtually wiped out.

4 The near-collapse of the company was one of the most spectacular in British corporate history. Formerly GEC, Marconi was an industrial giant built up by Arnold Weinstock, one of Britain's premier industrialists. At its zenith, it was worth more than £30bn. Problems began when Lord Weinstock's successor, Lord Simpson, decided to focus on telecommunications, selling

profitable defence businesses and dropping the name GEC in favour of Marconi.

5 Marconi ran into trouble three years ago when the hi-tech bubble burst. Demand for its products from customers such as BT dried up, and it was left with huge debts after an ill-timed acquisitions spree. Thousands of jobs were lost, and Marconi currently employs one third of its 12,400 global workforce at UK sites in Coventry, Beeston in Nottingham, Liverpool and Chelmsford.

The **Guardian**

US Airways vows to rise again

David Teather in New York

1 US Airways yesterday underlined its determination to stay airborne after filing for bankruptcy protection for the second time in as many years. Lawyers for the company said the management was intent on cutting costs and returning the airline to health, despite dire warnings that a second bankruptcy would spell the end for the business. 'The management team isn't here to preside over a liquidation,' US Airways lawyer Brian Leitch told the bankruptcy court.

2 US Airways shares went into free fall on Wall Street, dropping 45% to 81 cents in early trade. The seventh-largest airline in the United States filed for bankruptcy late on Sunday after failing to secure a further $800m (£440m) in annual savings from its workforce. The company said it was entering bankruptcy in order to conserve cash as it struggles with high fuel costs and competition from low-cost carriers. US Airways asked the court for permission to skip a $110m pension payment due this week, and said it might ask to terminate the plans for mechanics and flight attendants altogether.

3 Company chairman David Bronner last month warned that the probability of emerging from a second bankruptcy was 'about 1% to 2%'. Chief executive Bruce Lakefield on Sunday backed away

from those comments. 'We have come too far and accomplished too much to simply stop the process and not succeed,' he said. 'A US Airways with low costs and low fares will be a dynamic competitor.'

4 United Airlines remains in bankruptcy, and Delta Air Lines has warned it might face the same fate unless workers grant concessions.

*The***Guardian**

C Read both articles again. Use the context to help you choose the correct meaning of these words and expressions.

Marconi

1 returns (paragraph 2)
   a) rejected products   **b)** profit made

2 increase in confidence (paragraph 2)
   a) feeling that the economic situation is good
   b) need for secrecy

3 cashing in (paragraph 2)
   a) exchanging an investment for money
   b) profiting unfairly from a situation

4 staved off (paragraph 3)
   a) caused to happen
   b) prevented from happening

5 write off (paragraph 3)
   a) officially say that someone does not have to pay a debt
   b) send a letter

6 wiped out (paragraph 3)
   a) extremely tired   **b)** destroyed financially

7 acquisitions spree (paragraph 5)
   a) long time spent selling off parts of a company
   b) short time spent buying up other companies

US Airways

8 health (paragraph 1)
   a) good financial position
   b) not harmful or dangerous

9 dire (paragraph 1)
   a) cautionary   **b)** extremely serious

10 spell the end (paragraph 1)
   a) suggest a recovery   **b)** signify the closure

11 went into free fall (paragraph 2)
   a) went down very quickly   **b)** stayed stable

12 filed for bankruptcy (paragraph 2)
   a) informed the authorities that a business was unable to pay its debts
   b) informed the press that the company has financial problems

13 to skip (paragraph 3)
   a) to reduce   **b)** not to make

14 grant concessions (paragraph 4)
   a) agree to allow the company to pay less than it would normally
   b) give the company the right to conduct business activity

---

D Discuss these questions.

1 Which business sectors are doing well/badly at the moment? Do some research on the Internet to find out more.

2 Which business sectors and companies would you consider investing in nowadays and why? For example: the airline industry, car manufacturing, biotechnology, telecoms, construction or pharmaceuticals.

Business skills

Giving presentations

A 🎧 **7.3 Listen to an introduction to a presentation and complete the speaker's notes. What expressions does she use to engage the audience's interest?**

Good morning. My name's Diana Holden, I'm the Finance Director for BZ Systems. I'm here today .... [1], our shareholders, about the bright future ahead for our company. I'll .... [2] on last year's financial results. Then I'll talk about our recent performance in the past quarter. Finally, ... [3] our projections and the company's expansion plans for the future. .... [4] agree that BZ is growing from strength to strength. There'll be an opportunity at the end of my presentation to .... [5] you might have.

Presentation tips

Preparation
- Know your audience and visualise your presentation as a dialogue with them.
- Rehearse your presentation – it will help you to feel relaxed on the day.

Visual aids
- Make visual aids clear and simple. Label graphs and figures.
- Add a short sentence or two to a graph describing the conclusions to be drawn.

Delivery
- Pay special attention to your introduction – aim to engage the audience's interest.
- In the opening lines, establish who you are, what organisation you represent and why you are here.
- Briefly explain the purpose of your talk and provide an overview.

Describing financial performance

B 🎧 **7.4 Look at the graph below and listen to Mark Wyllie, CME's Vice President for Tax and Planning, presenting it. Complete this description of the company's performance and projections.**

What we've got here is a chart showing how our markets are expected .... [1] Western Europe over the .... [2]. The data comes from Zenith Optimedia, who do independent forecasting for TV ad markets, and what you can see from year one through to year seven is that Western Europe is expected to .... [3] in advertising terms, but that Eastern Europe, as shown here indexed to year one, by year seven will be .... [4] the year-one market, i.e. over the next five to six years, our sales are expected to double as well.

Central European Media Enterprises (CME) is an international television broadcasting company which operates eight networks in five countries across Central and Eastern Europe.

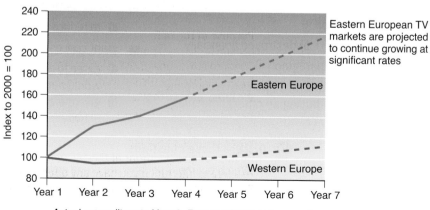

Eastern European TV markets are projected to continue growing at significant rates

Eastern Europe

Western Europe

Actual expenditure to Year 3. Forecast for Year 4 onwards.

 Grammar reference: Language of trends page 126

C 🎧 7.5 **Look at the chart on page 160. Listen to the next part of Mark Wyllie's presentation and correct the five errors in the chart.**

D **Look at these extracts from company performance reports in the financial press. What expressions are used to describe trends? Add them to the 'Language of trends' table on page 126.**

1 **The firm sank deep into the red during the technology slump.**

5 Shares in the company dropped sharply after it made losses of £3m this year.

2 Renault has seen profits leap due to worldwide demand for cars from its partner Nissan.

6 Passenger numbers climbed from 1.54 to 1.68 million in a month.

3 The retail chain is in crisis after its shares plummeted on Wednesday

7 Samsung Electronics' profit surged 81% in 2004 with profits almost tripling in the last quarter.

4 **Shares in oil giant have slipped after the company was hit by strikes.**

8 **Apple profits soar due to iPod sales. Apple has seen profits rise four-fold this year.**

Writing: introduction to a presentation

E **You are Vice President of CME. Write the introduction to your presentation about the company's financial performance for your investors. Use expressions from the Useful language box.**

Useful language

Introduction to presentations

Opening remarks
I am very pleased to welcome you all here this morning.
Thank you very much for coming along to today's presentation.
It's my (great) pleasure to be here today.
I'm here on behalf of . . . . , an organisation which ...

Purpose of the talk
My aim for today's presentation is to ...
I want to talk to you about ...
Our company is particularly proud of ...
We firmly believe that ...
As I'm sure you'll agree, ...

When to take questions
I'll answer any questions at the end of my talk.
Feel free to interrupt if you have any questions.
Please stop me any time you have a question or if you need clarification.

Cost-cutting at Erstaunliche Autos

'We aim to boost earnings by €10bn,' says new chief at Erstaunliche Autos

Background

Erstaunliche Autos (EA) is a medium-sized German car manufacturer based in Frankfurt. Workers have so far enjoyed a four-day week and high salaries, although production costs at EA are 40 per cent higher than similar car manufacturers. In addition, fierce international competition, including China, now poses a serious threat to Germany, where one in seven employees works directly or indirectly for the automotive industry.

EA is now facing a financial crisis. The new company chairman plans to boost productivity, which will require a drastic cost-cutting programme, and jobs may go. A group of financial consultants, Tompkins and Kosters, have been called in to help with the refinancing package.

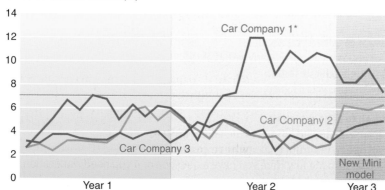

Share of Chinese market (%)

Car Company 1*

Car Company 2

Car Company 3

New Mini model

Year 1   Year 2   Year 3

Source: Asian Automotive Resources

*50% manufacturing joint venture with a US company

Listening 7.6

One of your colleagues from Tompkins and Kosters is being driven in a taxi to a meeting near London. Listen to the business news on the radio that he hears. What plans at Erstaunliche Autos have already been leaked to the press?

Task 1

You are from Tompkins and Kosters; you have been asked to present a cost-cutting package to management at EA. Look at the line graph on page 68. What has happened to competition in the Chinese car industry over the last two years?

Task 2

1 Work in groups of three. You need to devise a cost-cutting programme in order to reduce manufacturing costs and boost productivity at EA.

Student A: Turn to page 146.
Student B: Turn to page 153.
Student C: Turn to page 157.

2 Present your cost-cutting package to management at EA. Use figures and graphs where necessary.

Writing

Write a summary of your presentation for the board of directors with your cost-cutting proposals, including the productivity forecast for EA over the next three years. Use figures where possible to support your recommendations and describe market trends and forecasts for the car manufacturer.

➡ *Grammar reference: Language of trends* page 126

Consultants

> **❝** *Sometimes it takes an expert to point out the obvious.* **❞**
> Scott Allen (US technology entrepreneur and consultant)

Listening and discussion

A **Discuss these questions.**

1 Why do you think companies sometimes take on external consultants?

2 How can a company make sure the right kind of consultant or consultancy is recruited?

3 What do you think would be an appropriate sequence of steps when recruiting an external consultant for a company? Consider the following:

   a) Recruit the consultant.
   b) Negotiate contracts, terms and conditions for the consultancy.
   c) Define the problem, project or task.
   d) The consultant submits a written proposal.
   e) Write a brief for the consultant.
   f) Make a shortlist of possible consultants.

B 🎧 8.1 **Listen to the interview about recruiting consultancies with the consultant Michelle Geraghty from Business Today, a business advisory group. Check and compare your answers in the previous exercise.**

C 🎧 8.1 **Listen again and answer the questions for the different stages in recruiting a consultant.**

1 What are the SMART principles when defining a project or task?

2 List three things the brief could include.

3 List five things the consultant's written proposal should include.

4 List five items the written contract may contain.

5 What are the two types of possible contracts?

6 If the company is unsure about recruiting the consultant, what should they do?

▲ Michelle Geraghty, Business Today consultant

D 🎧 **8.2 Before you listen to the second part of the interview about managing consultancies, discuss these questions. Then listen and complete the answers.**

1 How can a company ensure the consultancy assignment or project is managed well?

You have to agree on several things: …

2 Why is it important that staff are involved early on in a consultancy project?

So that they are informed about …

3 How should the consultant's findings, recommendations and conclusions be communicated?

In a ………… and followed by a ………… .

Ask the consultant to produce …

E **Look at an extract from Michelle Geraghty's notes for the interview and complete the sentences using an appropriate word or phrase from the box.**

> brief   communication   deliverable   fees   managerial performance
> milestones   short-term   specialist tasks   T&M   timescale

1 Consultants can help you with ………… , manage projects and improve overall ………… .

2 Written contracts should include objectives, a specific ………… , how the consultancy will be managed, ………… and deliverables.

3 In a fixed-price contract, the consultant assumes most risk, but not all. In a ………… contract the client will assume most risk, but again, not all.

4 The client needs to set a ………… and a budget for the consultancy.

5 An agreement could include: how often you meet, tasks to be undertaken by you and your staff, definition of ………… goals, definition of ………… and agreement on deliverables.

6 Successful consultancy requires effective ………… ; that is to say, a good relationship with the client is essential.

7 The report is often the consultant's most tangible or evident ………… , but it must be in a suitable format and it shouldn't contain any surprises.

F **Discuss these questions.**

1 The radio presenter says: *Some critics say, consultants just snoop around and only produce a report telling you something you already knew!* Why do you think that is?

2 What do you think are some of the disadvantages of hiring external consultants?

3 What are the implied criticisms made about consultants in the comments below?

Top five things you'll **never** hear from your consultant

1 I don't know enough to speak intelligently about that.

2 How about paying us based on the success of the project?

3 Implementation? I only care about writing long reports.

4 Actually, the only difference is that we charge more than they do.

5 Everything looks OK to me. You really don't need me.

Reading and language

A Discuss these questions.

1 What are the possible benefits and drawbacks of working as a consultant?

2 Is the use of consultancy firms common in your country?

3 Which of these business sectors probably spend most money on consultants?

- manufacturing
- communications industry
- public sector
- banking and financial services
- retail industry
- utilities industry (e.g. gas, electricity and water)

B Read the article on page 73 and identify which paragraphs contain this information.

a) Lack of regulation of the consultancy industry
b) The possible benefits of becoming a consultant
c) The possible drawbacks of being a consultant
d) Problems consultancy firms sometimes have with clients

e) The businesses that spend most money on consultants
f) A failed consultancy project
g) A consultancy contract that gave good results
h) The reasons why more firms turn to consultants

C Match these definitions with words and expressions from the text.

1 one of the important people, companies, etc. involved in a particular industry, market, situation, etc. (paragraph 2)

2 a product, service or business that makes a profit (paragraph 2)

3 the department that does work connected with managing and organising the work of a financial institution, rather than actual work of trading, working with clients, etc. (paragraph 2)

4 remain competitive by trying to do things as well as other people, organisations, etc. (paragraph 2)

5 money paid to a professional person or organisation for their services (paragraph 3)

6 try to persuade people to buy goods or services you are offering (paragraph 3)

7 start to employ someone (paragraph 5)

8 gradually reduce in number or amount (paragraph 6)

9 done within the organisation, especially by the organisation's own staff (paragraph 8)

10 if a plan, business idea, etc. gets started or it starts to be successful (paragraph 9)

D Look at this extract from the article on page 73 and identify the negative prefixes used.

The industry is unregulated, and inexperienced clients can find themselves paying large fees for substandard work. (paragraph 5)

E Now read the extract on the left from an article about psychometric testing and complete these sentences using the correct prefixes.

1 Some executive search consultants think the assessments are .... used and .... necessary – particularly at senior executive level.

2 The tests can draw .... accurate, ... leading and potentially damaging conclusions.

3 It's possible to pass the tests and still be an .... competent manager.

4 Performance in a simulation is .... relevant, and what's more, it's .... possible to measure personality on a test.

5 Results from multiple-choice tests can be .... reliable. It's best to assess executives on what they have achieved during their career.

Testing times for Australia's psychometric outfits

Increasingly, corporations are turning to business psychologists and consulting firms to help select senior candidates. Sarah Kearney, managing director for Australia of SHL, the UK human resources group, says: 'Making mistakes at a senior level can be very expensive and damaging for a company, and they want to limit their risks as much as they can.'

FINANCIAL TIMES

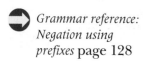

Grammar reference: Negation using prefixes page 128

Could it be you when they need an expert?

By Sara McConnell

1 So you want to be a consultant. It sounds good. In fact, it sounds like money for old rope. How can you fail when there are hundreds of stories about people who jack in their ordinary jobs with ordinary pay and return the following week to the same company, but with higher pay and a serious rise in status? Of course, it's not as simple as that. But public- and private-sector organisations alike are becoming increasingly enthusiastic users of outside consultants, be they large firms or individuals.

2 The total UK management consultancy market is worth an estimated £8bn (€12bn), and the industry's leading players collectively brought in fee income of £4.3bn, up 17% over the previous year, according to the latest figures from the Management Consultancies Association. The biggest consultancy money spinners were banking, insurance and financial services, says Sarah Taylor, deputy director of the MCA: 'They want an objective independent view of their business. Increasingly, they are looking at processes, like how they deal with their back office and how to improve productivity. They need to keep up with their competitors.'

3 It can be a cosy world of intimate relationships with old employers, or it can be a fiercely competitive business with firms staffed by high achievers desperate to bring in fee income. Firms attract graduates and more experienced staff with big salaries and give them large amounts of variety and autonomy. But in return, they're expected to work long hours and bring in the business. Sometimes this results in risky strategies like touting for business from clients in whose offices they're currently working or deliberately holding back on producing part of a solution to a problem in the hope of getting called in by the client again.

4 Consultants can be pressured by clients to achieve a specified solution to a problem before they start work.

'I'm often told, get this solution and you'll get the job,' says Rachel Jackson of the Hay Group. 'If I was unscrupulous, I would take it. But this isn't ethical.' Neil Paterson, general manager of Hay Group, which specialises in human resources, freely admits that the firm has accepted work which, with hindsight, wasn't suitable. 'There are times when we will have said yes when we should have said no. There are projects which may cripple you and some organisations are very what we call "high maintenance".'

5 Any firm can set itself up as a consultant and solicit for work. The industry is unregulated, and inexperienced clients can find themselves paying large fees for substandard work. Members of the Institute of Management Consultancy are bound by a professional code of conduct. 'The client/consultant relationship is a complex one,' says Ian Barratt, IMC's chief executive. 'The professional code will minimise the chances of an assignment going wrong.' But with just 4,500 individual members out of the UK's estimated 57,000 management consultants, the chances of businesses taking on a non-IMC member are huge.

6 Consultancy firms argue that it's up to clients as much as consultants to be clear about what they want, to be more certain of getting a satisfactory outcome. 'Problems can be laid at the door of the client as much as the consultant,' says IMC's Ian Barratt. Sometimes organisations need an objective expert to analyse why a part of their business is going wrong or to carry out a specific project. 'Twenty-five years ago, they had the luxury of spare bodies and used

them for new projects,' says Mr Barratt. 'Now more organisations have pared back and taken out redundant resources, which is why consultancy has grown.'

7 And organisations need new skills to find and recruit consultants, which is trickier than it looks. 'There are a number of people who don't know how to buy consultancy,' says Neil Paterson of the Hay Group. Experienced firms which use a wide range of consultants have developed sophisticated procedures for assessing and appointing consultants.

8 Even this isn't a failsafe way of avoiding the occasional mistake. Barclays Bank, which spent £130m on consultancy last year (an exceptionally large spend by the bank's standards because it was consulting on strategy development), successfully used a firm of consultants to build a customer database across its retail banking, Barclaycard and small-business divisions. 'At the time, we didn't feel we had the necessary skills to do it in-house,' says David Perry, portfolio management director, Operational Transformation, at Barclays. 'It was delivered on time, on budget and with the knowledge transfer to allow us to continue development in-house.'

9 But when the same consultancy was asked to develop a customer relationship strategy for the bank's affluent customer base, the strategy never got off the ground. 'It wasn't well integrated into our business, they didn't use high-quality people, and the bank didn't specify clearly enough what it wanted. So the strategy was just left on the shelf.'

*The*Guardian

Business skills

Negotiating sales

OK, I'LL MARRY YOU. BUT I GET TO KEEP THE DRAGON.

A Match the negotiating skills (1–4) with the sentences (a–d).

1 Explaining the value of a concession
2 Testing the situation
3 Responding to an unacceptable concession
4 Checking with a higher authority

a) I'd like to do business with you, but I'm afraid we're simply too far apart.
b) Let me run this by my boss and I'll get back to you tomorrow.
c) We'll pay for the delivery. In real terms, that's a saving of about €500.
d) What if I take 4,000 units? How much would that cost me?

B 8.3 **Listen to a sales manager giving a training session on sales negotiations to some sales trainees and say whether these tips are true or false.**

1 If you say to a future prospect, 'I'm going to have to check that with my boss,' it means you have limited authority and the potential customer won't take you seriously.

2 It's a good idea to negotiate for as long as possible, so that your customer finally gives in to your offer.

3 Professional negotiators start out with their largest concession first, then offer only very minor ones.

4 It's important in win-win negotiating that the customer gets the biggest discount possible.

5 A negotiation planning checklist should include the maximum amount of information about the potential buyer and all the salesperson's possible concessions and trade-offs.

6 Your bottom line, or BATNA, is the point in the negotiation when you may have to stop negotiating.

7 It's essential buyers value any concession that they are getting from the salesperson.

C Complete the sales manager's tips on making concessions with the words and phrases in the box.

> understands its full value   'take-it-or-leave-it'   big concession
> some sort of compensation   walk away from the negotiation
> willing to make concessions   you are giving one   ill-will   one by one

Sales negotiations: tips for making concessions

1 Don't give the first ....
2 Don't assume you have to match your customers' concessions ....
3 Don't give a concession away without ....
4 Never give away a concession without making sure the customer ....
5 The best time to get a concession from a client is when ....
6 Whatever you do, don't advertise you're ....
7 Make it clear that the .... offer is unacceptable. When facing this situation, restate your position and its benefits to the customer. Never use these words yourself. They only create anger and ....
8 If the customer is *not* planning to buy, it's pointless negotiating and you need to ....

D Sales negotiation role-play: the car deal. Work in pairs to negotiate the best deal.

Student A: Turn to page 146.
Student B: Turn to page 153.

Writing: terms and conditions

E Work in pairs. Use some of the expressions in the Useful language box.

Student A: Write an e-mail as the sales person of Fast Cars confirming the terms and conditions agreed upon in the previous negotiation.

Student B: Write an e-mail as the buyer confirming the terms and conditions agreed upon in the previous negotiation.

Useful language

Introducing the topic
Following our conversation / Further to our meeting on [date], ...

Confirming terms and conditions
We would be happy to offer you ...
Regarding terms and conditions of payment and delivery, ...
Where delivery charges are concerned, we would need to point out (that) ...
Our company policy regarding terms and conditions of payment is as follows: ...

Making a request
Could you please confirm your order in writing by ...?

Closing remarks
Should you require further information / be interested in ..., please do not hesitate to contact me.
We look forward to ...

F Check and compare your e-mails. Did you describe the same terms and conditions or were there any differences?

 Writing file page 137

Mobi-net: it's their call

Background

Mobi-net is a mobile service provider with more than 5 million subscribers in Austria, Slovenia and Croatia. With increased competition and the demand for the convergence of the Internet and mobile industries, Mobi-net needs to keep its lead in the Austrian mobile-phone market.

Mobi-net are therefore looking for a consultancy with extensive know-how in the industry and experience in new technologies to improve processes, offer better service to customers and help them maintain their lead in an intensely competitive industry.

Task 1

Student A: Look at the extract below from the proposal of Performance Consulting.

Student B: Turn to page 154.

What are the differences between the two consultancies and their recommendations?

Listening 8.4

Listen to a preliminary meeting between the Managing Director of Mobi-net, Cristoph Kahnwald, and a consultant from Performance Consulting. List four requirements that the mobile phone company has.

PERFORMANCE CONSULTING

Performance Consulting: mobile solutions that keep business moving

The UK consultancy group, Performance Consulting, provides consultancy in strategy and management, including information services and start-up support in the telecommunications and IT sectors.

Performance Consulting has developed its mobile-industry expertise through cutting-edge consulting assignments in international markets over the last ten years. Our range of expertise includes: advice on strategy, business planning, assessment of market opportunities and advice on key regulatory issues.

Performance Consulting can help you to devise long-lasting strategies that will shape the future of the mobile-communications industry.

Recommendations for Mobi-net

• A 'Family and friends' pricing package as an innovative package for subscribers.

• Centralisation of the call centre, which will improve customer service, make outbound marketing campaigns easier and allow expansion to new locations, giving Mobi-net more agility in the market.

• Training for customer service staff and management. These will be essential if Mobi-net is to increase cost-efficiency and improve sales.

Performance Consulting is a member of the Association of Management Consultancy (AMC)

Task 2

Mobi-net negotiates with each consultancy firm and then chooses the best proposal. Work in groups of three.

Student A: Turn to page 147.
Student B: Turn to page 154.
Student C: Turn to page 157.

Writing

Write a summary of the solution, fees and conditions as discussed in the meeting between Mobi-net and one of the consultancies.

 Writing file page 137

Strategy

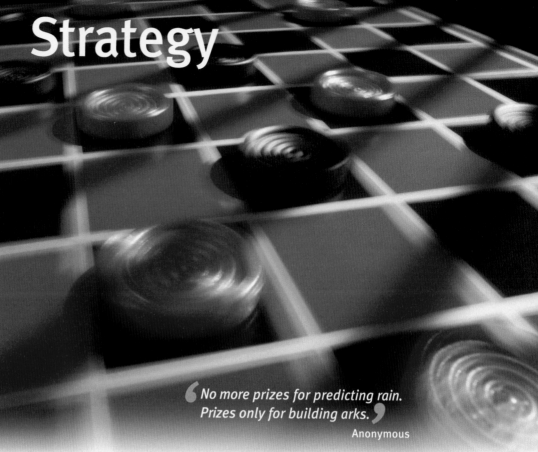

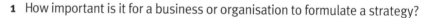

*No more prizes for predicting rain.
Prizes only for building arks.*
Anonymous

Listening and discussion

A **Look at these definitions and discuss the following questions.**

> **mission** the purposes and aims of a company or organisation

> **strategy 1** a plan or series of plans for achieving an aim; **2** the process of skilful planning in general

> **vision** knowledge and imagination needed in planning for the future

1 How important is it for a business or organisation to formulate a strategy?

2 How regularly should a company or organisation's strategy be reviewed and updated?

3 Who should be involved in deciding a company's strategy?

4 If a company wants to enter new markets, what kind of strategies can it adopt?

B 🎧 **9.1 Listen to the first part of an interview on strategy with Josep Valor-Sabatier. Choose the correct ending for these sentences.**

1 According to Professor Josep Valor-Sabatier, marketing departments are ...
  a) getting better at predicting market trends.
  b) not always better than other departments at predicting market trends.

2 A common practice of the clothing industry is to ...
  a) mass-produce seasonal collections in countries where labour costs are low.
  b) copy the market leaders, manufacturing clothes near the company's stores.

3 The Spanish clothing retailer, Zara, has its own production facilities, whereas other stores ...
  a) outsource manufacturing to countries like China.
  b) design seasonal collections six months in advance.

4 Zara chose not to have seasonal collections because it ...
  a) wanted to imitate retailers like Benetton and Gap.
  b) would take longer.

5 Zara's strategy was successful because it ...
  a) copied leading brands in the fashion industry.
  b) was different from leading brands in the fashion industry.

▲ Josep Valor-Sabatier, professor and Head of Information Systems, IESE Business School, Spain

C 🎧 **9.2 Listen to the second part of the interview and complete what Josep Valor-Sabatier says in your own words.**

1 The success of a company can be measured either by its ...

2 According to Professor Valor-Sabatier, companies need to concentrate on both ...

3 When implementing long-term strategies, it's easier to ...

4 When measuring success, the stock market tends to focus more on ...

5 It's very difficult to change a company's strategies because of the conflict between ...

6 Good strategic management consists of taking a company in the right direction for the future whilst ...

D **Match the words or phrases in the box with their definitions. Look at the audio scripts on page 170 if necessary.**

bottom line	innovate	margin	market follower
mass-produce	newcomer	profitability	reinvented

Audio 9.1

1 changed, improved and modernised (paragraph 1)

2 a business that has only recently started a particular activity (paragraph 1)

3 manufacture in large amounts (paragraph 2)

4 a company that is not one of the main ones in a market and that does not have a large market share (paragraph 3)

5 design and develop new and original products (paragraph 4)

Audio 9.2

6 the figure showing a company's total profit or loss (question 1)

7 the difference between the price of a product and the cost of producing it (answer 1)

8 the state of making a profit (answer 2)

E **Discuss these quotes and questions on strategy.**

Copyright 2001 by Randy Glasbergen.
www.glasbergen.com

GLASBERGEN

"I study the market research, analyze any changes in our customer base, then drink gallons of coffee until I hallucinate a big pink rabbit who tells me what to do."

1 Professor Valor-Sabatier describes Zara as a successful imitator in the retail fashion business. What other 'successful imitators' are popular in your country?

2 'The world is full of successful companies that did not create anything radical or new. Dell did not invent the personal computer, Airbus did not design the first wide-bodied passenger jet, Campbell's did not pioneer the concept of tinned soup and McDonald's did not invent the hamburger or the fast-food restaurant. Yet all four have been very successful.' (Morgan Witzel, *Financial Times*)
How have all/some of the four companies mentioned been successful imitators, rather than innovators?

3 'Any intelligent fool can make things bigger and more complex. It takes a touch of genius and a lot of courage to move in the opposite direction.' (Albert Einstein)
Think of some companies that have 'moved in the opposite direction'? Why were their main strategies (un)successful?

Reading and language

A What type of companies are Logitech, Giorgio Armani, Accor, Swissair and Marconi? Read the article quickly to find out about the ones you don't know.

B Read the article again and complete the following summary in your own words.

Adrian Slywotzky and other management gurus argue there is a growth crisis on the basis that ....[1].

Another consultant, Chris Zook predicts that ....[2].

However, Zook has found that many companies are forecasting ....[3].

.... , ... and ....[4] are three companies which have experienced healthy growth.

Zook believes that the secret of these companies success lies in ....[5].

Swissair's growth initiative involved ....[6] which may have led to ....[7].

In the 1990s, Marconi's decision ....[8] caused ....[9].

GROWTH MODE *Finding new ways to grow a company in today's tough climate isn't easy*

By Jason Karaian

1   The challenge for all companies: finding the next new source of growth will be more difficult than ever before. Traditional sources of revenue growth – such as product enhancements, grabbing market share or acquiring competitors – have been largely tapped out, says Adrian Slywotzky, a managing director at Mercer Management Consulting in the US. Slywotzky echoes other management gurus in calling this 'a growth crisis'.

2   In the hunt for growth opportunities, failure is rife. According to research overseen by Chris Zook, head of the global strategy practice at US-based consultancy Bain, only 13% of companies worldwide during the 1990s achieved 'even a modest level of sustained and profitable growth'. In today's hyper-competitive environment, he says he'd be surprised if that figure can reach 10%.

3   Yet that hasn't stopped companies from whipping up investor enthusiasm with magnificently ambitious growth plans. Zook notes that the average company sets a public target of revenue growth at twice its industry's rate, and earnings four times higher. Where will all that growth come from?

4   In many cases, finance might have the answer. Take, for example, these three very different companies, all renowned for their ability to tap into new avenues of growth: Logitech, a small start-up founded in 1981, made a name for itself as a maker of computer mice for PC manufacturers before expanding into the retail market to sell a vast range of accessories for computers, gaming consoles and entertainment systems; Giorgio Armani, the Italian fashion house, which, since its founding in 1975, has grown revenue organically to €1.3 billion through shrewd customer segmentation and brand control; and French hotel group Accor, which revolutionised its industry in the 1980s with a smart investment aimed at budget travellers and today is seeking to rekindle that innovative spirit.

5   Zook contends that the underlying strength in companies like these is in their ability to combine high growth and low risk by moving systematically into 'adjacencies' – products, services, geographies or customer segments that are highly related, or adjacent, to the company's core business. Other consultants offer variations on that theme. Richard Wise, another managing director at Mercer, for example, says that a successful growth strategy in his view is one that adds to, not detracts from, a company's core business. 'The idea is not to abandon the pillars of growth, but to add to the playbook,' he says.

6   Attempting to produce new growth via adjacency moves is not without risk. Chris Zook estimates that almost all of history's biggest business blunders were caused or made worse by growth strategies gone awry.

7   Swissair, for one, built a strong, if unglamorous, reputation for punctuality and efficiency since its founding in 1931. In the mid-1990s, a new management team launched a global growth initiative that involved investments in several regional airlines – Belgium's Sabena, Ukraine International Airlines and South African Airways, to name a few – and a clutch of travel-related ventures like airline caterer Gate Gourmet and airport retailer Nuance.

8   Was it distraction that caused Swissair's punctuality and baggage handling to worsen, hurting business, and its investments in the world's more marginal airlines to prove an additional drag on its finances? Hard to say, but in 2000 the company reported a mammoth loss of SFr3 billion (€2 billion at the time), and declared bankruptcy shortly after the September 11th 2001 terrorist attacks, SFr17 billion in debt.

9   Marconi is another example of growth strategy gone awry. A sprawling conglomerate with interests in products from lifts to semiconductors to defence electronics, the UK-based company (formerly known as GEC) made a big bet in the booming 1990s on telecoms equipment – a business in which it didn't actually have a toehold at the time. It sold all unrelated businesses and went on a spending spree to buy up telco equipment companies. When the tech bubble burst, the new Marconi was badly exposed and nearly collapsed. It trades as a shadow of its former self today. Adding insult to injury, Marconi's sale of its former 'core' defence-electronics business to BAE in 1999 turned that company into one of Europe's leading defence contractors.

10   At any given time, says Zook, a company with a strong core faces between 80 and 110 possible adjacency moves. Of these, 'only one in four, maybe fewer, will succeed in creating a stream of growing revenue and earn their cost of capital,' he says.

▲ Adapted from http://www.cfoeurope.com

C **Match the words and expressions from the text with the definitions and synonyms.**

1 revenue (para. 1)

2 target (para. 3)

3 start-up (para. 4)

4 range (para. 4)

5 core business (para. 5)

6 venture (para. 7)

7 retailer (para. 7)

8 booming (para. 9)

9 toehold (para. 9)

10 spree (para. 9)

a) someone's first involvement in a particular business activity from which they can develop and become stronger

b) activity that makes most money for a company and that is considered to be its most important and central one

c) very successful and growing

d) a result such as a total, an amount or a time which you aim to achieve

e) a new company

f) money that a business receives over a period of time, especially from selling goods or services

g) a set of similar products made by a particular company

h) a short period of time during which someone spends a lot of money

i) a business that sells goods to members of the public, rather than to shops, etc.

j) a new business activity or project that involves taking risks

D **Complete each sentence with the correct form of the words and expressions from Exercise C. There are two you don't need.**

1 British American Tobacco's decision to begin manufacturing in China gives the company a .... in the country.

2 Apple profits have risen four-fold on the back of .... sales of its iPod music player.

3 Survivors of the Bhopal gas leak tragedy are spending their compensation money on an unprecedented shopping ....

4 A community group planning to buy their local ferry service is set to hold talks with the local council to secure backing for the ....

5 .... from cash-machine charges has risen from £60m to £140m.

6 Ahold, the world's fourth-largest supermarket group, revealed ballooning annual losses, but said it was on track to meet all its .... this year.

7 Mr Gorman, CEO of Merrill Lynch, recalls that he was criticised for losing focus on the .... , but says the diversification was rewarded with a significant increase in revenue per client.

8 There is a wide .... of ethnic foods available in the local supermarket.

E **Discuss these questions.**

1 Do you think there is a 'growth crisis' in the global economy?

2 What is the 'core' business of each of these companies? Brainstorm the possible 'adjacencies' some of these companies could tap into:

- a publisher of children's books • a restaurant • a bicycle manufacturer
- a supermarket chain • a mobile-phone company

 Grammar reference: Idioms for giving examples page 130

Business skills

Brainstorming and creativity

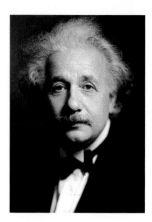

▲ Albert Einstein

A **Discuss these questions.**

1 Discuss the meaning of these quotes on creativity.

> 'If at first the idea is not absurd, there is no hope for it.'
> *Albert Einstein, American (German-born) theoretical physicist (1879–1955)*

> 'Exhilaration is that feeling you get just after a great idea hits you and just before you realise what's wrong with it.'
> *Anonymous*

> 'If you always think the way you always thought, you'll always get what you've always got.'
> *Michael Michalko, US creativity expert and author*

2 When are you most creative? Late at night? First thing in the morning? Working with a group of people or on your own?

3 Which of these statements do you agree with most/least? Why?

- The management in an organisation should be responsible for coming up with any new ideas.
- The typical work environment is not conducive to being creative.
- Whenever we have brainstorming meetings, any interesting ideas are usually dismissed by some of the more cynical team members.

B 🎧 9.3 **Listen to a trainer discussing brainstorming techniques with some staff from the British clothing retailer, Rose & Frankwright. Complete the brainstorming tips and the seven principles of Koinonia. Do you know of any other brainstorming techniques?**

Brainstorming tips
- Think of as many ....[1] as possible.
- There shouldn't be more than ....[2].
- ....[3] all ideas, however absurd.
- Don't spend too long ....[4].
- Be enthusiastic and ....[5] of other people's ....[6].
- Clearly define the ....[7].
- ....[8] ideas after the session.

Seven principles of Koinonia
1 Establish ....
2 Exchange ....
3 Don't ....
4 Don't ....
5 Listen ....
6 Clarify your ....
7 Be ....

C **Look at the information below about Rose & Frankwright. In groups, brainstorm some more marketing strategies to help the company with its current difficulties. Use some of the brainstorming expressions and remember to write down all ideas. When you have finished, evaluate the ideas and decide which strategies will best help the company recover from its present crisis.**

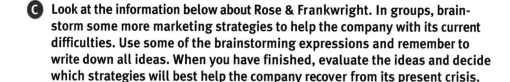

R&F, Rose & Frankwright, is a well-known British retailer that specialises in clothing for women over 45 at the upper end of the market. The outlook for the retailer and the industry is, however, bleak with higher costs, from rents to wages, and fierce competition. R&F is currently one of the poor performers on the British high street, with sales having fallen consecutively over the last six quarters.

The management team is currently reviewing R&F's marketing strategy, with the vision of 'attractive clothing at attractive prices'. Strategic goals may include: diversification, emphasis on quality products, competitive pricing ...

Useful language

Expressions for brainstorming

Would anyone like to start/get the ball rolling?
I've got one! What/How about ...?
That's a great/fantastic/interesting/unusual idea!
I think that's been done / we've done that before.
Let's just get lots of ideas down at this stage.
I was thinking (more) along the lines of ...
I was just going to say that!
You've taken the words out of my mouth!
Has anyone else got a contribution to make?

Writing: mission statements

1 Avis
2 Avon
3 Kodak
4 International Committee of the Red Cross
5 World Bank

D Look at parts of some mission statements and match the statements to the companies and organisations on the left. Which ones seem the best/worst/most creative/(in)sincere?

a) To fight poverty and improve the living standards of people in the developing world.

b) To grow more rapidly than our competitors by providing customers with the solutions they need to capture, store, process, output and communicate images – anywhere, any time ...

c) We try harder.

d) To protect the lives and dignity of victims of war and internal violence and to provide them with assistance.

e) To be the global beauty leader ...

E Write four criteria for writing mission statements based on this text.

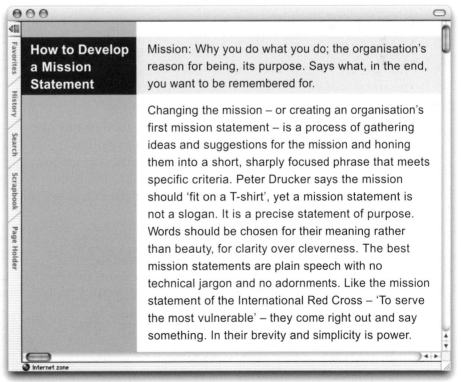

How to Develop a Mission Statement

Mission: Why you do what you do; the organisation's reason for being, its purpose. Says what, in the end, you want to be remembered for.

Changing the mission – or creating an organisation's first mission statement – is a process of gathering ideas and suggestions for the mission and honing them into a short, sharply focused phrase that meets specific criteria. Peter Drucker says the mission should 'fit on a T-shirt', yet a mission statement is not a slogan. It is a precise statement of purpose. Words should be chosen for their meaning rather than beauty, for clarity over cleverness. The best mission statements are plain speech with no technical jargon and no adornments. Like the mission statement of the International Red Cross – 'To serve the most vulnerable' – they come right out and say something. In their brevity and simplicity is power.

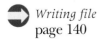

Writing file page 140

F You are developing the mission statement for your organisation. Set your criteria – see Exercise E – and brainstorm some ideas using the expressions in the Useful language box to help you. Write the first draft using the Writing tips on page 27.

The company makeover

Background

Hazel is one of the world's largest direct sellers of cosmetics and beauty products, a position it has held for over 50 years. Until the mid-1980s, the company was one of the leaders in the global cosmetics, fragrances and toiletries (CFT) industry. By the 1990s, Hazel's sales in the US and Western Europe had begun to decline, as fewer women bought products sold door-to-door. In addition, Hazel's products had little appeal with teenagers and young women.

Hazel's cosmetics business has achieved only modest revenue and earnings growth throughout the last ten years. The company now has serious problems, with annual sales growth of less than 1.5%. Given this climate, a new CEO has been appointed to devise a new strategic vision for the company.

Global sales cosmetics, fragrances and toiletries $140 billion

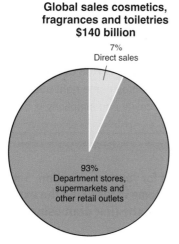

7%
Direct sales

93%
Department stores, supermarkets and other retail outlets

Hazel's percentage of company sales by key sectors

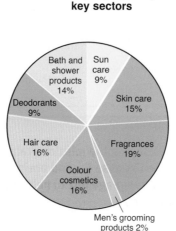

Bath and shower products 14%

Sun care 9%

Deodorants 9%

Skin care 15%

Hair care 16%

Fragrances 19%

Colour cosmetics 16%

Men's grooming products 2%

Hazel's net sales by geographical region

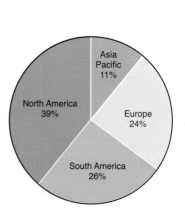

Asia Pacific 11%

North America 39%

Europe 24%

South America 26%

Cosmetics and Toiletries: World Market Overview and Key Trends

Manufacturers increasingly target specific consumer groups defined by age, sex, race and particular physical conditions, such as sensitive skin. The ageing of populations underpins an ongoing increase in the demand for products claiming to counter the visible effects of ageing. At the same time, new product launches tap into the unprecedented spending power of teens and pre-teens.

Sales increases in the global CFT industry are being driven primarily by product innovation in varying degrees. Anti-ageing products now account for most of the 2 per cent annual growth in the overall CFT industry and for much of the growth in such categories as hair care, cosmetics and skin care. However, the teen and pre-teen market rivals that of the baby boomers. Skin care is a particularly attractive product category in the teen market, since nearly 80 per cent of teen girls use complexion-care products on a daily basis.

Listening ∩ 9.4

During her first month as CEO, Angela Lang decided to get some first-hand experience as a member of the direct sales team. Listen to part of her summary presentation of her findings to the senior management team and make notes about the problems she highlights from a) the customers and b) the sales reps.

Task

You are the senior management team at Hazel, responsible for devising a new strategic plan for the company. Use a SWOT analysis and brainstorm ideas to help you prepare your new strategic vision for the company.

Strengths (Internal)	Weaknesses (Internal)
Opportunities (External)	Threats (External)

Writing

Prepare a report summarising your proposals to present to the company board of directors.

Here are some options you might want to consider:

- Rebrand or rebuild and improve Hazel's image with consumers around the world (e.g. new packaging, new logo, new advertising campaign with celebrity endorsements, etc.).
- Develop innovative new brands and products that can be marketed globally.
- Enter the retail sector to fuel future growth.
- Use of the Internet and e-commerce as a link in Hazel's direct-selling business model.
- Pursue market opportunities by entering new market segments and new countries.

Writing file pages 138–139

7 Finance and banking

Vocabulary
business idioms

Which of the words in column B does *not* collocate with the word in column A?

	A	B
1	credit	account card equity
2	savings	interest account bank
3	write off	a debt shareholder a loan
4	acquire	an interest a stake an ATM
5	return on	accounting investment capital
6	pay off	a loan creditors price
7	capital	share fixed asset
8	cash	bankruptcy flow machine
9	make	profits assets forecasts
10	financial	flow analyst year

Business skills
presentations

Match these sentences for introducing a presentation.

1	I am very pleased to	**a)**	any time if you need clarification.
2	Thank you very much for	**b)**	your questions at the end of my talk.
3	My aim for today's presentation is	**c)**	welcome you all here this morning.
4	Our company is particularly proud	**d)**	to give you an overview of the company.
5	Please feel free to interrupt me	**e)**	of our excellent track record.
6	I will be happy to take any of	**f)**	coming along to today's talk.

Describing financial performance

Complete this newspaper extracts about a US car manufacturer with the words and phrases in the box. Two are not used.

> consecutive quarter   dragged CH shares down   have improved
> higher steel costs   growth   net loss   poor results   recordèd a profit
> recovery plan   reducing costs   the next four years   the same period last year

CH Autos lost more than $1bn in its automotive business for the second ....[1], dragging one of the world's biggest car maker to an unexpected ....[2] and forcing it to promise faster cost cuts.

CH Autos admitted it was not ....[3] fast enough and raised the prospect of further factory closures to remove 500,000 units of production capacity – ten per cent of its North American total. It had previously said it would cut the US blue-collar workforce by 25,000 over ....[4].

The surprise second-quarter $286m net loss compares with a net income of $1.38bn in ....[5]. The analyst forecast was for a profit of three cents per share, but CH said a combination of lower output, a soaring healthcare bill and ....[6] had set it back.

The car maker's ....[7] follow unexpectedly bad performance at Ford, CH Autos' US rival, on Tuesday, and ....[8] 1.7 per cent to $36.21 in early New York trading.

'Things have deteriorated more quickly than expected,' said a credit analyst at JP Morgan in London. He said factory capacity needed to be reduced more quickly, and the ....[9] 'doesn't seem to be addressing the issues'.

The car maker's European operation, meanwhile, ...[10] of $37m, its first in five years, before a charge of $126m as part of the layoff of 12,000 staff.

FINANCIAL TIMES

Writing
introduction to a presentation

You are one of the financial directors at CH Autos. Look again at the information in the article and prepare the introduction to a presentation at a shareholders' meeting. Present the company's performance in as positive a way as possible, including the projected forecast.

8 Consultants

Vocabulary
word-building

Complete this advice on contracting a consultant using the word in brackets in its correct form.

1 It's crucial you take on a consultant with the right experience and (expert) .... in the industry.
2 It's best to recruit a (reputation) .... consultant or one that is a member of a recognised consulting body or association.
3 Bear in mind that smaller (consult) .... firms tend to charge less than the larger and better known ones.
4 The (allocate) .... of time and money should be clearly set out in the client's brief.
5 Make sure the consultant's (deliver) .... are clearly defined before the project starts.
6 The consultant's (propose) .... should also include the fees, terms and conditions of the project.
7 Use SMART when evaluating the feasibility of a project or task: is it specific, measurable, (achieve) .... , relevant and time limited?
8 Some firms experience problems with (recruit) .... and retention of consultants as many leave because of the demands of the job.

Grammar
conditionals

Say whether each conditional sentence (1–6) is a first, second, third or a mixed conditional and match it to its correct function (a–f).

1 Were the completion date to be brought forward, we could not guarantee quality of service.
2 Had I listened to you, we wouldn't have gone over budget.
3 We wouldn't be having these problems now if we hadn't contracted your firm!
4 Should you be interested in our training solutions, we can arrange a meeting.
5 Unless you specify milestones in the contract, the project will overrun.
6 You're going to be disappointed if you take on that firm.

a) Making an offer
b) Emphasising something is unlikely to happen
c) Stating a necessary condition
d) Giving advice
e) Describing a hypothetical situation in the past
f) Expressing complaint or criticism

Business skills
negotiating

Imagine you are a consultant negotiating with a potential client that could bring in a large amount of income on an important IT project. What could you say to them in the following situations? Take some notes and then role-play the dialogue with a partner.

1 We would need the project to be completed in five months' time.
2 We want you to use your best, senior consultants.
3 Your fees would be calculated based on a T&M contract, not an hourly pay rate. I'm afraid that's not negotiable.
4 It's not possible for you to have access to all company information.
5 We want your deliverables to include a presentation of your final report to the board of directors and any consequent implementation work.
6 We have plenty of other proposals from competing firms if you're not interested.

Writing

putting it in writing

Look at this letter following a contract agreement between Unicorn Consulting and a new Slovenian client. In most of the lines (1–12) there is an extra word that doesn't fit. Write the extra word or put a tick (✔) if the line is correct.

Unicorn
CONSULTING

Dear Mr Dimitrij Cuk,

Further to our meeting yesterday in Ljubljana, I am writing   1 ....
to confirm the terms and conditions of our agreement.   2 ....
With respect to the implementation of an IT systems in your   3 ....
company and subsequent staff for training, we would be happy   4 ....
to assign two high specialist consultants with expertise in SAP   5 ....
systems. Fees will be paid according to a T&M contract: please   6 ....
refer within to the attached document for a description of   7 ....
timescale and deliverables for the project, including fee pay   8 ....
details. If should you require further information about our   9 ....
consultancy proposal, please do not to hesitate to contact me.   10 ....
We thank you once again for your generous hospitality in   11 ....
Ljubljana and we very much look forward to working with you.   12 ....

Best regards,

Anna Belmont

Senior Consultant

9 Strategy

Marketing strategies

Complete these sentences describing different marketing strategies with the expressions in the box.

adapting their products or services	develop their products and services
downscaling their operations	integrating them both at an early stage
more responsive and flexible	

1 Every time companies interact with a customer, they can find out about customer needs and satisfaction, enabling them to further ....

2 Companies are now working more effectively with customers and suppliers, ... in the product-development process.

3 Multi-domestic marketing involves companies thinking globally, but .... to various local markets.

4 Companies are moving away from large economies of scale and .... within different marketplaces.

5 Large companies are now increasingly copying the approach of small and medium-sized companies by becoming ....

Reading
communicating the brand

Complete this extract of an interview with marketing consultant Paul Byrne with the words in the box.

advertisements	advertising	brand	communicating	competitors
core values	creative	differentiating	innovative	leveraging

'What companies are looking at doing now, because they have become increasingly conscious of the reduced effectiveness of the traditional forms of ....[1], is they're looking for new, innovative and creative ways of ....[2] their brand.

We are constantly being bombarded by ....[3] in all their forms, and we can be subjected to up to 2,000 different advertising communications on a daily basis. Therefore, companies are looking for new and ....[4] ways of attracting our attention to their brand. A new approach has been developed, referred to as a through-the-line approach, whereby companies are integrating different media to achieve a consistency in their ....[5] message.

Another strategy which has been developed is that of ....[6] the brand, whereby companies are looking at ways of distinguishing, ...[7] and communicating the ....[8] of their brand in a more effective and ....[9] way which will differentiate them from their ....[10].'

Vocabulary
strategy

Professor Josep Valor-Sabatier (see page 78) is talking about factors that affect a company's strategy. Complete the extracts from the interview with the phrases in the box.

change the rules	customers and suppliers	entering the market
future competitor	goals and objectives	management systems
market position	planning systems	significant impact	the same vision

'The *external* factors affect everything related to the business environment *outside* the company. What is its ....[1] within the industry? Who are its ....[2]? Which companies are having a ....[3] on the market? These companies include those that have decided to sell the same products as you, even though they are not doing so now, but are planning on ....[4] and becoming a ....[5]. Then there are technological improvements in other industries: if they were to be applied in *your* industry, how would they ....[6]?

The internal factors have to do with how ....[7] are implemented in order to attain a company's ....[8]. Management systems consist of compensation or reward systems, ...[9], and ensuring everyone in a management position shares ....[10] and is working towards the same goals.'

Writing
mission statements

Look at your notes for a turnaround strategy for the British retailer Rose & Frankwright, as discussed on page 82. Using ideas that were brainstormed, write up a press release outlining the company's new strategy in no more than 100 words.

Doing business online

> *To err is human, but to really foul things up you need a computer.*
> Paul R. Ehrlich, US biologist

Listening and discussion

A **Discuss these questions.**

1 How often do you shop online?

2 What goods and services do you buy online?

3 What other goods and services do you or would you buy online?

B ∩ **10.1** **Listen to three speakers. What types of online shopping are they describing?**

C **Match the words related to online shopping (1–10) with the definitions (a–j) on the next page.**

1 (shopping) cart	6 browse
2 back-end systems	7 hacker
3 cookie	8 B2B
4 banner	9 dotcom
5 pop-up ad	10 e-commerce

a) online retailer or Internet business

b) exchange of services, information and products between businesses via the web

c) buying and selling goods and services and doing other business over the Internet

d) piece of software that acts as an online seller's catalogue and ordering process

e) small advertisement for one website displayed on other sites; by clicking on it, the user is taken to the new site

f) someone who secretly gets into another person's computer system in order to use the information or damage the system

g) advertisement that automatically opens a new browser window and covers the window the user was intending to read.

h) hardware and software applications that manage order processing, billing, sales, inventory and shipping

i) • move from place to place on the Internet, searching for topics of interest
   • look at goods in a shop without wanting to buy any particular thing

j) piece of data that can be used to recognise an online customer and personalise the webpage

▲ Maija Pesola, IT Correspondent for the *Financial Times*

D 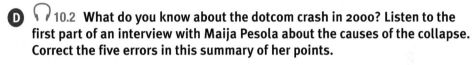 10.2 **What do you know about the dotcom crash in 2000? Listen to the first part of an interview with Maija Pesola about the causes of the collapse. Correct the five errors in this summary of her points.**

The problem was that there was too much investment money coming into the market too quickly. Therefore funding was given to dotcom companies that didn't have particularly enthusiastic business plans and didn't necessarily have the advertising revenue to carry out their plans. Another factor was that the market wasn't ready for Internet shopping in the way that it is today, and in 2000, not many people had Internet browsers. The positive outcome of the dotcom collapse is that it's improved some of the weaker companies, and those companies that are still in existence today have refined their B2B systems.

E 10.3 **Listen to the rest of the interview and answer these questions.**

1 What was the first type of Internet advertising used, and why was it unsatisfactory?

2 How did consumers react to the second model of advertising on the Internet?

3 What form of advertising appears to have had more success in recent years?

4 Why is this model of advertising more popular with companies?

5 Which products and services are/aren't selling well on the Internet, and why?

F **Discuss these questions.**

1 Will there come a time when we will do all of our shopping online? Why (not)?

2 Are you concerned about Internet security and using your credit card to purchase goods online?

3 What are governments and companies are doing to stop so-called 'cyber crime'? What else could they do?

4 How can and do online retailers use the information they collect about their customers?

5 As a customer, how does online shopping compare to the real thing?

6 What are the benefits to a company of doing business online?

Reading and language

A Which of these is most important for you when you're considering buying something online: cheap prices, an easy-to-navigate website, quick delivery service, good customer service?

B Read the first part of the article and find out the difference between success and failure for online companies.

Net gains on the shop front
by Gareth Chadwick

1 Cyberspace is increasingly the location of choice for many retailers. It is not hard to see why; online retailing – or e-tailing – is big bucks. The e-tail market, worth £14bn (€21bn) a year in the UK alone, is growing at an annual rate of between 30 and 40 per cent. In the six weeks leading up to Christmas, over £3.5bn (€5bn) was spent online – almost 7 per cent of the total retail spend during the same period.

2 It is not just online retailers such as Amazon or eBay that have built successful businesses in cyberspace. A huge number of retailers have some kind of presence on the Internet. Most high-street names have fully transactional online operations. But many smaller retailers are nervous about the potential of e-tailing, often perceiving it as a risk and an expensive distraction as much as an opportunity.

3 'It is not a question of building a nice website and waiting for the money to come rolling it. It calls for a new business model, which seamlessly connects e-tail with the rest of the business.' says Ian Bathgate, a principal lecturer at the University of East London Business School. 'It only takes one mistake, one oversight online, to not only lose huge volumes of sales, but cause serious damage to your brand and reputation.'

4 Research shows that e-tail customers are more demanding, less forgiving and more fickle. The Web is fiercely competitive, and customers have access to unprecedented amounts of information. It takes more than a flashy website to convince them to part with their cash. An up-to-date and user-friendly website is taken as standard. The issues that are decisive in whether an online sales operation is a success – and which can create that vital competitive advantage – are around good old-fashioned customer service and order fulfilment.

5 An online operation that amounts to printing the e-mail orders at the end of the day, manually checking they are in stock and popping them in the post, probably costs more in time and effort than it earns and is unlikely to meet customer expectations in terms of accurate information on stock availability and delivery times. 'You have to manage expectations from the very beginning. It's often assumed that e-tail is all about finding the cheapest product. Yes, price is important, but probably not as important as delivery or customer service. Paying a rock-bottom price is no good if the product doesn't get delivered when it should,' says Andrew McClelland, head of projects and marketing at the Interactive Media Retail Group, the trade body for e-tailers.

C Read these sentences and choose the correct options. Read the first part of the article again and check your answers.

1 The majority of well-known shops *still haven't invested in / now offer* online sales operations.

2 Many small businesses appear to *be enthusiastic / have mixed feelings* about e-tailing.

3 The consequences of a problem with your website are loss of sales and the *high costs of finding a solution / repercussions for the company's good name*.

4 When online customers see a stylish website, they are *no longer impressed / more willing to make purchases*.

5 Manually dealing with online orders is *unlikely to be cost effective / a good low-cost option* for some businesses.

D **Read the second part of the article and decide whether these statements are true or false.**

1 A company's website doesn't have to be designed to integrate with the company's existing systems.

2 A website could lose repeat customers if it doesn't give correct information about what is available.

3 The White Company's online sales are growing at more than double the rate of the rest of the business.

4 The White Company's website receives the latest information about sales made in all areas of the business.

6 Rather than the website being a separate, self-contained part of the business, e-tail needs to be fully integrated into the support systems and infrastructure that drive every other part of the business, such as stock control, storage, delivery, customer returns and order picking. If it can't be fitted into the existing framework, then the framework needs to change to fit the website. The back-end systems – taking the order, taking payment, processing the order, despatching it –have to be geared up to make the online purchasing process as smooth as possible.

7 'Take stock availability,' says Oliver Spark, managing director of The White Company. 'A few years ago, people were more accepting if you had an item on the website that turned out not to be in stock. They are not any more. They shop online because it is quick and convenient. If your website says one thing and the stock room another, they are not going to invest their time with you again,' he says.

8 The White Company started out as a mail-order company in 1994, moved on to the Web six years ago and on to the high street in 2001. And after a slow start, the e-tailing side is booming. 'We launched our first website in 2000, and this year it will bring in sales of about £8m (€12m). It's about 20 per cent of total sales and is growing twice as quickly as the rest of the business. Overall growth is about 40 per cent, but the online side is up 86 per cent on last year,' says Spark.

9 The company's website is integrated in real time into its stock management database, the same database which feeds its shops and mail-order business. It means that when an item is sold, whether through a shop or mail order, the website is automatically updated. All its stock is stored in one warehouse and fulfilment centre in west London. During the day, mail order and online orders are picked and packed for delivery, while at night it is the stock orders for shops that take priority.

10 It is not taking the orders online that causes the problems for e-tailers, it is the operational costs of fulfilling those orders. Getting the website up and running and taking the orders is the easy part. It is meeting the higher expectation levels of the e-tail consumer where it gets tricky.

▲ Adapted from http://news. independent.co.uk

E **Find the following word partnerships in the article.**

1 Two phrasal verbs which collocate with *cash* or *money*. (paragraphs 3 and 4)

2 Three adjectives that collocate with *website*. (paragraph 4)

3 Three adjectives that collocate with *customer* and a noun phrase using *customer*. (paragraph 4)

4 Two verbs and an adjective which collocate with *expectations*. (paragraphs 5 and 10)

5 A verb phrase, a verb and five nouns which collocate with *stock*. (paragraphs 6, 7 and 9)

6 Four verbs which collocate with *order*. (paragraphs 6 and 10)

F **Use the correct words from Exercise E to complete the sentences.**

1 It isn't easy for e-tailers to persuade consumers to .... their money.

2 We need those parts today if we're going to .... this order from our Belgian client on time.

3 Our manager has very .... expectations of all her staff.

4 I'm sorry, the red ones won't .... stock until next week. We've got a black one left though.

5 It's a really .... website with lots of moving images, but the content isn't very .... – it only goes up to last year's Tour de France.

6 Supermarket customers are very .... nowadays. They'll go where the prices are most competitive, regardless of the quality of the customer ....

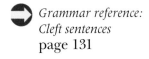

Grammar reference: Cleft sentences page 131

Business skills

Presentations:
summarising and
dealing with
questions

A **Look at the website extract and the definition of *usability* and discuss these questions.**

1 Which website(s) do you use most frequently?

2 Rate three websites for usability, giving a score out of ten. Give reasons for your scores. Consider the following: content, navigation, overall design and effectiveness of the website(s).

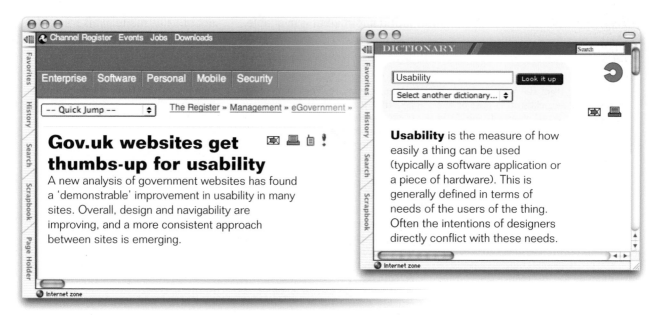

Useful language

Summarising your talk
Right, that really brings me to the end of my talk/presentation.
Let's take a look again at the key issues/points/factors …
Let's just recap …
As we've seen today, …
My main point is that …
So, to sum up, …
You'll find a summary of … in the handout.

Asking questions politely
I'd like to know what/when/where/why/how/if/whether …
I'd be interested to know (more) about …
I was just wondering what you thought about / with respect to / regarding …
Yes, but I was wondering if/whether …
I mean to say, could you tell us / explain to us …?

Dealing with questions
I'm glad you asked me that question.
I'm often asked that question. What I (usually/often) say is …
As I've said/mentioned before, …
Do you mind if we deal with that later?
I'm actually coming to that point later in my talk.

Dealing with difficult questions
I'm not sure if I entirely understand your question. Do you mean …?
What I would say is … I hope that answers your question.
I'm afraid I don't have that information at hand, but …
I'm sorry, but that's not really my field/department/sector.
I'm not really an expert on … My colleague will be talking about that later.

▲ Sophie Rawlings, Head of Web Services and Content Management for a UK government department

B 🎧 **10.4 Listen to Sophie Rawlings giving a talk about creating web pages for small businesses. How does she deal with each of the five questions?**

a) She replies positively to the question.
b) She deals with the question in a humorous way.
c) She implies she's already talked about it.
d) She says the next speaker will address the issue.

C 🎧 **10.4 Look at the expressions in the Useful language box on page 94. Listen again to Sophie dealing with questions and complete the expressions used to introduce the audience's questions.**

1 .... were the main differences between government websites and those in the private business sector?

2 .... how a company can actually improve its online sales through web-page design.

3 .... about copy writing. .... what kind of language you think work wells in websites?

4 .... whether there was any kind of language that you would avoid using?

D **Work in pairs. Ask each other questions related to the Internet and new technologies.**

Student A: Turn to page 147.
Student B: Turn to page 155.

E **You are going to give a five-minute talk on a topic. Look at page 161 for possible topics. Prepare the main points for the summary of the talk and make a note of any questions you anticipate. Tell your audience when you will take questions: either during the presentation or at the end.**

Writing: presenting information on a website

F **Sophie's colleague, Peter Adams, is giving a talk on doing business online for small businesses at the local Chamber of Commerce in London. Look at his notes from the talk which he has posted on the Chamber's website on page 161. In small groups, discuss how you could best present this information on a website, making the information clear, effective and easy to follow.**

G **Write up the main points of your talk for your company's or organisation's website. Use the Writing tips below and on page 27 to help you.**

Writing for websites

- Keep each page **short and simple**. Write 50 per cent less text than you would in hard copy, so that online users can scan information quickly.
- **Split up** long information into multiple pages.
- Use **one idea** per paragraph when writing for websites.
- Write in an **objective style**. Web users are busy and want to get straight to the facts.
- An **informal style** is also in keeping with the Web's immediate nature.
- **Update** pages regularly to reflect all possible changes, e.g. statistics, numbers and examples.

 *Writing file page 141*

CASE STUDY

Background

Audio Wire Incorporated is a leading manufacturer of professional microphones, earphones and other audio electronics based in New York. Audio Wire has hired a web design company, Online Experience, to improve sales of the earphones section of Audio Wire.com, where they sell high-quality earphones directly to consumers.

Audio Wire wants to improve online business by improving its website and is looking to increase conversion rates* and overall sales by 100%.

The deliverables for the project required of the web consultants are as follows:

- E-commerce analysis of the customer experience and the website's usability
- Analysis of online sales data
- Recommendations for redesign: content, navigation and copywriting

* The percentage of users who are browsing that end up purchasing goods or services online.

Listening 🎧 10.5

Look at Audio Wire's website below and listen to a discussion between team members at Online Experience. Ed is the Managing Director, Larry is the Online Sales Analyst and Kirstie is the Designer and Copywriter. What are the main problems with the client's website? What are their recommendations and deliverables?

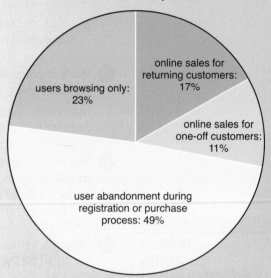

**Sales conversion rates for
Audio Wire Incorporated**

- users browsing only: 23%
- online sales for returning customers: 17%
- online sales for one-off customers: 11%
- user abandonment during registration or purchase process: 49%

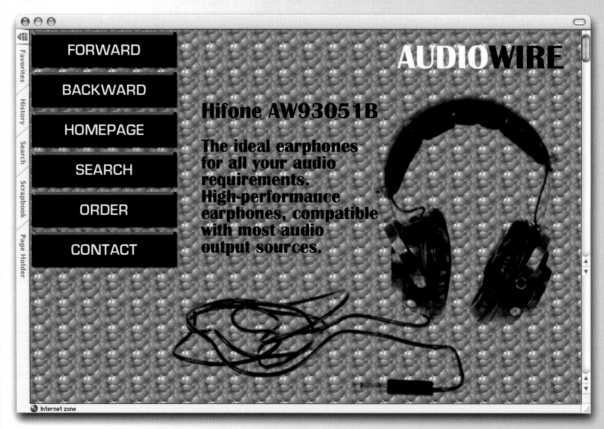

FORWARD

BACKWARD

HOMEPAGE

SEARCH

ORDER

CONTACT

Favorites · History · Search · Scrapbook · Page Holder

AUDIO WIRE

Hifone AW93051B

The ideal earphones for all your audio requirements. High-performance earphones, compatible with most audio output sources.

Internet zone

Task 1

Work in groups. You work for the web design company, Online Experience. Hold a meeting to discuss the relaunch of Audio Wire's website. How can it be more effective, and how can the business improve its online sales of audio electronics? Consider these points:

- analysis of the online customer experience: usability, navigation, content and copy-writing
- recommendations for more effective web design
- analysis of sales data
- recommendations for a more effective customer-experience strategy
- delegation of tasks and deliverables for the project

Writing

Write up a brief proposal of the recommendations for your client, Audio Wire Incorporated. Include the following information:

- executive summary (background to the project)
- key findings
- recommendations for redesign
- description of deliverables, e.g. relaunch of website

 Proposal writing page 39

Online Experience specializes in increasing online sales by improving the customer experience.

Case study

After working with Online Experience, DTV Television Networks' store saw a 50% increase in its already above-average sales conversion rate. Online Experience typically generates 40% to 150% improvements in key operating metrics, such as profit margins, conversion rates, and cost savings.

Client testimonial

"We are very happy with the impressive results from this project. Online Experience quickly and effectively delivered recommendations that led to significant, measurable improvements in our business."

DTV Television Networks

Task 2

1 In groups, present a summary of your recommendations to Audio Wire and deal with any questions they may have.
2 When you have given your presentation, listen to the other presentation(s) and ask your colleagues about their recommendation(s).
3 Decide which group put forward the best proposal.

New business

> *Whenever you see a successful business, someone once made a courageous decision.*
> Peter F. Drucker, writer and management consultant

Listening and discussion

(A) Discuss these questions.

1 Would you like to run your own business? If you wanted to start your own business, which, if any, of these sectors would most interest you?

- Hotels and catering
- Retail
- Personal-care services
- Financial services
- Tourism and leisure
- Manufacturing
- Training and education
- Publishing and printing

2 If you have a hobby that you're passionate about, could you start a business around it? Would you? Why (not)?

3 According to some business experts, to be a start-up entrepreneur you need to have huge self-confidence. You also have to be willing to risk your capital and, to an extent, your career. Do you agree with this view? What other qualities might you need?

▲ Max Benson, a director of Everywoman

(B) Everywoman is a UK consultancy which provides advice and support to women running their own businesses. Read this description of the company. Can you predict what Max Benson will say?

Search

everywoman

Favorites
History
Search
Scrapbook
Page Holder

How can Everywoman help you?
We can advise you on where to get help and we encourage you to network, to learn key ....[1] and to learn from others. We can signpost you to the people best ....[2] to help you start up. We also provide ....[3] for women, so that you can get advice from others and discuss the ....[4] and the ....[5] that you are facing in your business. We do this both via our website and hold ....[6] networking events where women can meet ....[7]. We also run ....[8] to help you develop business skills you haven't learnt in a ....[9] or because you haven't been in the ....[10].

Internet zone

C ⌒ **11.1 Listen and complete the description in Exercise B.**

D ⌒ **11.2 What sort of barriers might exist specifically for women starting a new business? Listen to the second part of the interview with Max Benson and correct the following information.**

> Research has shown that there are three specific barriers that woman face when starting a new business. Firstly, they don't know how to get access to advice. Secondly, a lot of business networks are set up and dominated by men. Another major barrier is their lack of experience. Furthermore, women are not reaching high positions in corporations and they therefore lack the range of qualifications of many men starting their own businesses. It also appears that women are slow to adopt techniques that can be used to help a business to grow.

E ⌒ **11.3 Listen to the next part of the interview and tick (✔) the main types of businesses that attract women entrepreneurs in the UK. Listen for examples of jobs and note them down.**
- Travel and tourism
- Health and personal care
- Retailing
- Computer consultancy
- Catering services
- Training and development

F ⌒ **11.4 Listen to the final part of the interview. What are the two main problems for both men and women starting their own business?**

G **Discuss these questions.**
1 Do organisations like Everywoman exist in your country? What other types of networking organisations exist for small or new businesses?
2 What are the barriers and challenges for someone starting a new business in your country?
3 What are some of the problems and risks facing small businesses generally?

H **Complete the sentences with the words and expressions in the box.**
There are two expressions you don't need.

business grants	business plan	entrepreneur	franchise
out of business	partnership	red tape	venture capital

1 I wanted to run a business, but didn't want to go it alone, so I went into . . . . with my brother.
2 Government statistics show that most small companies go . . . . before their first anniversary.
3 When looking for finance, many local and central governments offer . . . .
4 One of the biggest headaches for small business owners is the amount of government . . . . – it's very time-consuming.
5 . . . . firms and business angels are other sources of finance for small businesses.
6 Buying an existing . . . . can be a lower risk way to start your own business.

Reading and language

A Discuss these opinions about starting new businesses before you read the article.

A = agree   D = disagree   DK = don't know

1 Investors are more likely to provide capital for a great idea with a mediocre team than a great team with a mediocre idea.

2 Leadership skills in an entrepreneur are more important than experience in the field.

3 One common way of starting a business is to gain experience and knowledge in a small company and then set up a rival company in the same sector.

4 Who you know is as important as what you know when starting a new business.

5 New innovative companies usually upset the power of more established ones.

6 It is generally thought to be bad business to start up in a mature market.

7 If an entrepreneur is researching a new business idea and finds a lot of data about a specific market, it usually means it is a great business opportunity.

8 Smaller businesses are often more successful than larger ones because they can focus more on customer needs.

B Work in pairs. Student A read paragraphs 1–5 and Student B read paragraphs 6–10, then review your answers to Exercise A together.

C Find words or phrases in the article that are similar to or mean the following.

1 to start doing or saying or saying something that a lot of people are already doing or saying (paragraphs 1 and 7)

2 people who invest money in new businesses (paragraph 2)

3 something belonging to an individual or a business that has value or the power to earn money (paragraph 2)

4 the amounts of money coming into and going out of a company, and the timing of these (paragraph 2)

5 rival companies created using the knowledge and experience gained at larger companies (paragraph 4)

6 practical ability, knowledge and skill in a technical area (paragraph 5)

7 the ability to change or adapt to new ideas or trends quickly (paragraph 6)

8 very few companies who control all or most of the business activity so that others cannot easily compete with them (paragraph 6)

9 new business activities or projects that involve taking risks (paragraph 8)

10 significant because it's never been done before (paragraph 9)

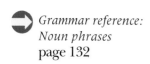
Grammar reference: Noun phrases page 132

D Find five examples of noun phrases in paragraphs 2, 3, 4, 5 and 7 of the article.

E Discuss these questions.

• To what extent do you think an entrepreneur's personal qualities are as important as their ideas?

• Who are the leading entrepreneurs in your country? Why have they been successful?

The bruises of the bandwagon

By Paul Tyrrell

1 Is there a way to tell whether a business idea will fly rather than die? Everyone, it seems, wants to run their own business, but many are failing to prepare thoroughly before scrambling on to the bandwagon. The most widespread trait is a failure to appreciate that an entrepreneur's personal qualities are just as important as their ideas.

2 Venture capitalists and business angels have always been more inclined to back a great team with a mediocre idea than a mediocre team with a great idea. They attach a lot of importance to what they term 'scar tissue' – evidence that the person has learned from experience. Even high-street banks now focus more on individuals than their convertible assets when assessing applications for business loans. If a prospective entrepreneur applies for less than £50,000 – enough for about 90 per cent of UK start-ups – the lending decision is likely to depend on an analysis of their account history, and to a lesser extent on the cashflow predictions for their business, rather than the value of their property.

3 Ultimately, the success of a business idea rests on the ability of the entrepreneur. They must have basic business skills or acquire them via personal development or hiring. They must also have leadership qualities and, of course, their chances of success will also improve in proportion to the level of relevant knowledge they bring to their chosen market. This is particularly clear in product development situations – for example, where an engi-neer takes the knowledge he gains at a large company and uses it to set up a rival.

4 Research led by Dr Rajshree Agarwal, associate professor of strategic management at the University of Illinois, suggests 'spin-outs have a survival edge in the market over other entrants, as the result of a combination of entrepreneurial flexibility and inherited knowledge'. Dr Agarwal surveyed the disk-drive industry between 1977 and 1997 and found that 25 per cent of new entrants were started by individuals leaving larger companies in the same sector.

5 Ultimately, though, what distinguishes successful entrepreneurs is their ability to spot commercially exploitable patterns where others cannot. Herbert Simon, winner of the 1978 Nobel Prize in economic sciences, suggests this process is intuitive: a good business idea stems from the creative linking, or cross-association of know-how and contacts.

6 Radicalism has always been the domain of small businesses because they can move faster than larger rivals, and venture capitalists talk of looking for opportunities that are 'disruptive' because they offer the best growth opportunities. The idea of the entrepreneur as a disruptive force dates back to 1934, when the economist Joseph Schumpeter argued that entrepreneurs were essential to long-term economic growth because they subjected monopolies or oligopolies to what he called 'creative destruction'. Innovation – whether in the form of a new product type, production method or marketing medium – is a temporary source of market

power that erodes the profits and position of old companies. This creates a new, competitive market that draws in other entrepreneurs until consolidation is required.

7 Subsequent research by Dr Agarwal, in collaboration with Professor Michael Gort, has shown that timing is critical for entrepreneurs wishing to benefit from such a market: 'Early entry during the growth phase helps survival, but is disadvantageous during the mature phase,' the pair suggest. In other words, jumping on a bandwagon is almost always a bad idea. Entrepreneurs should, in fact, be encouraged when they find there is very little data available about their chosen market. '[It] is frequently inversely related to the real potential of an opportunity,' says Jeffry Timmons, author of *New Venture Creation*.

8 This idea of combining ideas to find new solutions has become important over the past 20 years. As it has become harder to launch genuinely different products, consumers have become more value-conscious and less brand-loyal, while retailers have become increasingly powerful. 'Many entrepreneurial ventures – derived from customer knowledge – can be considered as the "consolidators" of goods and services,' suggests Richard Scase, a UK futurologist. 'Today, consumers want to be different ... Meeting these more focused consumer needs gives small firms greater competitive advantage over their larger counterparts.'

9 So if you have an idea that you think is sufficiently ground-breaking, how should you assess it? Popular benchmarks include an annual growth potential of at least 20 per cent; gross margins of at least 35 per cent; and free cashflow characteristics. Other positive qualities include: clear routes to market, the ability to create 'post-entry barriers' (measures that prevent competitors from imitating your idea once it is commercialised); and comparatively low capital requirements.

10 Yet nothing is as important as demonstrable value to customers. As Daniel Muzyka, dean of the Sauder School of Business in Vancouver and a commentator on entrepreneurship, has written: 'Opportunities are about creating value, not necessarily lowering cost ... the failure of some entrepreneurs who believe they haven't come in at the right cost is that they have not communicated value.'

FINANCIAL TIMES

Business skills

Telephone strategies

A Work in pairs. Can you predict the missing information in these telephone tips? Ask your partner questions to complete the tips.

Student A: Turn to page 147.
Student B: See below.

Student B

Telephone tips for dealing with customers and suppliers

1 Always give your name and use the other person's name. It helps to establish . . . .

2 Quote any relevant account/customer/invoice numbers and have . . . . to hand.

3 Listen actively and show that you are listening. Connect with the person by apologising, or empathising as appropriate.

4 Restate the details you are given to . . . .

5 Confirm the follow-up action that you and/or the other speaker have agreed to.

6 Make sure you agree dates or set . . . .

B 🎧 11.5 Listen to a telephone conversation between the Accounts Manager at Dyson Kitchenware and a supplier, Fenwick Plastics. What is the call about? Make a note of the good telephone strategies each speaker uses. Is there any room for improvement?

C 🎧 11.6 Listen to another telephone conversation in which the supplier, Fenwick Plastics, is chasing Dyson Kitchenware for payment. What follow-up action does each speaker agree to?

Useful language

Identifying yourself
Hello. This is [*name*] from [*company (and country)*].
This is [*name*] calling on behalf of [*company (and country)*].
I'm calling from [*company (and country)*]. Please call me [*name*].

Clarifying understanding
Sorry, I didn't get that / I missed that.
I'm sorry. I didn't quite catch that.
Would you mind repeating that, please?
Could you explain that (to me) again?
Could you go over that again?
Could/Can you spell that for me, please?

Checking details
Let me see if I have this right …
Did you say that …?
Are you saying that …?

Reaching agreement
I think we can work with that.
That seems reasonable.
Yes, that's do-able.

Confirming follow-up action
Can I just check/confirm that?
You're saying that …
I'll get back to you when/if/at/on …
As I say/said, I'll need to …
Can you tell me when that will be?
When will you call me back?

Being polite but firm
I'm sorry, (but) we'd like/expect/ want to …
(Under the circumstances), we're considering …
(Given the situation), we'll have to consider …
(You see), we may have no alternative but to …

Chasing payment

D **Complete the tips with the words and expressions in the box.**

> account/invoice   deadline   ~~debt recovery~~   delivery notes
> payment terms   recipient   reminder letter   withholding payment

---

Tips for chasing payment

- Define a structured approach to *debt recovery* [1] and stick to it with every customer. Be reasonable, firm and consistent.
- Quote any relevant .... [2] reference numbers in correspondence and on the telephone.
- Be specific and stick to the point – quote dates and any relevant agreements, such as .... [3] and credit limits.
- Include/attach copies (not originals) of any relevant documents, such as .... [4], purchase orders and invoices.
- Be clear about what you want the .... [5] to do.
- Set a .... [6] by which time you want the matter to be resolved and stick to it.
- Be persistent – write a .... [7] or follow-up on the telephone if you don't get a reply to your first letter or e-mail.
- If the client is .... [8] due to a problem with your goods or service, try to rectify the situation as soon as possible.

E **Role-play. Work in pairs. Look at your information and make the telephone call about the outstanding payment.**

Student A: See below.
Student B: Turn to page 155.

> - You are Wendy Taylor from the Accounts Department at Fenwick Plastics. You have to chase up payment at Dyson Kitchenware every month. Your company has a good working relationship with Dyson, and they place big orders, but they have recently become late payers. You suspect they may be having cashflow problems.
> - It's now July, and payment is still outstanding on invoice 17124 dated 8 June.
> - What's more, there are two new invoices issued in June which are now overdue for payment: 17289, dated 15 June, and 17356, dated 22 June. You want to get immediate payment of the invoice dated 8 June and may allow up to 15 days for the other two bills.
> - You'd also like to find out subtly if the company are having financial difficulties – it could have adverse effects on your business, too.
> - Decide what your best course of action is and phone Darren Bailey at Dyson.

Writing: a letter chasing payment

F **You are Wendy Taylor from the Accounts Department at Fenwick Plastics. Write a reminder letter to Darren Bailey, the Accounts Manager at Dyson Kitchenware. Use some of the expressions given on page 102. Include the following information:**

- Explain that payment is overdue for invoices 17289, dated 15 June, for €2,915, and 17356, dated 22 June, for €2,675.
- Remind the company about your terms and conditions of trade – payment is due 30 days from date of invoice.
- State your decision not to despatch further goods until the account is settled.
- Advise Dyson Kitchenware that you may reduce their credit limit to €6,000.

11 Copisistem: the next step

CASE STUDY

Background

Copisistem, a DVD copying and printing company based in Valencia, Spain, was set up ten years ago. At that time, VHS was the main format, but the company's founders, Doug Halliwell and José Ramón García, coming from an electronics multinational, could see the future would be digital.

The start-up costs were high, as they invested heavily in the latest data-duplication equipment and leased some light industrial space in a business park. Among their first clients was a major publisher which launched a DVD collection of wildlife documentaries.

Copisistem also worked for a national newspaper which sold DVDs with its Sunday edition. Despite this, the turnover was low in the first couple of years, as relatively few people had DVD players. But they were working with good margins and, more importantly, had managed to capture some of the biggest potential clients in the country.

Listening

🎧 **11.7** A local radio station transmits a short programme in English every morning, which is very popular with commuters. The show interviews Doug and José Ramón about their company. Listen and take notes about how the company is doing under the following headings.

- Staffing
- Threats and competition
- Turnover
- Future plans

Financial position in last three years

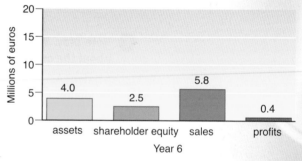

Year 6: assets 4.0, shareholder equity 2.5, sales 5.8, profits 0.4 (Millions of euros)

Year 7: assets 6.1, shareholder equity 2.9, sales 8.8, profits 0.6 (Millions of euros)

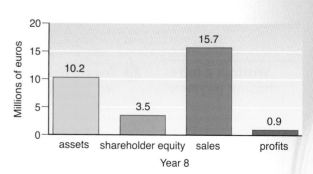

Year 8: assets 10.2, shareholder equity 3.5, sales 15.7, profits 0.9 (Millions of euros)

To: Doug Halliwell
From: Miriam Cartier
Subject: Our order no. RB673-06

Dear Mr Halliwell
I'm writing to confirm our initial order for 50,000 copies of our Natural World documentary. Our purchase order is in the post to you. You agreed in our conversation that this order could be dispatched within five working days. Could you confirm that in writing?

Doug
I've just checked, and there's no way we can fulfil this order on time. We'll have to work overtime or start doing 24-hour shift work if the orders keep coming in at this rate!!

José

Problems Copisistem's growth has also led to a number of constraints:

- Order books for this year are very full, but customers generally pay up to four months after delivery. To meet the demand, the owners need to decide if the company should stop taking orders or find a way of meeting the demand, which means raising finance. It could potentially damage the company's reputation and cost them clients if the goods aren't delivered on time. Even if the company does manage to raise some capital to buy new equipment, it wouldn't be in time to meet all this year's orders.

- The level of borrowing from banks has reached a stage where they aren't prepared to extend much more credit. The logical step is to raise finance from elsewhere, e.g. factoring, a venture capital firm or even try to negotiate faster payment from clients.

- Another major concern is that DVD technology will almost certainly soon be replaced, and they'll be left with a lot of expensive equipment.

Task 1

Work in pairs. You are the owners of Copisistem; you decide to investigate venture capital firms.

Student A: Turn to page 148.
Student B: Turn to page 155.

Task 2

You now try to find a solution to Copisistem's problems.

1 Brainstorm your options for dealing with your order book for this year and devise a plan.
2 Decide which options for raising finance you want to pursue and what you are prepared to negotiate on.
3 Decide what your strategy should be for getting the most out of your expensive equipment before its value depreciates.
4 Decide who you need to recruit to your management team to help with the expansion of your business and a possible move into other European markets.

Writing

Write a job advert for a new position in your company. See page 12 for a model if necessary.

Checklist
- job title
- employer and location
- description of business, market position and aims
- indication of where the role is in the structure
- outline of job role and purpose (expressed in the second-person: you, your, etc.)
- indication of scale, size, responsibility, timescale and territory of role
- outline of ideal candidate profile, qualifications and experience required (expressed in second person)
- salary or salary guide
- application instructions
- contact details, for example, address, phone, fax, e-mail, etc.

Project management

> *Nothing is ever built on time or within budget.*
>
> Cheops, pharaoh responsible for the
> Great Pyramid at Giza (c. 2550 BC)

Listening and discussion

A Do the following quiz about project teams. Discuss and compare your answers.

What makes a good project team?

1 A good project manager …
  a) is always friendly and easy-going.
  b) must be the most senior person on the team.
  c) spends time developing a team spirit.

2 For decisions to be reached in a project team, …
  a) there needs to be total consensus.
  b) majority rule is an efficient and fair system.
  c) what the project manager says goes.

3 In terms of timing, a successful project …
  a) will always stick to schedule.
  b) may run over schedule if the need arises.
  c) always takes much longer than expected.

4 The biggest problems for a project team are …
  a) competing goals between team members.
  b) unclear team roles and overlapping duties.
  c) lack of clearly defined objectives for the project.

▲ Michael Sawyer, Vice President of Supply Chain and Purchasing for the Sara Lee Bakery Group

B 🎧 **12.1 Michael Sawyer and Rob Jackson are two different types of project manager. Listen to their individual answers to the question:** *What are the qualities of a good project manager?* **Who mentions these points, Rob, Michael or both?**

A good project manager …	Michael	Rob
1 has good communication skills.	☐	☐
2 clarifies people's roles on the team.	☐	☐
3 knows how to organise and motivate people.	☐	☐
4 avoids acting like a boss.	☐	☐
5 includes members of the team in decisions.	☐	☐
6 knows how to delegate work.	☐	☐
7 can deal with many tasks at the same time.	☐	☐
8 is able to take a global view of the project.	☐	☐
9 ensures everyone is clear about the project aims.	☐	☐

▲ Rob Jackson,
Operations Manager for
Bachy Soletanche

C 🎧 12.2 **Listen to the next part of the two interviews and complete the notes in your own words.**

In Michael's company, it's the project sponsor's responsibility to:

- make sure that departmental goals aren't interfering with overall company goals
- make sure that the project leader has all the ....[1] needed for the project
- set ....[2] and be involved in establishing the ....[3] of the project
- attends ....[4] meetings to make sure that results are being produced and acts as a ....[5] at these meetings.

If a project isn't producing the results you wanted, Michael says you may have to ....[6]. In his experience, you need to act ....[7] you aren't getting the results.

When a project isn't on track, Rob always distinguishes between ....[8] and ....[9] issues. If the problem is an external one, you need to involve ....[10]. When's it's an internal problem, you often end up ....[11] your team.

D 🎧 12.3 **Michael Sawyer and Rob Jackson talk about what makes a project a success. Listen and complete the information.**

Michael says it's important to ....[1] at the first project meeting for two reasons:

- If you don't do that, you aren't going to have adequate ....[2].
- If the whole team agrees from the beginning, then the ....[3] is much easier.

Rob tracks the success of a project by measuring:

- Time against the ....[4]
- Costs versus ....[5] to make sure you ....[6]
- ....[7] – making sure that safe systems of work are in operation
- whether the client will return and give you ....[8]

E **How do these phrases relate to project management? Use them to complete the project managers' weblog.**

> celebrate the major milestones   face setbacks   get a quick progress report
> have a strong sponsor   miss a deadline   reach a consensus
> renegotiate budgets and timescales   take on a project

Project managers have many roles and we need support. My advice is not to ....[1] that doesn't ....[2] who is committed to seeing the project succeed. From the start, I always make sure he or she knows that you may need to ....[3] as planning progresses.

Meetings take a long time at the start of a project. You can't set the goals and make decisions without involving all team members and trying to ....[4]. It's also vital to have regular, short meetings throughout the project to ....[5] every so often.

We all know that getting through a project is hard work, and the team can easily get discouraged when they ....[6]. That's why I think it's important to ....[7] and to keep morale up. For me, whether you meet or ....[8], it's a team issue, and every member needs to feel accountable for his or her work.

Reading and language

A Rate these jobs on a scale of 1 to 5, according to which ones you think are the most difficult and thankless (5), and which ones that you think are the most enjoyable and rewarding (1). Discuss your answers.

estate agent   teacher   air-traffic controller
nurse   trader   accountant

B Read section 1 of the web article on page 109. Why do you think these firms don't have enough project managers? Read sections 2–4 and check your answers.

C Read the rest of the article and match the following headings to the different sections. There is one extra heading.

a) Project managers have to be tethered to the office

b) Technical expertise above communication skills

c) The higher education system doesn't do the job

d) Project manager is a very difficult job

e) Make the job of project manager easier

f) Not enough good project managers?

g) Project manager – sometimes a thankless job.

D Find words and expressions in the article with these or a similar meaning.

1 underachievers (section 2)

2 praised by everybody (section 3)

3 complaining (section 3)

4 extremely satisfying (section 3)

5 annoying interruption (section 4)

6 being contactable via e-mail/Internet (section 4)

7 practical (section 5)

8 constraining (section 6)

 Grammar reference: Cohesion page 133

E What or who do the highlighted words in the article refer to?

1 it (section 1)

2 it (section 2)

3 it (x2) (section 2)

4 they (section 3)

5 this (section 4)

6 that (section 5)

7 we (x2) (section 6)

8 them (section 6)

9 stuff (section 6)

10 they (section 6)

F Discuss these questions.

1 To what extent do you agree that the higher education system doesn't turn out competent project managers?

2 How could projects be the most exciting work of companies?

3 Research claims that people only consistently perform at high levels when they are appreciated at least once every seven days. Do you agree? Why (not)?

ABOUT   PUBLICATIONS   LIBRARY   NEWS   LINKS   HOME

PROGRAMMES
Design Review
Enabling
Policy
Research
Regions
Skills
Education

SEARCH THE SITE

The Zweig letter

The voice of reason for architecture, engineering and environmental consulting firms

1 . . . .

Instead of lamenting the lack of good project managers, leaders should focus on why that's the case.

My theory is that no firm is completely happy with how it handles project management. There are always problems. And one of the common complaints heard is, 'We don't have enough good project managers.'

While I will accept that as fact – i.e. architectural, engineering and environmental firms DON'T have enough good project managers – it may be helpful to explore the question of WHY that's the case. Here are my thoughts:

2 . . . .

There's no doubt about it – being a PM is a tough role. As a PM, you may get responsibility for completing a job you didn't start. A lot of bad decisions could have been made that you will have to live with. The fee allocated to do the work may be too low. The client could be impossible to please, yet your job is to please them. You could be stuck with a team of low performers and not have the authority to get rid of them. The job you are assigned to manage may be one of ten jobs that you are responsible for managing. Your computer system may not support moving the work around the firm to get it completed by those best qualified to do it. There just isn't enough time, money or manpower to do the job properly. The fact is, project manager is probably the most difficult job in the firm to do well for any number of reasons.

3 . . . .

Not only is being a PM a tough job, but you get very little appreciation from your firm for doing it. If the budgets are routinely exceeded, deliverables late or quality lacking for any number of reasons, it's no wonder PMs are not universally lauded in our firms. The fact that many, if not all, of these things were not/are not under the control of the PM is not usually brought up when top management is griping about it, or when other employees who aren't project managers are looking for someone to blame about their lack of a bonus. The good news for PMs is that they can at least get some positive feedback from the client. As the lead person handling the project from the architectural, engineering or environmental firm, they are also in the best position to see the firm's successes from the client's point of view. That's tremendously gratifying.

4 . . . .

While most everyone these days in any position of responsibility in a design or consulting firm has to accept more intrusion of work time into personal time (especially if we let personal time intrude on work time occasionally!), project managers probably face more of this than anyone else. Clients expect an immediate response to every question. Team members need to be informed of changes in direction immediately. Contractors with questions in the field need an immediate response. The need for rapid-fire response requires that the cellphone be turned on and e-mail be constantly checked. And this level of connectedness can create stress in your personal life.

5 . . . .

What the system does tend to turn out are experts (if you can call anyone with a technical degree an 'expert'). What I mean by 'expert', is someone with specific technical knowledge in a particular engineering/design/scientific discipline.

NO amount of technical knowledge, however, is a replacement for being able to communicate, being able to work well with others or being able to solve complex problems.

These are the skills that are essential to being a good project manager, and they really are not emphasised in the typical engineering, architecture or science education. The reasons for that are many. Employers want people with certain training, accreditation boards drive higher-institution curricula in certain directions, and academics often lack real-world work experience.

6 . . . .

If we want to solve the problem of not enough good project managers in our firms, we are going to have to do some things differently. That includes making the job as easy as we can for our PMs by giving them some permanently assigned staff resources, fixing accounting policies that don't encourage resource sharing, and building intelligent wide-area networks.

We need to thank our effective PMs for the amazing job they do, and we need to get those who don't do so well into roles that they can be successful at doing. We need to make sure we don't have overly restrictive policies on work hours or absences during the day if we expect on-call response from the PMs 24/7.

And we need to make sure we can tell people what the PM role is and provide some good guidance to those who want to succeed as project managers, not allowing them to go on with a dysfunctional idea that it is less important than the technical stuff they do. All of these things will help!?

Business skills

Writing: briefing multinational teams

A 🎧 **12.4 Listen to three people describing different aspects of their own cultures. Where do you think each person is from? What type of misunderstandings and conflicts could arise if you were working in a team with these people and didn't know about the issues they mention?**

B **Read these tips and try to predict the missing information. Then fill the gaps with the expressions in the box.**

frank and direct	loss of face	perceptions	senior staff
sharing information	sticking to deadlines	working practices	

Tips for working with multinational teams

- The first step is to be aware of your own behaviour, values, ...[1], ways of working and preferences. Remember, what's 'normal' for you isn't for everyone.

- Have patience. Try to learn as much as you can about the ....[2] customs, and nuances of the culture(s) that you're working with, but at the same time recognise that you're never going to know everything.

- Pay particular attention to your own attitudes and those of others in terms of
  - time (e.g. are punctuality and ....[3] highly valued?)
  - relationships (e.g. how you relate to older or ....[4])
  - communication (e.g. are people ....[5] / is there a culture of ....[6]?)
  - social values (e.g. attitudes to risk, ...[7], individuality, etc.)
  - meetings (e.g. do you expect to be involved in decision-making?)

- Know what positive and negative perceptions people from other cultures have about you and your culture.

- Adapt your communication style to work effectively with people from other cultures.

C **Look at the third tip in Exercise B. You are about to work with a multinational team. Write a brief for the other team members, explaining the standard working procedures you think are 'normal' in your country and any other information you think it is important to point out before you start working together.**

Teleconferencing

D 🎧 **12.5 Discuss these questions about teleconferencing. Then listen and decide what the problem is in each of the three conference calls.**

1 What are the technical options available for teleconferencing?
2 What are the pros and cons of teleconferencing?
3 What sort of advance planning is required?
4 What suggestions do you have to make teleconferences effective?

E Look at this advice for running a successful teleconference. Fill the gaps with the phrases in the box, then match the two parts of each phrase.

> the agenda   basic rules   an eye on   get feedback
> go over what was discussed   keep track of   take a roll call

1 Always .... at the beginning
2 Then outline ....
3 Quickly go over the .... and guidelines
4 Remember to keep .... the clock
5 Don't forget to .... who
6 Then pause periodically to ....
7 Before ending the teleconference, briefly .... and

a) and the objectives of the meeting
b) for the call, such as speaking time limits.
c) to make sure the telecon doesn't overrun.
d) is contributing to the discussion and who is not.
e) clarify any action the participants need to take.
f) and take questions from the other participants.
g) so that everyone knows who is involved and listening.

Useful language

Presentations
Let's start by taking a roll call.
Attending today's teleconference are our colleagues in the Rome office.
Otto Peterson is also joining us today. He is our chief engineer.
Who do we have with us today?
Hannah Murphy will be with us shortly.
Christine Emerson has just joined us.
Hello. This is Teresa Sousa from R&D, Lisbon.

Making a contribution
May I ask Otto a question?
I'd like to direct a question to Hannah.
I'd like to add to what Christine Emerson said.
That's something I'd like to comment on.
May I make a comment at this stage?

Checking action points
Can I just check who's doing what?
Is it correct to say that Christine is in charge of the trials?
Could we go over the action points again?

F The product development team for Archibald, a multinational food group, is holding a teleconference to discuss progress on a project. Look at the agenda and your notes for the meeting. Work in groups of three.

Student A: Turn to page 148.
Student B: Turn to page 156.
Student C: Turn to page 158.

Background
Archibald is a multinational food group. The company has been trying to break into the Chinese market, initially with its famous tinned-soup brand, but without much success. Now the company plans to hit the Chinese market with its Toto biscuits, a best-selling brand worldwide.

CASE STUDY

Leatty Shanghai: a construction project

Background

There is a building boom in residential, commercial and institutional buildings all over China. The country is currently using 54 per cent of the world's production of concrete and 36 per cent of its supply of steel. Predictions suggest that this building boom will continue for at least the next 20 years.

Leatty, a major property developer, has already been involved in several projects in China. The company's latest project, in Shanghai, aims to create a new generation of buildings based on low energy consumption, comfort and environmental protection using the most advanced technologies in the world. The project includes a three-phase housing development, as well as a shopping and leisure centre. The team is multinational, with the developer based in Canada, the architects in Germany and the multinational team of structural engineers and contractors in Shanghai.

The completion of the first phase was due 12 months after the start date. The team are now nine months into the work, and conservative estimates suggest that the project is 16 per cent over budget and two months behind schedule. A new project manager has been called in to rescue the troubled project.

Construction Phase One Milestones	Dates
Demolition and site-preparation start date	Nov 1
Building-excavation start date	Dec 15
Foundations completion	Feb 9
Underground parking complete	Mar 6
Phase 1 external steel structure complete	June 26

Report

Read this report about the delays in the project. What types of strategy might the new project manager employ to solve these problems?

UTC-time	Toronto	Berlin	Shanghai
	Mon 12:00	Mon 18:00	Tues 0:00
	Mon 15:00	Mon 21:00	Tues 3:00

The World Clock Meeting Planner

DELAYS TO THE CONSTRUCTION PHASE

SUMMARY OF FINDINGS

The building phase of the project is suffering from multiple delays.

Redesign

Initial work was delayed by design reviews on the part of the developer. The architect's redesigned plans took over three weeks to reach the contractor. Construction finally got underway on 21 January. These late design changes also delayed delivery of structural steel for the project.

Road works

Further delays were caused by the lack of access to the site. Government road building work meant that larger equipment could not reach the site until late December, and this held up the start of the site excavation.

Building contractors

One sub-contractor responsible for the foundation work was unable to comply with the new start date. Two main issues arose: they were having financial difficulties, and there was slippage on another project they were involved with, which meant they did not have the manpower or equipment necessary to start the work.

Suppliers

Because the foundations were not going to be ready on schedule, the building contractors postponed steel delivery. Indeed, on-time delivery of the steel would have caused a storage problem. Since the demand for structural steel in China far outstrips the supply at the moment, the knock-on effect has been an increase in the cost of steel and delays in delivery, which has also added to project costs.

Weather conditions

Building work was planned on a 24-hour schedule. However, there was a heatwave for part of the summer months, which hampered efforts to work around the clock.

Listening 🎧 12.6–9

There are also problems with relationships between the client and the various contractors and consultants and morale is rock bottom. The new project manager has held a number of confidential one-to-one meetings with the client and the other project team members. Listen to their views and make a note of the problems they mention.

- 🎧 **12.6** The developers
- 🎧 **12.7** The architects
- 🎧 **12.8** The building contractor
- 🎧 **12.9** The structural engineers

Task

Work in pairs. You are the project manager and the project sponsor. Hold a meeting to discuss the problems and devise a strategy to rescue the project.

1 What can be done to improve the information exchange and co-ordination of tasks?
2 What needs to be done to improve communication, team morale and working practices?
3 How can you create a safe atmosphere in the project so that team members will talk openly about problems and risks?
4 What lessons can be learnt from the first phase of the project which should be applied to the second and third phases?

Writing

Write a short assessment report of your main findings and a list of action items for the sponsor, team members and other project stakeholders. Include the following information:

- Background of project
- Reasons for this review
- Key findings
- Recommendations
- Immediate action plans

 Writing file pages 138–139

10 Online business

Reading

Read this article and complete it using the correct options.

Latest figures show a sharp growth in Internet shopping in the decade since the launch of Netscape Navigator, the first widely available Internet ....[1]. While Internet shopping accounted for just €450 million of retail sales in the UK in 1999, by last year, consumers were spending over €22.5 billion online.

Most people are now on the Internet, with 56 per cent of homes in the UK having an Internet connection and an estimated 5 million people with high-speed ....[2] access.

When the ....[3] boom took off in the 1990s, Tesco, the UK's largest supermarket group, was quick to embrace ....[4] as an alternative channel for its business and began tri-

alling online shopping in 1996. Tesco says its ....[5] is now the world's most popular online grocer and ....[6] about 120,000 ....[7] a week.

However, as consumers opt for the ease of shopping online, ...[8] crime is flourishing, with ....[9] stealing people's credit card and bank details.

The Internet has also

become one of the fastest-growing sectors of the advertising market, with spending expected to grow 20 per cent this year. With this increased activity, some of the business models discredited during the ....[10] in 2000 are now producing results, not least online shopping.

FINANCIAL TIMES

1	**a)** browse	**b)** browser	**c)** search	**d)** B2B
2	**a)** wide band	**b)** big band	**c)** broadband	**d)** browser
3	**a)** bubble	**b)** cookie	**c)** cart	**d)** dotcom
4	**a)** e-commerce	**b)** banner	**c)** back-end	**d)** hacker
5	**a)** website	**b)** cart	**c)** pop up	**d)** e-tail
6	**a)** part with	**b)** takes	**c)** deals	**d)** picking
7	**a)** petitions	**b)** buys	**c)** orders	**d)** stock
8	**a)** web	**b)** net	**c)** hyper	**d)** cyber
9	**a)** pop ups	**b)** hackers	**c)** browsers	**d)** e-tailers
10	**a)** fall	**b)** booming	**c)** crash	**d)** burst

Vocabulary

e-commerce

Which of the four words in column 2 does NOT collocate with the word in column 1?

	Column 1	Column 2
1	damage to their	reputation fickle brand stock
2	part with	cash money time goods
3	customer	expectations flashy returns service
4	stock	room availability back-end management
5	order	fulfilment picking store processing
6	launch a(n)	product website campaign order
7	online	retailer shopping website sales
8	business	model plan channel selling
9	user-friendly	website software price system
10	take	a mistake an order payments priority

Cleft sentences

Choose the correct alternative to complete each sentence.

1 *It is the increased /What has increased* access to the Internet that has made online shopping a success.

2 What caused the business to fail *was their poor /it was poor* website design.

3 *The reason why /The thing that* attracts people to online shopping is the convenience.

4 *All that has /What has* forced many large retailers to have a presence on the Net is consumer demand.

5 *Queuing /It was queuing* in busy shops was what made her decide to do the rest of her Christmas shopping online.

6 The reason why I like eBay *is that it's /is why it's* fun to take part in an auction.

Presentations

summarising and dealing with questions

Match the functions (1–7) to the expressions (a–g).

1 Summarising your talk
2 Asking questions politely

3 Dealing with questions
4 Dealing with difficult questions

5 Delaying giving an answer

6 Referring to a previous point

7 Offering to take questions

a) I'm actually coming to that point later.
b) I'm glad you asked me that question. What surprises me is the growth in revenue.
c) Let's take a look again at the key points.
d) Just feel free to interrupt if you have any questions.
e) I'm not sure if I understand your question. Do you mean how to advertise online?
f) I was wondering what you thought about online advertising.
g) As I mentioned before, most people now have Internet access

Writing

You are responsible for Audio Wire's website (see page 96). Your company has implemented Online Experience's proposals for improving the website. Write a report for your manager explaining how online sales have been affected by the relaunched website.

11 New business

Reading

Look at the following web page which provides information for people wanting to start their own businesses. Complete the spaces with the words and expressions in the box.

| business plan | an entrepreneur | franchising | go out of business |
| going into | grants | loan | red tape | running | venture capital |

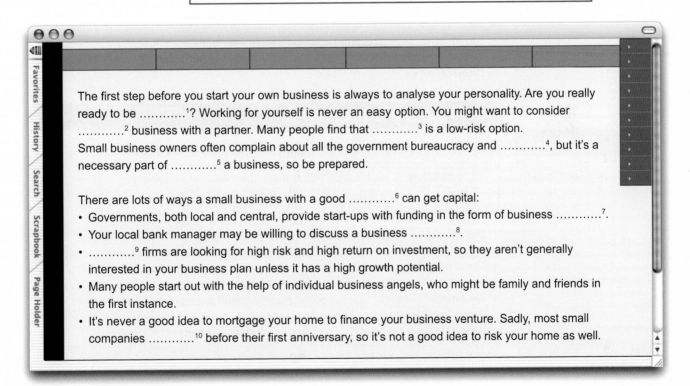

The first step before you start your own business is always to analyse your personality. Are you really ready to be ....[1]? Working for yourself is never an easy option. You might want to consider ....[2] business with a partner. Many people find that ....[3] is a low-risk option.
Small business owners often complain about all the government bureaucracy and ....[4], but it's a necessary part of ....[5] a business, so be prepared.

There are lots of ways a small business with a good ....[6] can get capital:
• Governments, both local and central, provide start-ups with funding in the form of business ....[7].
• Your local bank manager may be willing to discuss a business ....[8].
• ....[9] firms are looking for high risk and high return on investment, so they aren't generally interested in your business plan unless it has a high growth potential.
• Many people start out with the help of individual business angels, who might be family and friends in the first instance.
• It's never a good idea to mortgage your home to finance your business venture. Sadly, most small companies ....[10] before their first anniversary, so it's not a good idea to risk your home as well.

Telephone language

Match the function (1–5) to the expressions (a–e).

1 Identifying yourself
2 Clarifying understanding

3 Checking details
4 Reaching agreement
5 Confirming follow-up action

a) As I said, I'll get back to you this afternoon.
b) Let me see if I have this right. You can deliver within 24 hours.
c) I'm sorry, I didn't quite catch that.
d) This is Jill Barnes calling on behalf of Fenwick Plastics.
e) I think we can work with that.

Chasing payment

Look at this letter demanding payment. In eight of the lines (1–12) there is an extra word that doesn't fit. Write the extra word on the line provided or put a tick (✓) if the line is correct.

We are writing to inform you that, despite earlier requests	1 ....
for payment, invoice no. 908.06, dated 18 March for	2 ....
€1,688.50, remains outstanding. Please you find attached	3 ....
a copy of the invoice for your information.	4 ....
In the view of our good commercial relationship to date,	5 ....
we would have like to resolve this amicably. We ask	6 ....
that you to settle this account within seven days of today's	7 ....
date. In the event that you have already been paid this	8 ....
invoice, please ignore that this reminder.	9 ....
We'd be grateful if you could give this matter your urgent	10 ....
attention. Unless payment is not received by this date, we	11 ....
may have no alternative but to do review your account with us.	12 ....

Presentation

Look at the Copisistem case study on page 104. You are one of the company directors and you have sent your business plan to a venture capital firm. They want you to do a ten-minute presentation that will include your priorities and vision for the company.

Outline

- Begin by giving the backgrounds of key management members and what it is about your management team that makes them uniquely capable.
- Outline the primary risks facing this opportunity and how the potential rewards justify the risks.
- Describe any alliances or partnerships that you have entered or plan to enter.
- Say how you plan to expand your workforce and management team.
- Conclude with a brief presentation of your financial performance, projections and capital needs.

12 Project management

Vocabulary

Complete the sentences with the correct word or phrase from the box.

deadline	multitask	on track	over budget	sponsor
	reach a consensus	safety	setbacks	

1 The project .... has been extended to 31 January.
2 It's going to be impossible to .... on this issue. We'll have to go with majority rule.
3 There have been a number of .... due to the bad weather conditions.
4 The increasing cost of raw materials means that we're running completely ....
5 We have an excellent .... record. There haven't been any accidents on site.
6 A good project manager knows how to ....
7 Despite delays, we're still .... to open the new hospital in March.
8 The .... isn't involved in the day-to-day running of the project, but she attends our weekly progress meetings.

Cohesion

Read this article and substitute the underlined phrases with the words in the box.

both parties	by then	it	it	the other
the project	them	they	this	this

In 1995, a global software house had been contracted to develop a crew scheduling project for a large airline. The project[1] was due to take 18 months with 300 full-time staff. When I was asked to review the project in 1998, the project[2] was already 18 months late. In 1998[3], the airline and the software house[4] were on their fourth project manager, and each side was blaming the other side[5].

It became clear during the review that the software house and the airline[6] had a vested interested in letting the whole thing[7] fail. The supplier had realised that their software design was fundamentally flawed, and wanted to hide their design flaw[8] by blaming the failure on the customer's frequent design changes. The customer, however, had identified a better solution and wanted to sue the existing supplier as incompetent, in an effort to recover costs.

In other words, a project can encounter problems because someone deliberately created these problems[9], in addition to poor planning, incompetence, coincidence or a host of other reasons. The good project manager has to be constantly on the alert for this situation[10], particularly if trouble is already brewing elsewhere.

Reading

Complete the article with the words or phrases in the box. There are two extra ones you don't need.

around the clock	confronting	direct style	face-to-face
meeting times	milestones and deliverables		overruns
teamwork	telecon	setbacks	speak up	workload

When US clients and Indian firms work together, the biggest challenge is cultural integration. 'Indians do not ....[1] in meetings and do not like ....[2] the client, which sometimes leads to awkward situations like project delays and cost ....[3]. The client often wonders why those things were not stated in the first place,' says Girish Paranjpe, president, Wipro Technologies. 'North Americans typically employ a bold, ...[4] of communication. Indians, on the other hand, are often more ambiguous in their verbal communications, and in how they interpret what is being said.' To avoid these pitfalls, team managers insist on writing out the exact expectations of a project, with concrete ....[5].

Then there are differing working styles, which can create more tension. Indian managers tend to prefer ....[6] meetings and speaking in person, so they don't like leaving voicemails. Also, Indians are used to working ....[7], whereas in the West, the balance between work and personal time is seen as very important. There are even problems when fixing ....[8]. A senior manager at an IT development centre in India says: 'The time for a ....[9] was set when the US team came to work in the morning, which is late at night for us.'

Indian companies now hire a lot of expatriates in sales and business development roles. Given that they understand both Indian and American cultures, they can rapidly identify potential pitfalls in ....[10] and intercultural communications.

Writing

Imagine a colleague of yours is going to work on an international project with Indian and North American team members. Write an e-mail to him/her giving them some advice about some cultural issues such as: communication style, meetings, working practices.

Teleconferencing

You are Bob Frasier, a marketing manager for the Archibald Food Group (see page 111). Write the action minutes from your last teleconference and a short status report for your project sponsor.

Grammar reference

1 Business idioms

There are many metaphors and idioms related to sport and gambling used in the business world.

*British business leaders say they face **an uneven playing field** in Europe.* (= unfair competition)

*What time does the sales workshop **kick off**?* (= start)

*Let's **kick around** a few ideas around for a new marketing slogan.* (= discuss or brainstorm)

*You may not like his methods, but he's really **on the ball**.* (= quick to understand)

*Can you give us **a ball-park figure**?* (= an approximate number)

***The ball's in our court now**.* (= it's (our) turn to do something about a situation)

*The sales are **on track** for another quarterly improvement.* (= likely to achieve)

*The meeting is starting to **get off track**.* (= not focus on the essential)

*The company has **a good track record** in running projects.* (= shown how good they are in the past)

*The company has been **gaining ground** on **the bigger players** in the industry.* (= reaching a similar level to; important companies or people)

***The stakes are high** in venture capitalism.* (= it's risky)

*Salaries will increase by 3 per cent **across the board**.* (= for everyone in the company)

*This could be a very lucrative deal **in the long run**.* (= at a much later time)

*This strategy seems like **a long shot**.* (= it will have little chance of success)

***The odds are** that our competitors will lower their prices soon.* (= It's likely)

● **Look at the business idioms in *italics* and choose the correct meanings.**

1 Let's *get* this meeting *back on track*.
   a) postpone for a later date
   b) return to the main subject

2 Shall we *go over* the figures on the handout?
   a) examine
   b) ignore

3 Well, we *are running out of* time. So let's have one final question.
   a) have lots of
   b) don't have much

4 Could you *stick to the point*?
   a) give an example
   b) talk about what's relevant

5 Can we *get your input on* this?
   a) hear what you think about
   b) ask you to stop talking about

6 Would you like to *kick off* the discussion?
   a) stop
   b) start

7 It's hard to *keep track of* what she's saying. She talks so fast.
   a) decide what's relevant
   b) follow and understand

8 Why don't we *kick around* a few ideas?
   a) discuss
   b) reject

2 Multiword verbs (see also Unit 6)

We form multiword (or phrasal) verbs using a verb, e.g. *set*, with a prepositional particle, e.g. *up*, or an adverbial particle, e.g. *back*. There are four types:

1 **Intransitive multiword verbs**

   These have no object.

   Please ***go on***.

2 **Transitive multiword verbs**

   The noun can go before or after the particle. Note: if a pronoun is used to substitute a noun, it can only go before the particle.

   We've ***called*** the meeting ***off***.
   We've ***called off*** the meeting
   We ***called*** it ***off***.
   ~~We called off it.~~

3 **Prepositional verbs**

   The object can only go after the particle.

   *It isn't easy persuading online shoppers to **part with** their cash.*

4 **Three-part (phrasal-prepositional) verbs**

   The object goes after the particles.

   *Let's see if the packing department can **come up with** a solution.*

There are various multiword verbs related to education, training and research, e.g. *break away from, bring in, catch up (with), cope with, drop out, fall behind with, follow up, look into, put someone through, read up on, start up, set up, write up*:

*I found it difficult to **cope with** the heavy workload. I **fell behind with** my background reading and **dropped out** of the MBA course before the final test.*

*Giovanni is employed by a business school because of his contacts with companies abroad. They expect him to **bring in** more overseas students.*

*He's **following up** his postgraduate economic research by writing articles in specialist journals.*

*Simone is a management trainer and is **looking into setting up** an online course for busy managers.*

● Complete these sentences using a verb from the box in the correct form.

break away from   catch up   cope with
drop out   fall behind with   follow up
look into   put someone through

1 Blended learning is one way of .... more traditional educational methods but not everybody enjoys studying online after a day at work.

2 We've really .... our training and development in recent years; some of the staff haven't done any courses for three years now.

3 I couldn't attend the course last week. Do you mind lending me some of your course notes so that I can .... ?

4 Unless you .... every course programme in detail, it's impossible to tell which ones are the best.

5 I was very disappointed when my mentor .... of my programme; it's so difficult to find a replacement.

6 She was very bright and talented and managed to get a sponsor to .... an MBA at a prestigious Parisian business school.

7 The course trainer was excellent; he made us work hard, and we enjoyed learning about techniques for .... stress at work.

8 Our HR director has always .... on the benefits of investment in training by insisting that participants put into practice what they have learnt.

3 Dependent prepositions

1 Many verbs go with dependent prepositions. Here are some examples:

- *allow, apply, argue, ask, bid, budget, charge, opt, pay, provide (something)* **for**

- *believe, delay, experiment, invest, result, train* **in**

- *advise, (dis)agree, build, collaborate, depend, improve, insist, rely, research, spend* **on**

- *admit, allocate, allow, connect, decide, decline, encourage, expect, fail, forbid, force, forget, help, hesitate, hope, intend, lead, learn, like, listen, mean, need, offer, persuade, prefer, present, propose, recommend, sell, speak, submit, supply, talk, tend, try, want* **to**

- *(dis)agree, collaborate, consult, contrast, discuss, meet, negotiate, provide (someone), supply, work* **with**

*We are **depending on** the government to improve local transport services.*

*The management of the London Underground eventually **opted for** a public private partnership to run the trains.*

*The public sector has to **collaborate with** the private sector if the public is to be **provided with** hospitals, schools and transport.*

2 Some verbs may be followed by more than one preposition, sometimes with a corresponding change in meaning.

*A private construction firm **negotiated** successfully **with** the government and won the contract.*
(= reached agreement with)

*Workers in the public sector have **negotiated for** a salary increase this year.* (= asked for and obtained)

*They **forgot to allow for** inflation, so the cost of the project went up by two per cent.* (= did not budget for)

*The British government **allowed** the country's railwork network **to be** privatised.* (= gave permission)

Note: We can *provide someone with something*, but we *provide something for someone*:

*The NGO **provided** people in the affected area **with** emergency food, water and medical supplies.*

*The NGO **provided** emergency food, water and medical supplies **for** people in the affected area.*

3 Nouns related to the previous verbs can also have corresponding dependent prepositions.

- *allowance, application, argument, bid, budget, charge, need, preference, proposal, provision, recommendation, request* **for**

- *belief, delay, experiment, improvement, investment, research, result, training* **in**

- *advice, (dis)agreement, building, collaboration, dependence, improvement, insistence, spending, work* **on**

- *admittance, allocation, attempt, connection, decision, expectation, failure, hesitation, hope, intention, persuasion, presentation, proposal, recommendation, sales, supply, tendency* **to**

- *(dis)agreement, collaboration, comparison, contrast, discussion, meeting, negotiation, supply* **with**

***Delays in** the region's infrastructure development have led to significant **loss of** foreign trade.*

*We fear the **decision to** increase government spending will result in higher taxes.*

*It was the third time the city had lost the **bid for** the Olympics.*

*Construction **work on** the airport was very slow.*

***Provision for** public services in Scandinavian countries is generally very good.*

4 Sometimes the verb and noun use different prepositions.

*The government **needs to** build more hospitals.*

*The **need for** hospital construction has resulted in various public private initiatives.*

● **Write the following verbs and nouns in the correct column, according to which preposition they can be followed by. Some can go with more than one.**

advise build forbid persuade prefer provide supply

to	on	with

3 Passive

We use the passive when the person who performs the action is unknown, unimportant or obvious.

1 The passive can be used in all tenses and with modal auxiliaries.

   *A new station **is being** built.*

   *The project **was going to be completed** last week.*

   *He **had been asked** to rewrite the report.*

   *Construction workers **may be required** to work Sundays.*

   *The best proposal **should be presented** to the board of directors.*

   *The public **would have been informed** eventually of the plans.*

2 If we know who performed the action (the agent), we use *by*.

   *The secret plans were revealed **by** an undercover TV journalist.*

3 Passive constructions are common in formal contexts, for example in reports or action minutes, and help to create an impersonal style. Using *it* as a subject avoids mentioning the person responsible for saying or doing something.

   *It **was considered** to be the best option.*

   *It **was felt** that a public private partnership would receive criticism.*

   *It **was agreed** that the motorway should be built by an Italian firm.*

Passive use of *get* and *get something done*

1 Look at these examples of *get* for (informal) passive use from the text on pages 24–25.

   *Companies **got badly burned** in Latin America.* (paragraph 5)

   We can also say *Companies **were badly burned** ...*

   *'... if nobody pays for this stuff, it **doesn't get built**,' says Mr Klein.* (paragraph 7)

   We can also say, *... if nobody pays for this stuff, it **isn't built** ...*

2 We can also use *get* in a similar way to *have* in the expression *have something done* when you ask someone to do something for you.

   *The Austrian government **had/got a new toll road system designed and built** by Autostrade of Italy.*

3 We also use *get* (not *have*) in the expressions *get someone interested/involved*, etc. instead of saying *interest/involve someone*.

   *We're trying to figure out how to **get projects' sponsors interested** again.* (paragraph 6)

   We can also say, *We're trying to figure out how projects' sponsors could be interested again* or *... how to interest projects' sponsors again.*

● **Rewrite these active sentences, changing the underlined verbs into the passive.**

1 Several US states have recently involved the private sector in international marketing campaigns.
   The private sector ...

2 How much money should private enterprise put into public projects, when there is an existing government budget?'
   How much private money ...

3 The state of Alabama has partly solved the problem by giving the private sector an almost free hand.
   The problem ...

4 But critics say it is hard for the private sector to know how far it should involve itself when government funding exists.
   But critics say it is hard for the private sector to know how far it ...

5 Vice-president of the Economic Development Partnership of Alabama says 70 businesses privately funded his department last year.
   Vice-president of the Economic Development Partnership of Alabama says his department ...

6 The public-private Indiana Economic Development Corporation provides another model.
   Another model ...

7 The IEDC president says it has encouraged companies to locate to Indiana, and the state now handles export promotion.
   The IEDC president says companies ...

8 The state of Indiana has already closed twice as many deals compared with the same period last year.
   Twice as many deals ...

4 Discourse devices: linking expressions

Type	Expressions	Examples
Adding extra information	*in addition to*, too, also, as well (as), what's more, on top of this, moreover, with regard to, with reference to, furthermore**	*Quarterly results yesterday showed a 3.6 per cent improvement.* **Furthermore,** *demand remains strong. The alleged bribes threaten to damage the reputation of company's vice-chairman,* **as well as** *the chairman.*
Contrasting information	*however, nevertheless*, despite (this), in spite of, although, yet, (even) though, but, on the other hand*	*The company had set itself modest targets for this year. Now,* **however,** *there is a chance it might deliver better than expected results. Acquisitions in Latin America boosted the profits of the telephone company,* **despite** *declining revenue in its home market.*
Introducing the result of previous information	*as a result, so, consequently*, as a consequence*, given*, due to, because of, thereby*, therefore*	*Profits may soon fall* **due to** *weak demand and high prices.* **Consequently,** *growth could drop to two per cent again next year.*
Giving the reason for something	*as, since, because, in order to*, so that, that's why, for this reason**	*Generating electricity using renewable sources costs more.* **For this reason,** *government subsidies are needed* **in order to** *compete.*
Expressing a sequence of events	*firstly/secondly etc., in the first/ second/etc. place, then, after (that), finally, the final point/step/issue, some time later*	*The CEO resigned* **after** *the riotous shareholders' meeting.*

* Formal written language rather than speech

⬤ **Complete the second sentence so that it has a similar meaning to the first. Use between one and five words, including the one in brackets.**

1 If petrol prices increase a lot, people might buy smaller cars.

   People are unlikely .... petrol prices increase a lot. (*unless*)

2 The oil supply is running out. Consequently, we'll soon have no option but to use other forms of energy.

   We'll soon have no alternative but to find other sources of energy .... running out. (*since*)

3 Although the villagers had reservations about the wind-farm project, they accepted it.

   The villagers accepted the wind-farm project .... about it. (*spite*)

4 The company is organising an energy saving drive in order to cut fuel bills.

   The company is promoting energy saving .... reduce fuel bills. (*so*)

5 Wind energy is expensive because of the high cost of the turbines.

   Wind energy isn't .... a lot to build the turbines. (*because*)

6 Given the low rainfall this spring, the government is going to restrict water supplies.

   The government plans to place restrictions .... the low rainfall this spring. (*because*)

5 Cohesive devices

We often refer back or forwards to something in the text to avoid repetition and so that it is easier to understand.

1 This is an example of **forward** reference.

*I looked at the big headline on the e-mail and hesitated before doing **what I usually do** with **this sort of stuff**: **press delete**. **The message**, from a consultancy called Rapporta, stood out for its sheer stupidity.*

What I usually do refers forwards to *press delete*.

This sort of stuff refers forwards to *The message*.

2 These are examples of **backward** reference, i.e. they refer back to a previous word in the text.

***General Electric** pioneered the India 'offshoring' model in the 1990s, when **it** hired staff in Delhi to perform simple data-processing tasks.*

*India now employs **more than 300,000 people** in call centres, many **of whom** work at other in-house – or 'captive' – centres owned by foreign investors.*

*When you move certain processes offshore to a country like India**, your cost-savings** are one-off – **they** tend to diminish pretty quickly.*

*What we hear increasingly loudly is **international companies** saying: '**We** don't want to do **this** ourselves any more. If **others** can provide a better value proposition and we can still retain some control, then **that's the way** we should go.*

In this last extract, *We* refers back to *international companies*.

Others refers to other international companies.

That's the way refers to the idea of other companies doing the job.

3 A writer sometimes refers to an idea **outside the text.** In the previous example, the writer assumes the reader knows what the writer is referring to; in this case, *this* refers to outsourcing call-centre work.

● Look at this extract from the article where *others* refers back to and substitutes the phrase *some companies*:

*'Some companies have introduced salsa classes. **Others** have moved to multi-cuisine canteens.'* (paragraph 5)

What do these words and phrases in the article refer to? Do they refer forwards or back to something in the text? Do they substitute or omit another word or phrase?

1 such anxieties (paragraph 1)
2 This (paragraph 2)
3 **This** is particularly true (paragraph 3)
4 Almost all (paragraph 5)
5 them (paragraph 5)
6 More seriously (paragraph 6)
7 for **those** (paragraph 6)
8 At the same time (paragraph 10)

5 Using inversion for emphasis

1 Not only ... (but) also

Not only have the trends towards outsourcing and offshoring offered India and China huge opportunities, **but** they have **also** provided companies around the world with new markets.

Based on current trends, **not only** will the US have five per cent fewer people of working age by 2015 than it does today; it will **also** need 15.6m more workers.

2 Only ...

Only when I get difficult customers.**do I** get stressed at work.

(= I only get stressed at work when I get difficult customers.)

3 Rarely / Never / Hardly / Scarcely / No sooner

Rarely is call-centre work interesting or varied.

(= Call centre work is rarely ...)

4 Under no circumstances / On no account

Under no circumstances were we allowed to make personal calls at work.

(= We were not allowed to make ... under any circumstances.)

● **Rewrite these sentences using the words or expressions given.**

1 Call-centre work is repetitive and it's stressful too.
   Not only ...

2 The company increased salaries and created recreational facilities for staff.
   Not only ...

3 Paul worked in IT for two years before realising he wasn't cut out for the job.
   Only when he had ...

4 I had never found a job so rewarding until I started working for myself.
   Never ...

5 He had just started interviewing candidates for the new job vacancies when three more people handed in their notice.
   Hardly ...

6 She will never accept a cut in salary.
   On no account will ...

6 Multiword verbs (see also Unit 2)

Here are some common multiword verbs:

1 Telephone language

call/phone/ring back, hang up, put (someone) through, get back to (someone)

2 Meetings

bring (something) up, carry (something) out, deal with (something), fill (someone) in, fix (something) up, get down to (something), get though (something), look into (something), move on to (something), put (something) off, point (something) out, see to (something), send for (someone or something), set (something) up, sit down, stick to (something), turn up

3 Negotiations

back out of (something), fall through, get back to (someone), set (something) out, take (something) over, take up (something), talk about (something), think about (something), turn (something) down, walk out on (something or someone)

1 Complete the following questions using the correct multiword verb. Then discuss the questions.

1 Do you think it's important that companies *set up /set out /follow suit* their commitment to CSR in an annual report?

2 How can corporations be *held to account / carried out /fallen into* by governments, consumers and employees?

3 What types of products and practices might companies *set out /phase out /fall into* in the interests of social responsibility?

4 Why might a company *follow suit /hold to account /shy away from* difficult questions in their CSR reports?

5 If a multinational decides not to employ child labour, do you think smaller companies will *follow suit /carry out /phase out*?

2 Complete the sentences using the correct multiword verb.

1 I'm sorry, I don't have that information. I'll .... to you later today.
   a) get through
   b) get down
   c) get back

2 This isn't time to do this today. Can we .... making a decision until next week?
   a) put off
   b) put through
   c) get through

3 The government has agreed to .... an investigation into the food-poisoning incident.
   a) carry out
   b) drop out
   c) point out

4 A committee was .... to co-ordinate the company's social responsibility effort.
   a) turned up
   b) set up
   c) brought up

5 It was .... at the shareholders' meeting that our safety record had improved tremendously.
   a) walked out
   b) phased out
   c) pointed out

6 The deal .... when we discovered that their employment practices were unethical.
   a) fell through
   b) put through
   c) got through to

7 We have .... the consultant's recommendation to sponsor a local sports event.
   a) turned up
   b) taken up
   c) hung up

8 The company is prepared to .... contracts with suppliers which are not disposing of industrial waste in a responsible manner.

7 Language of trends

In the Since the	first/second/ etc.	month/ quarter/year	
Over the	short term, medium term, long term, next ... months, next ...years,	we are expecting a ... there will be a ... we'll see	
There was a There has been a There will be a We expect a	gradual slight slow steady	increase recovery upturn growth decrease	in demand. in share prices. in sales. in advertising revenue.
	unexpected sudden	downturn	
	rapid huge		
Profits have	doubled. tripled. recovered. improved. rocketed.		
	increased risen gone up jumped grown	by 25%. by a third. threefold. slightly. gradually. suddenly. etc.	
	decreased dropped fallen gone down declined dipped		
	stabilised levelled off		
Sales are expected/ projected to	increase, etc.		

1 **Look at the graphs and choose the correct option to describe the trend.**

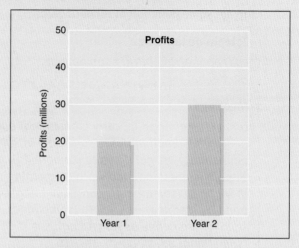

1 Profits have ...... since last year.
   a) jumped by 50%
   b) gone up by a third
   c) risen slightly

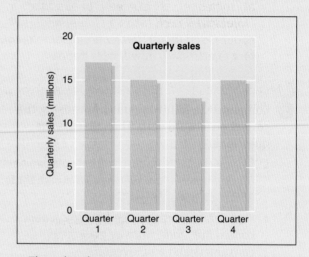

2 There has been a ....
   a) huge leap in sales since the first quarter of this year
   b) slight recovery in sales in the last quarter
   c) sharp drop in sales between the third and fourth quarters

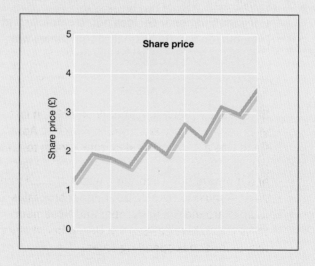

3 Shares in the company have ...... since the takeover was announced.
   a) almost doubled
   b) levelled off
   c) gone up almost threefold

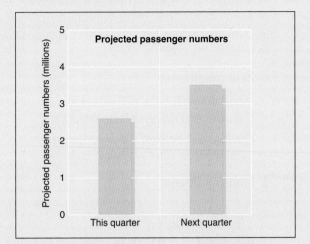

4 Passenger numbers are ...... in the next quarter.
   a) up this quarter at 3.5m, but expected to return to 2.6m
   b) expected to grow by 0.9m
   c) projected to leap by 2.6m to 3.5m

2 **Look at the graph and complete the sentences with one of the words or expressions in the box.**

falling from	gradually declined	rapid upturn
recovered	slight drop	soar to	stabilised at

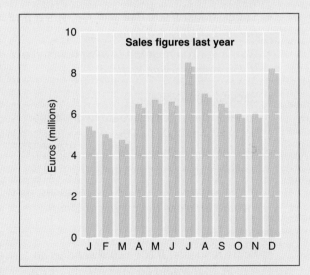

Sales ....[1] between January and March last year, ...[2] 5.4m to 4.25m. In March to April, there was a ....[3] in sales from 4.75 m to 5.5m. July saw sales ....[4] 8.5m thanks to the launch of our new range. Then there was a ....[5] from 7m in August to 6.5m in September and sales ....[6] around 6m in October and November. Sales ....[7] well at 8.2m in December, thanks to the Christmas spending spree.

8 Negation using prefixes

We can make nouns, verbs and adjectives negative with a negative prefix.

	Prefixes	Examples
Nouns	anti-	*anti-business lobby, anti-nuclear campaign*
	de-	*deregulation of the industry, company decentralisation*
	dis-	*dishonesty, dissatisfaction, disadvantage*
	in-	*incompletion, inconvenience*
	non-	*non-executive director, non-dollar assets, non-core businesses*
Verbs	de-	*decentralise, decommission, deregulate, devalue*
	dis-	*discontinue, disagree, disinvest*
	mis-	*misinterpret, mismanage, misrepresent, misunderstand, misuse*
	un-	*unbundled, unbalance, uncover, unload*
Adjectives	dis-	*dishonest, dissatisfied, disqualified*
	il-	*illegal, illegible, illicit*
	im-	*impossible, imperfect*
	in-	*incompetent, inactive, incompatible*
	ir-	*irrelevant, irresponsible, irrecoverable*
	mis-	*misleading, misused*
	un-	*uneconomic, unreliable, unscrupulous, unemployed*

● **Complete the second sentence so that it has a similar meaning to the first sentence. Use the words in the box with a suitable prefix.**

compatible	continued	convenient	core
informed	interpreted	leading	legible
loading	regulated	satisfied	used

1 I'm sorry, you were not given the correct data.
   I'm sorry you have been ....

2 We are not at all happy with your customer-service department.
   We are very .... with your customer-service department.

3 Monday's not a good day for me to meet.
   It's .... for me to have the meeting on Monday.

4 The machine is broken because it hasn't been operated properly.
   The machine is broken because it's been ....

5 The company decided to sell off everything that was not central to their business.
   The company decided to sell off all .... business.

6 This colour is no longer available.
   This colour has been ....

7 I don't think I have understood what you meant.
   I think I may have .... you.

8 A consignment of glasses were broken while being taking off the truck.
   A consignment of glasses were broken when they were .... them.

9 His handwriting is impossible to read.
   His handwriting is totally ....

10 The consultant warned that the two company cultures might not work together.
   The consultant warned that the two company cultures might be ....

11 This advertisement does not give a true description of the product.
   This advertisement gives a .... description of the product.

12 The government has reduced its control of the energy sector.
   The government has .... the energy sector.

8 Conditionals

Conditional sentences usually have two clauses: a conditional clause and a main clause. There are four basic conditional forms. The pattern we use depends on the time of the condition and how possible or impossible the event is. It is possible to reverse the order of the clauses.

1 **Zero conditional**

   Form: *If/When* + present, present

   Use: General rules, universal truths.

   *Obviously it **helps** to have some capital **if** you **want** to start your own business.*

2 **First conditional**

   Form: *If/Unless* + present, *will* (other modal verb or *going to*) + infinitive

   Use: likely or possible situations or events, now or in the future.

   *Heavy industries **could shut down** temporarily this winter **if** a cold period **leads** to a gas shortage.*

Related uses:

- Offers: *I'll **send** you some of the literature **if** you **like**.*

- Orders: ***Switch** off the air conditioning **if** it **gets** too cold in here.*

- Requests: ***Will** you **send** that e-mail today **if** you **have** time?*

- Suggestions: ***If** you **like** seafood, you'**ll find** the monkfish is delicious.*

- Warnings: *You'**re going to burn** yourself out **if** you **keep** working so hard.*

3 **Second conditional**

   Form: *If* + past tense, *would/wouldn't* (or other modal) + infinitive

   Use: unlikely or improbable situations or events, now or in the future.

   ***If** they **wanted** to acquire the company, they **would increase** their share holdings.*

Related uses:

- Polite requests: ***If** you **could send** us an e-mail, that **would be** the best approach.*

- Giving advice: ***If** I **were** you, I'**d start** applying for a new job.*

- Desires and regrets: ***If** we **had** more time, we **could** fine-tune this proposal.*

Inverted forms:

   ***If** we **needed** more time, would that be a problem?*

   ***If** we **were to need** more time, would that be a problem?*

> ***Were** we **to need** more time, would that be a problem?*
>
> ***Should** we **need** more time, would that be a problem?*

4 Third conditional

Form: *If* + past perfect, *would/could* + *have* + past participle

Use: unreal or hypothetical situations or events in the past.

> ***If** we **had signed** the deal a week earlier, we **would have saved** some costs.*

Related uses:

- Expressing criticism: ***If** you **had told** me sooner, we **could have avoided** this problem.*

Inverted form:

> ***Had we signed** the deal a week earlier, we **would have saved** some costs.*

● **Look at this extract from the article on page 73. Then identify the conditional in each example (1–6) and choose an option (a–f) to explain why a conditional is being used.**

'I'm often told, get this solution and you'll get the job,' says Rachel Jackson of Hay Group. '**If I was unscrupulous, I would take it**. But this isn't ethical.'
Second conditional: describing a hypothetical current situation

a) Making a polite request
b) Stating a necessary condition
c) Giving a warning
d) Expressing complaint or criticism about a past action or event
e) Describing a hypothetical situation in the past
f) Emphasising that something is unlikely to happen

1 If we hadn't employed an outside consultant, we could never have got the project off the ground.

2 If we could postpone the meeting until next week, it'd be more convenient.

3 Were we to need more time to complete the study, would that be a problem?

4 Had they given us enough time and resources, we could have done the work in-house.

5 Shareholders will accept the new strategy, provided it increases the bottom line.

6 Unless we get some results soon, they're going to shelve this project.

9 Idioms for giving examples

- *for one*
  Several people haven't seen the presentation yet. The VP, **for one**.

- *take for instance*
  Many food manufacturers are now moving into the Chinese market. **Take for instance** Archie, maker of the famous Toto brand.

- *to name (just) a few*
  The list of speakers at the forum was impressive: Mary Summer, Brian Nobel and Jill Rogers, **to name just a few**.

- *a good example is*
  Some multinational companies provide information on their website in many languages. **A good example is** Johnson & Johnson.

- *a case in point is*
  Many Asian banks do not have an 'optimal' currency mix. **A case in point is** Japan, which is believed to hold up to 85 per cent of its reserves in dollar-denominated assets.

- *alone*
  All areas of the business have seen improved sales. Sales of soft drinks **alone** rose by 9% in the last quarter.

- *a typical/classic case*
  Fenwick Plastics' decline was **a typical case** of poor strategic planning.

- *illustrative of this is*
  If cities can become creative capitals, they can also fall off the map. **Illustrative of this is** Florida, which seems to be attracting less creative talent than it used to.

- *like*
  National airlines **like** British Airways and Air France face stiff competition from budget carriers.

- *such as*
  Chinese companies, **such as** Nanjing Automotive, are now moving into European markets.

Complete the sentences with the phrases from the box, used for giving examples. There are two phrases you do not need.

Alitalia for one
Take, for instance, Arnott's
Halls, to name a few
A good example is Tesco's 'Finest'
a case in point is Burger Max
such as British Airways and Iberia
cars alone
Nissan and Renault are typical cases
illustrative of this is Burberrys
like Lindt and Sprüngli

1 Many fast-food companies – .... – are now promoting healthy eating.

2 Airlines, ... , have formed strategic alliances to beat other competitors.

3 Several national carriers, ... , have received state aid to help with restructuring plans.

4 Experts predict that the levels of CO_2 will continue to increase. Emissions from .... are expected to jump in the next decade.

5 Given falling profit margins and stiff competition, many supermarkets now promote their own brands. .... own-label.

6 Food manufacturers are keen to break into the Chinese market. .... , the Australian biscuit manufacturer, which is now six months into an ambitious project.

7 Manufacturers of quality confectionery, ..., are experiencing record sales, as consumers in the UK and the US discover the delights of premium chocolate.

8 Cadbury Schweppes' sales growth was helped by its confectionery brands – including Cadbury, Trident and ....

10 Cleft sentences

In cleft sentences, information is divided into two clauses, each with its own verb. This technique is used to emphasise new information, to give explanations or to contrast ideas.

*Taking orders online **doesn't cause** problems for e-tailers.* (one verb)

***It is not** taking the orders online **that causes** the problems for e-tailers.* (two verbs)

- *It* clefts are used to emphasise the subject, or object, or an adverbial or prepositional phrase:

  It + a form of *be* + emphasised phrase + *that/which/who* clause.

  ***It is not** just online retailers such as Amazon or eBay **that have built** successful businesses in cyberspace.*

- *Wh-* clefts highlight the action in a sentence:

  Wh- clause + a form of *be* + emphasised word or phrase.

  ***What** Amazon has done **is** successfully adopt a new online business model.*

  It is possible to reverse the parts in *wh-* cleft sentences.

  ***What they did next was** move into toy and music sales.*

  *Moving into toy and music sales **was what they did next.***

- *Wh-* clefts are used with *when/where/who/ why* to highlight a person, place, time or reason:

  *The day (**when**) I called was last Thursday.*

  *The hotel **where** we stayed was near the company offices.*

  *The one/person **who** edits our web page content is on holiday at the moment.*

  *The reason (**why**) we've called this meeting is to discuss our quarterly sales.*

- *The (only/last) thing* or *All* are also used to emphasise a noun or verb phrase:

  The thing /All + *that/which/who* clause + a form of *be* + emphasised word or phrase.

  ***The thing that** made them successful **was** their adoption of a new business model.*

  ***All (that)** we need to do **is** improve our web page.*

● **Rewrite the following as cleft sentences using the word(s) given in brackets.**

1 Meeting the expectation of online shoppers is very difficult. (*It*)

2 The rapid spread of broadband Internet access has had a huge impact on e-commerce. (*What*)

3 They contracted Amazon to help them improve their online sales. (*why*)

4 They just print off the orders and deal with them manually. (*All*)

5 Delays in delivery damaged the company's reputation and sales. (*It*)

6 We like the simplicity of the online ordering process most. (*thing*)

11 Noun phrases

We use noun phrases to give extra information about the noun.

1 The main noun of a noun phrase can be modified, using usually adjectives, but also adverbs, other nouns or a prepositional phrase before or after it. Look at the noun phrases in this sentence from the article on pages 100 and 101:

*Dr Agarwal surveyed **the disk-drive industry between 1977 and 1997** and found that **25 per cent of new entrants** were started by individuals leaving **larger companies in the same sector**.* (paragraph 4)

a) *the disk-drive industry + between 1977 and 1997*
noun phrase + prepositional phrase

b) *25 per cent + of new entrants*
noun phrase + prepositional phrase

c) *larger companies + in the same sector*
adjective + noun + prepositional phrase

2 We can often combine nouns with other nouns, where the first noun functions as an adjective, e.g. *business angel, business venture, business opportunities*. These are often referred to as noun compounds or word partnerships. Sometimes three or more nouns occur together, in which case the first two are often hyphenated:
disk-drive industry
supply-chain management

1 Complete these sentences using a suitable noun phrase from the box.

---
a) long-term economic growth
b) the profits, power and position of older companies
c) a rapid entry of firms
d) the ability to see how an idea can be commercially exploited
e) a certain industry or business activity
f) this idea of the entrepreneur as a disruptive force
g) a stabilisation in the number of competitors
---

1 According to the economist Joseph Schumpeter, innovation is the temporary source of market power that erodes ....

2 It was Schumpeter who discovered .... and said that entrepreneurs help to foster .... because they upset the monopolisation of larger companies.

3 A monopoly is when one company dominates .... and it is difficult for other companies to compete.

4 When determining the number of competitors any given market can sustain, economists Michael Gort and Steven Klepper have shown that after a product is 'born', there is .... , then a mass exit and finally .... at a level of about 40% below the peak number.

5 What distinguishes successful entrepreneurs is their business intuition, or ....

2 Match the nouns (1–5 with a–e, and 6–10 with f–j) to form word partnerships.

1	prize	a)	station
2	space	b)	gravity
3	zero-	c)	flight
4	space	d)	version
5	21st-century	e)	money
6	ticket	f)	TV show
7	video	g)	engineers
8	home	h)	sales
9	reality	i)	computers
10	aeronautics	j)	games

3 Complete this article from the *Financial Times* using the correct noun combinations from Exercise 2.

Peter Diamandis, the entrepreneur who put together $10m in ....[1] for the first successful private ....[2], is selling another outlandish idea. Over the past two decades, he has started an International Space University, a company that offers ....[3] travel, another company that brokers private trips to the international ....[4], as well as the X Prize, awarded to the first private manned spacecraft.

Mr Diamandis now says the next big thing is his new Rocket Racing League. The basic idea is that ten rocket-propelled aircraft will race at speeds of up to 300mph on an aerobatic circuit, in a ....[5] of Formula 1. It will start in the US, but hopes to go international soon after.

The plan is to make money through TV rights, ...[6], sponsorship and merchandising, but also by tying in with the current boom in online ....[7]: offering fans the chance to compete head-to-head with the pilots on their ....[8].

Many of the pilots will be chosen through a ....[9], so by the time they race, they should be familiar to potential fans. ....[10] will vie for the money and prestige, designing ever-faster airframes and split-second pit-stop technology.

12 Cohesion (see also Unit 5)

Grammatical cohesion is needed in a text to 'bind it together'. Cohesion can be used to avoid unnecessary repetition by substituting or omitting words so that the writing is clear and reads well. These examples are taken from the Reading on pages 108 and 109.

*Instead of **lamenting the lack of good project managers,** leaders should focus on why **that's** the case.* (section 1)

In this sentence, *that* refers back to *the lack of good project managers*.

Textual referencing is used to refer to words or ideas that have previously been mentioned in a text (**anaphoric reference**); that are going to be mentioned (**cataphoric reference**); or that are simply not mentioned in the text because the writer assumes the reader will understand (**exophoric reference**).

- **Anaphoric reference**

  *We need to thank **our effective PMs** for the amazing job **they** do.*

  They refers back to *effective project managers*.

- **Cataphoric reference**

  *... and we need to get **those** who don't do so well into roles that they can be successful at doing.*

  In this sentence, *those* refers forwards to those project mangers that don't do so well.

- **Exophoric reference**

  *Not only is being a **PM** a tough job, but you get very little appreciation from your firm for doing it.*

  The reader assumes *PM* stands for *project manager,* but it is not explained in the text.

  *What **the system** does tend to turn out are experts (if you can call anyone with a technical degree an 'expert').*

  The reader assumes *the system* is the educational system or technical training project managers receive, but it is not clarified in the text.

● Complete this text on intercultural communication, either replacing the underlined words with a suitable cohesive device from the box or omitting them. Two of the items are not needed.

it	ones	they	they	this is why	those

When working in an international context, communication can break down for a variety of reasons. These <u>reasons</u> include differences in business practices and management styles such as multi-tasking or prioritising which may be open to misinterpretation <u>in an intercultural setting</u>.

International teams may get frustrated if team members are not given specific guidelines or if <u>team members</u> are not given sufficient independence to carry out tasks. On the other hand, middle managers can find it difficult to adapt to the challenges of living and working in a different culture.

These problems <u>of living and working in a different culture</u> may consist of not only lack of language skills, but more complex misunderstandings concerning attitudes to hierarchy, national humour and loss of face. <u>All of these difficulties when working in an international context mean that</u> project managers particularly need to realise that understanding local systems is essential when <u>project managers</u> communicate internationally. Western cultures, for instance, do not tolerate ambiguity as readily as non-Western <u>cultures</u>, whereas establishing trust and relationship-building are paramount in many non-Western societies.

Formal letters: accepting an invitation

McEwan Training Solutions
68 Old Court Road
Bristol BS22 7QR
Tel: 01799 597 3442
E-mail: jmcewan@compuserve.com
www.mcewantraining.com

Francine Vergé
IBWA
International University of Nice
6 avenue Prince Albert
Nice

18 June 20—

Dear Ms Vergé,

With reference to your letter of 3 June, I would like to thank you for inviting me to speak at the networking conference organised by the International Business Women's Association in Nice this October.

It will be my pleasure to attend, and I am planning to talk on the following topic: Networking for women starting up new business. Please find enclosed a brief outline of the proposal for my talk as requested. Could you confirm how many people you expect to attend the talk?

As I am planning to book my flight in the next few weeks, I would also appreciate it if you could confirm travel details and accommodation arrangements. Finally, I would like to confirm that I will be attending the conference dinner on the Friday evening.

I look forward to hearing from you.

Best regards,

J. McEwan

Joanna McEwan
Training Consultant

Encl. Proposal for presentation

This is a British English form of date. American English always puts the month first, i.e. June 18 or 6/18/20—

Salutations

Dear Sirs
if you are writing to a company or organisation

Dear Sir/Madam
if you don't know the person's name

Dear [name]
if you know the person's name

Common titles

Mr   for men
Mrs   for married women
Ms   for women if you don't know, or prefer not to specify, marital status
Miss for unmarried women

Note: in the US, *Mr, Mrs* and *Ms* require a full stop/period, e.g. *Mrs. Vergé*.

Endings

Yours sincerely if you know the person's name
Yours faithfully if you don't know the person's name
Yours truly   American English

The style of this letter is similar to a formal e-mail, although *(Best) regards* or *Best wishes* is more usual as an ending in e-mails.

Sign your name, then print your name and position under the signature.

Common abbreviations

Re.   regarding
pp.   when you sign the letter for another person (per pro = on behalf of)
encs. }
encl. } document(s) are enclosed with the letter
cc.   copies: the names of the people who receive a copy are included in the letter

Effective e-mails

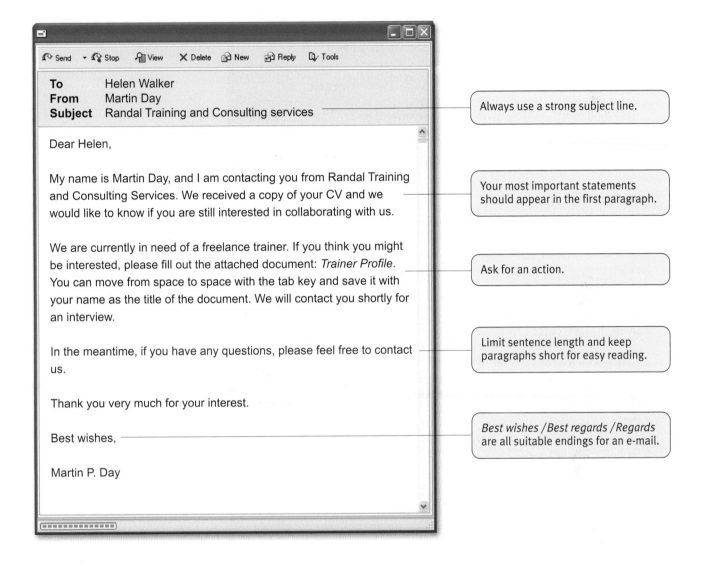

To	Helen Walker
From	Martin Day
Subject	Randal Training and Consulting services

Always use a strong subject line.

Dear Helen,

My name is Martin Day, and I am contacting you from Randal Training and Consulting Services. We received a copy of your CV and we would like to know if you are still interested in collaborating with us.

Your most important statements should appear in the first paragraph.

We are currently in need of a freelance trainer. If you think you might be interested, please fill out the attached document: *Trainer Profile*. You can move from space to space with the tab key and save it with your name as the title of the document. We will contact you shortly for an interview.

Ask for an action.

In the meantime, if you have any questions, please feel free to contact us.

Limit sentence length and keep paragraphs short for easy reading.

Thank you very much for your interest.

Best wishes,

Best wishes / Best regards / Regards *are all suitable endings for an e-mail.*

Martin P. Day

Action points/minutes

Minutes of meeting on our commitment to corporate responsibility

Date:	8 February
Venue:	Bath Crescent
Present:	Erika Koning, Matthew Meehan, David Gibbs, Siobhan Peters, Simona Viccoli

> For most business meetings, action minutes or action points are more useful and more concise than full minutes. Action minutes are intended to make sure that decisions of the meeting are understood and carried out.

	Action	By
1 Overseas visits: Stitch Wear manufacturers Following recent complaints of varying standards in our factories overseas, we agree that more frequent visits are essential for standardisation and quality assurance. Matthew suggested drawing up a series of guidelines for these visits.	MM/EK	Mar 8
2 Supplier screening policy The Purchasing Department will review the current supplier-screening policy and send an e-mail report before the next meeting.	SV	15 Feb
3 CSR (Corporate Social Responsibility) programme Various ideas were discussed. The most popular was sponsorship of a local project involving young people. Marketing will look into the proposal. To be discussed further at the next meeting.	DG	22 Feb
4 New position of CSR officer It was agreed that Erika will take on the new role of Corporate Social Responsibility Officer and would co-ordinate any subsequent actions of the CSR team. Decision on Erika's request for a full-time assistant is pending. It was stressed all company directors and managers need to assume responsibility for their respective areas.	EK	22 Feb

> There is a summary of the discussion for each item on the agenda.

> The initials of the person responsible for carrying out any action required are given in the margin, along with any deadline.

Next meeting confirmed:	22 February, 10.00 a.m.
Venue:	Sefton Place offices, room 21
Purpose of meeting:	marketing proposals for CSR programme

> The date, time and place of the next meeting are given.

A formal e-mail summarising terms and conditions

To   andreapfeifer@chautos.de
From   jpacek@pacekmachines.pl
Subject Pacek Machinery order no. 11892006

Dear Ms Pfeifer,

It was a pleasure to meet you at the trade mission organised by the Chamber of Commerce in Warsaw on 20 May. Further to our meeting, I am writing to confirm the terms of our sales agreement as follows:

1   Pacek Machinery will provide CH Autos with industrial machinery, ref. no. X127H49.
2   Twenty per cent of payment will be paid on delivery, with the remainder paid three months after delivery following supervision and approval of your engineers.
3   Expected delivery date is 5th April, subject to confirmation.
4   Please refer to the attached document for details regarding transport, installation and our cancellation policy.

If you should require any more information, please do not hesitate to contact me.

Best regards,

Jan Pacek
Managing Director

This style of e-mail is similar to a standard business letter. This kind of summary should be formal but brief, particularly if further details or a contract agreement are attached.

Opening
Alternative formal openings:

Following our meeting/phone conversation …
With reference to …
Regarding our …
I am writing to confirm …

Main points in the summary could be numbered or listed.

Further details may need to be attached to avoid making the e-mail too long.

Ending
Alternative formal endings:
For additional information, please …
We look forward to doing business with you.

Layout and organisation of a report

The format used here is suitable for most formal reports:
- title
- executive summary
- introduction
- findings
- conclusion
- recommendations

Title of report

The **executive summary** is a summary of the main points and conclusion of the report. It gives the reader an overview of the situation.

The **introduction** shows the main points that will be looked at.

Headings and sub-headings help to make layout and organisation clear.

The **findings** are the facts discovered. This is often the main body of the report.

(Note: Findings are not reproduced here in full, as this is only a summary of the main points of this report. A complete report may be over 100 pages in length.)

Formal language such as the passive is frequent in reports.

Building Better Partnerships
by the IPPR

Executive summary

The Institute for Public Policy Research (IPPR) calls for a rethink of 'flawed' public private partnerships (PPPs) in the UK. This report, Building Better Partnerships, states that lessons need to be learned from the private finance initiative, the system for building new public buildings with private capital. It says that there may be a case for giving greater protection to employees transferred to the private sector; and adds that PPPs should be more innovative and more accountable to the public. In many cases this report has found that there was simply a 'private-sector default' situation, in which there was no alternative to the PPP on offer.

Introduction

This report will look at:

- examples of Public Private Partnerships in various sectors in the UK

- the role of the Private Finance Initiative (PFI) in public-private projects

- recommendations for successful Public Private Partnerships

Findings

Health

The health sector is where PPPs are most prominent in the UK. One Private Finance Initiative (PFI) has been created to build new hospitals and doctors' surgeries. An agreement also exists with private healthcare providers to encourage the National Health Service (NHS) to send patients to private hospitals for treatment in order to reduce waiting lists.

Under the NHS plan, more than 100 hospital schemes will be delivered over the next ten years, and private-sector investment under PFI will rise to £7bn. A further £1bn worth of private investment in primary-care health centres is planned through PPPs.

Transport

One of the biggest controversies involving PFI is the proposal to use the private sector to refurbish and modernise London Underground's tube transport system. This report has found that the Tube did not require a special PPP because it had a revenue stream from which it could have raised capital in the markets.

The PPP scheme to upgrade air-traffic control in the UK has also come under criticism. The NATS (National Air-Traffic Services) project went ahead without using a public-sector comparator to see whether there was a better public-sector alternative.

Other sectors for PPPs
Elsewhere, private sector providers are running prisons; local authority revenues and benefit services; the majority of residential homes for the elderly, and even schools.

Council white-collar jobs in education, human resources and administrative functions have also been outsourced to private firms, as well as services such as refuse collection and street cleansing.

In housing, a quarter of all councils have sold off their homes to housing associations, which can raise private money to meet repair bills and build new homes. So far, housing associations have raised £20bn on the private financial markets in this way.

Recommendations

The private finance initiative (PFI):

- The evaluation of a project's suitability for PFI must be improved to ensure it offers value for money

- Government departments should be set an overall budget that covers both public spending and the capital value of PFI spending – and avoid seeing PFI as extra investment

- Public authorities must have a clear planning policy that fully integrates PFI with traditional public forms of investment and service provision – otherwise services will be fragmented

Protecting employees:

- The government must promote good employment practices within PPPs.

- There is little evidence that PPPs lead to new recruits receiving poorer terms and conditions than those transferred from the public sector.

- If the Office of Government Commerce report shows that PPPs create a two-tier workforce, then the government should ensure that new employees are properly protected.

Fostering public enterprise:

- As an alternative to PPPs, successful public bodies should be able to work with less successful ones to improve performance.

- Public bodies should have greater freedom to raise capital and trade with each other, allowing some public enterprises to 'opt out' of Treasury financial controls.

- Government should consider transferring the ownership of a public enterprise to a non-profit-making trust, especially where there is a natural monopoly and where safety is a key concern.

Improving accountability:

- The National Audit Office should have statutory authority to examine information on all significant public contracts.

- Partnership agreements should establish boards – which include public officials and service users – that have a say over the terms of service provision in a project and the hiring and firing of service providers.

- The Cabinet Office and the Office of Government Commerce should provide guidance on how to conduct community consultation on PPP projects.

New models of partnership:

- Public managers should have more discretion to design PPP deals that incorporate the services that best meet the needs of local users.

- More innovative partnerships should be developed, e.g. allowing the public sector to provide investment for a project while the private sector designs, builds and operates services.

- Profit-sharing and joint decision-making bodies between the public and private sectors should become the norm.

Conclusion

This report concludes that the public finance initiative (PFI) has proved value for money in roads and prisons, but not in hospitals and schools. Furthermore, the government's determination to use PPPs has led to shortcomings in the proposed schemes for London Underground and air-traffic control (NATS).

PPPs should be used to improve standards and not just to lower costs at the expense of quality. This report signals a new era for the debate over public-private partnerships. The future will decide how far the private sector will move from the margins into 'core' areas, transforming the nature of public services.

Mission statements

Crystal
THE CHEMISTRY IS RIGHT

Our mission and values

Crystal Mission

We aim to be the leading company and the preferred partner in the specialty chemicals industry. We combine leading-edge technology and innovation with superior applications and customer-service skills.

Crystal Values

- **Customer focus:** We concentrate our efforts on the individual requirements of our customers.
- **Personal engagement:** We achieve results through individual commitment, continual skills development and entrepreneurial behaviour.
- **Team spirit:** We rely on the strength of teamwork to realise our full potential.
- **Innovation:** Using extensive know-how and experience throughout the company, we continuously endeavour to bring new services, applications and products to the market.
- **Shareholder commitment:** We strive for creating value for the benefit of our shareholders.
- **Integrity:** We are a trustworthy, loyal and respectful partner in all our internal and external relationships.
- **Sustainability:** We contribute towards sustainable development by finding the best balance between environmental, social and economic needs.

> A mission statement describes the overall purpose or aims of the company; it should be short and concise.

> The values are the principles and practices that a business or organisation thinks are important and which it tries to follow. Company values include commitment to corporate social responsibility and stakeholders.

Agendas

Product Development Team meeting

AGENDA

Date: Monday 25 July 20—
Time: 10 a.m.
Venue: Meeting room C, third floor, Palmer Building

1 Apologies for absence

2 Minutes from the previous meeting

3 Status report

4 Next round of trials

5 Product labelling

6 Production capacity

7 Consumer testing

8 A.O.B

> Always give the date, time and place.

> It is usual to send your apologies if you can't attend a meeting. These are noted in the minutes of more formal meeting.

> Everyone should receive a copy of the previous minutes before the meeting, sometimes with the agenda.
>
> The chairman usually asks if everyone agrees with the minutes of the previous meeting and notes any changes or additions that have to be made to the minutes.

> The issues for the meeting are then dealt with in priority order.

> The chairman asks towards the end of the meeting if anyone has any other business they want to discuss, which is related to the subject of the meeting, and isn't on the agenda.

Writing for websites

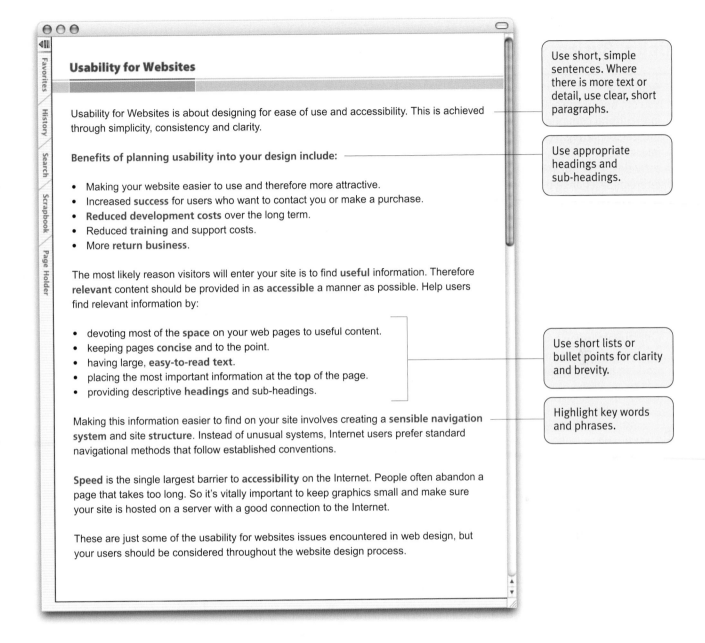

Usability for Websites

Usability for Websites is about designing for ease of use and accessibility. This is achieved through simplicity, consistency and clarity.

Benefits of planning usability into your design include:

- Making your website easier to use and therefore more attractive.
- Increased **success** for users who want to contact you or make a purchase.
- **Reduced development costs** over the long term.
- Reduced **training** and support costs.
- More **return business**.

The most likely reason visitors will enter your site is to find **useful** information. Therefore **relevant** content should be provided in as **accessible** a manner as possible. Help users find relevant information by:

- devoting most of the **space** on your web pages to useful content.
- keeping pages **concise** and to the point.
- having large, **easy-to-read text**.
- placing the most important information at the **top** of the page.
- providing descriptive **headings** and sub-headings.

Making this information easier to find on your site involves creating a **sensible navigation system** and site **structure**. Instead of unusual systems, Internet users prefer standard navigational methods that follow established conventions.

Speed is the single largest barrier to **accessibility** on the Internet. People often abandon a page that takes too long. So it's vitally important to keep graphics small and make sure your site is hosted on a server with a good connection to the Internet.

These are just some of the usability for websites issues encountered in web design, but your users should be considered throughout the website design process.

Use short, simple sentences. Where there is more text or detail, use clear, short paragraphs.

Use appropriate headings and sub-headings.

Use short lists or bullet points for clarity and brevity.

Highlight key words and phrases.

Activity file

Unit 1, Business skills, Exercise D, page 10

Student A

You are one of the speakers at an international conference in Vienna, Austria, on intercultural communication. It is now the coffee break. Start a conversation with the person sitting beside you, as her/his company may be interested in intercultural training. You should describe your company's or organisation's activities, your job and responsibilities or studies in brief. Find some common interests, exchange business cards and arrange a future meeting, e.g. for a game of tennis or golf. Be careful to address her/him using her/his surname or family name.

Unit 1, Case study, Task 2, page 13

Student A

These are your incomplete notes for the country-orientation session as, unfortunately, you had to leave early. Ask the other trainee to explain to you what you missed. When you have finished, discuss how useful these notes are for working and living abroad.

1 • *Don't underestimate culture shock; initial excitement can soon turn to criticism*
   • *Find a balance between finding out about the new culture and spending time with people from your own culture.*
   • *When you return home, don't expect family/friends to be interested in all your stories. It is important, however, to find people that you can talk to who have had similar experiences.*
2 • *Building relationships is highly important in many non-Western cultural contexts; make sure you spend some time getting to know local people.*

Unit 1, Case study, Task 3, page 13

Student A

Last year, you were working as an office manager for a transport company in Argentina when you lost your job due to cost cuts and re-structuring. You are now living with friends in Amsterdam. When you saw the job advert for Logistaid in the newspaper, you thought it would be an opportunity to get back into the job market. In the past year, you have travelled to Mozambique and Nigeria for short periods as a volunteer on emergency aid projects. You haven't found the course particularly useful, as you already have plenty of experience in intercultural communication.

1 Network with the other course participants and find someone who:
   • took the job for the same reason as you
   • has found the course useful
   • has some basic medical knowledge
   • has been to the Indonesian jungle.
2 Think of some hobbies or interests you may have; find someone with similar hobbies/interests.
3 Agree to a further meeting before being relocated and promise to keep in touch when you are in Indonesia.

Unit 2, Case study, Task 1, page 21

Student A
You are Kamal Satinder, IT Manager at SmileCo. Phone Geraldine Parker at Pollack Learning Alliance. You've worked with her company before and you know her. Explain the problem with the sales team's existing information-gathering system and your solution. Explain what you'd like her company to do for you.

Unit 2, Case study, Task 2, page 21

Student A
You are Kamal Satinder. You'd like to raise these points with Geraldine when you discuss her training proposal.
- How the training programme will meet your company needs.
- How the system will be tested.
- Sales people get bored sitting in a classroom. Any on-the-job training?
- Few staff on the IT help desk. Who will provide post-training support?
- Documentation to support the training programme?

Unit 3, Business skills, Exercise E, page 26

Student A
1 You are a buyer for the chainstore, Deco-fittings. You are negotiating with a new supplier, Taps and Pipes. Agree on the price per unit for some chrome taps.
   - Maximum price you want to pay is €25 per unit for 100 units.
   - Delivery within three months is required.
   - You hear Taps and Pipes has been selling this product at reduced prices – ask for confirmation.
2 You are a junior member of a sales team and want to go to a conference on negotiating techniques in Brussels in May. Negotiate the trip with your boss and justify the expense. Remember to ask specific questions and use expressions for being precise.

Unit 3, Case study, Task, page 29

Student A

You represent Polish Airports and the Ministry of Infrastructure in the PPP negotiations. Negotiate a PPP agreement with the German construction company Laumann and the Weber-Merkel bank using the notes below. Make notes about what was finally agreed under the same headings.

Financing	• Total cost: €120m. • 90% of funds borrowed from Weber-Merkel bank. • Loan agreement €108m, preferably interest rate of 2.5%. • Guarantees given by the Polish Government. • Remaining 10% will be financed by Polish Airports.
Operation and management	Ownership of assets and operation of airport services remain with Polish Airports.
Repayment terms	• Loan will be repaid over 20 years. • Repayments begin on full completion of works and will be on a quarterly basis. • Polish Airports will collect take-off and landing charges from foreign airlines and overflight fees (charges for planes flying through Polish airspace). • These charges and fees will be used to make loan repayments. Excess funds will belong to Polish Airports.
Building schedule	• Construction project will take 24 months. • Laumann will sub-contract work to and cooperate with Polish construction companies.
Risk allocation	• Commercial risks, e.g. delays in the building schedule and low air-traffic volumes, transferred to the private contractor. • Delays in building programme will incur penalty fines of €0.5m for each week's delay.

Unit 4, Business skills, Exercise E, page 38

Student A

1 You are the Regional Manager of a large insurance company in Europe. The staff turnover and sickness levels are significantly higher in your Rotterdam branch. The branch manager reports that there is a heavy workload there. The situation is costing your company a lot of money in recruiting and training new staff. Discuss the problem with the Human Resources Manager and suggest what could be done to find a solution. Try to use some phrases from Exercises B and D.

2 You are the co-owner of an electrical goods shop. It is a very hot summer, and your store has already sold out of air-conditioning units. Suppliers are completely out of units and can't get any more to you until the end of the summer, by which time it'll be too late for this year. You could order more units for next summer, but you also have a storage problem (which was what prevented you from ordering more units than you did this year). Discuss the problem with your partner and suggest some solutions. Try to use some phrases from Exercises B and D.

Unit 4, Case study, Task 1, page 41

Student A
You recently received this government literature. Report the information to your colleagues.

Energy Efficient Lighting in Shops

Maximising the use of daylight reduces the need for electric lighting, as does linking the control of the display lighting in the window areas to day lighting levels, automating the switching-off or dimming of the lighting to match the ambient lighting level outside the store.

Painting the surfaces of the rooms, including the ceiling, with light/bright colours maximises the effectiveness of the light output. Light/bright colours can reflect up to 80 per cent of incident light; dark/deep colours can reflect less than 10 per cent. Where there are large spaces that need to have a large number of lamps switched on for extended periods, energy-limiting devices can be very effective. These devices automatically reduce the voltage/current to the lighting circuits by 10–20 per cent when the lamps have been switched on and are stable. The consequent reduction in light output is only 5–10 per cent. Savings typically of 30 per cent are achievable, with a payback period of two to three years. This strategy is particularly suited to supermarkets and wholesale stores.

Unit 5, Business skills, Exercise E, page 47

Student A
You are Orsolya, a sales rep in a direct-banking organisation in the Ukraine. You work in the SME lending division, giving loans to small and medium-sized companies. There is very strong competition between teams and individual bankers. There are things that you don't like about the job; one of those is the cheating that goes on between colleagues.

The company rule is that if you get a first visit, then the client is yours and no other banker can approach that client. You discover that Bohdan, one of your colleagues, has lied and stolen a client from you by phoning and arranging a visit after you'd made first contact. You decide to confront him about it.

You feel the company encourages this kind of underhand behaviour by your colleague because, although it's common practice, the company does nothing to stop it happening. You've come to the conclusion that the only way to stop your colleague is to argue and fight for your clients, even though you can't prove you'd got there first.

Talk to Bohdan in order to resolve your differences. Use some of the active listening expressions.

Unit 5, Case study, Task 1, page 49

Student A

You are Mira Biswas, a Team Manager. Tricia Monroe is one of your agents. She has worked for the company for almost three years and, as such, is one of the longest-serving agents. She is a very competent worker and a popular member of staff. However, she is off sick with minor ailments at least eight times a year, and all her sick days tend to fall on either a Friday or a Monday. Until now, you've decided to turn a blind eye to this situation, but management have asked you to conduct one-to-one interviews with all staff members with high levels of sickness leave in an attempt to monitor the situation and reduce absenteeism. Think about what you're going to say to Tricia and hold a meeting with her.

Unit 6, Case study, Task, page 57

Student A

You are Head of PR and will chair the meeting. Look at the agenda before the meeting, take notes and add some of your own points:

- Item 3: to include former child employees under 14
- Item 7: either you or one of your team are interested in the new position of Corporate Responsibility Officer.

Unit 7, Case study, Task 2, page 69

Student A

You are one of the financial consultants at Tompkins and Kosters. Look at the pie chart showing projected productivity over the next three years. You propose the following measures to boost profits by €4 billion in three years:

- Savings of €7 billion over three years: a €2 billion saving in improved sales and a €5 billion saving with cost-cutting measures such as redundancies.
- An improved productivity plan that involves replacing the current four-day week with a five-day week with the option of a sixth day for overtime, paid at time and a half the normal rate.
- One of your own proposals, for instance, asking suppliers to lower their costs over the next two years.

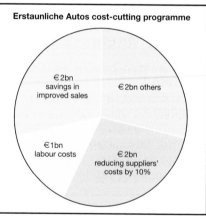

Erstaunliche Autos cost-cutting programme

Unit 8, Business skills, Exercise D, page 75

Student A

You are a sales person working for Fast Cars showroom. Look at the following facts and negotiate a deal with the potential buyer. Use some of the expressions from Exercise C on page 74.

Seller's facts

- You have to sell the new Audi model. You need to earn a minimum commission of €1,000 in the next few days in order to pay for your family holiday, a world cruise. This is your bottom line, but you could use more money, as the holiday is expensive.
- The Car Book of the Year values the car between €9,000 and €13,000, depending on special features.
- Your seller's reservation point (RP), or bottom line, below which you do not want to go, is €10,000.

- You make only €50 for cars sold *under* €10,000. You make a commission of €100 per car sold between €10,000 and €12,000. You make €150 commission for cars sold *over* €12,000.
- If you have not made a deal by the end of the week, you will reconsider your bottom line.
- This is the second time the buyer has visited the showroom. If the buyer's first offer is lower than you would like, persuade him/her to buy a more expensive model with special features.

Unit 8, Case study, Task 2, page 77

Student A

You represent the UK consultancy firm, Performance Consulting. Meet with the representative(s) of Mobi-net, answer their questions about your proposal and negotiate the best solution, fees and conditions for the project.

Contract and fees

You want a T&M (time and materials) contract, including an hourly consultant rate of €150; €120 for junior consultants. You would prefer *not* to accept a fixed-price contract, as you think it's a complex project that may overrun. If the client says they have lower quotes from other consultancies, point out the added value of your reputation, ten years' expertise in the industry and quality of service.

Schedule

All your senior consultants are currently very busy. They will not be available for another three weeks, although you are able to offer junior consultants who can start immediately at a reduced rate. You could complete the project in four months' time, less if they choose a senior consultant.

Competition

You think Mobi-net would be willing to pay you more than your competitor, Unicorn Consulting, a smaller consultancy group that are less established but cheaper. Request **exclusivity of the project**. You also require access to **company information**, especially the customer-service department.

Unit 10, Business skills, Exercise D, page 95

Student A

Ask your partner these questions, paraphrase them using expressions for indirect questions. Add two of your own indirect questions. Then answer your partner's question using expressions for dealing with questions.

1 Should all university and higher education exams be administered online?
2 How can access and use of the Internet be improved in developing countries?
3 Should there be stricter control of the Internet regarding security?

Unit 11, Business skills, Exercise A, page 102

Student A

Telephone tips for dealing with customers and suppliers

1 Always give your name and use the .... It helps to establish a good working relationship.

2 Quote .... and have the paperwork to hand.

3 Listen actively and show that you are listening. Connect with the person by .... as appropriate.

4 Restate the details you are given to check that you understand what's been said.

5 Confirm .... that you and/or the other speaker have agreed to.

6 Make sure you agree dates or set a deadline for follow-up action.

Unit 11, Case study, Task 1, page 105

Student A

You are Doug. Read the information about ownership and control issues and summarise it for your partner. Ask questions about annual charges and the final objectives of venture capital firms.

WHAT VENTURE CAPITALISTS WANT AND EXPECT

Ownership

The partners of the venture firm buy a portion of the business's equity in exchange for their investment. Most VC firms, at least initially, don't want a position of more than 30% to 40% because they want the owner to have the incentive to keep building the business.

Control

The VC firm, regardless of its percentage of ownership, usually wants to leave control in the hands of the company's managers.

However, the VC firm does want to participate in any strategic decisions that might change the basic product/market character of the company and in any major investment decisions that might divert or deplete the financial resources of the company. They will, therefore, generally ask that at least one partner of the firm is made a director of your company.

VC firms also want to be able to assume control and attempt to rescue their investments if severe financial, operating or marketing problems develop. So they will usually include clauses in the agreements to allow them to take control and appoint new officers if financial performance is very poor.

Unit 12, Business skills, Exercise F, page 111

Student A

You are Bob Frasier, the Marketing Manager for Archibald, based in Sydney, Australia. You are in charge of this project. You've arranged a teleconference with Francesca Russo, the R&D Manager, based in Rome, Italy, and Gao Shan, the Production Engineer, based in Guangzhou, China.

It's now 4 p.m. in Sydney, 2 p.m. in Guangzhou and 7 a.m. in Rome. Remember to take a roll call and go over the agenda at the start of the call.

These are the notes you've made on your agenda:

Agenda

Status report: ask Fran to report on the last round of product trials.

Next round of trials: Ask Gao and Fran when they're due.

Product labelling: Fran – is the problem solved or will there be delays?

Production capacity: Ask Gao Shan to report on this. Will there be extra costs which I need to alert the sponsor to?

Consumer testing: These tests can go ahead provided the trials produce good results. My people in marketing can start consumer testing as soon as the next round of trials are finished.

Unit 1, Business skills, Exercise D, page 10

Student B
You are attending an international conference in Vienna, Austria, on intercultural communication. It is now a coffee break. You are the marketing manager of ATC, a family company providing market research to client companies wanting to enter or expand in your home market. Respond to the person talking to you. You think he/she may be a useful contact for intercultural training in your company, but you need to talk to your boss, your father, before arranging any future meetings. If you were to meet her/him again, you would prefer a business lunch or a formal visit to your company. You have run out of business cards.

Unit 1, Case study, Task 2, page 13

Student B
These are your incomplete notes for the country-orientation session as, unfortunately, you arrived late. Ask the other trainee to explain to you what you missed. When you have finished, discuss how useful these notes are for working and living abroad.

4 • *Apart from obvious language problems, misunderstandings often arise due to differences in attitudes to time and punctuality, dress codes, importance of loss of face and so on. Be respectful of the traditions, customs and behaviour of the people you are working with.*

• *Be careful when using humour; what is funny in one culture may be offensive in another.*

5 • *Do not jump to conclusions about work practices; you may have only a superficial understanding of why things are done the way they are.*

• *Go into your project with the philosophy 'What am I going to learn from this experience?' rather than 'What am I going to teach the locals?' You will have a less stressful time, frustrate fewer people and build up long-lasting work relationships.*

Unit 1, Case study, Task 3, page 13

Student B
Until recently, you have been working in the logistics department of an American computer company in London. When a friend told you that Logistaid were looking for logisticians, you thought it would be the perfect opportunity to combine your experience in logistics with helping people in developing countries. You went to Indonesia and Thailand a number of years ago on a family holiday. You have found the course interesting, but think it's not enough before going to work abroad.
1 Network with the other course participants and find someone who:
  • took the job for the same reason as you
  • is worried about being relocated to Indonesia
  • has previously done similar work in Nigeria and Mozambique
  • has worked in Germany.
2 Think of some hobbies or interests you may have; find someone with similar hobbies/interests.
3 Agree to a further meeting before being relocated and promise to keep in touch when you are in Indonesia.

Unit 2, Case study, Task 1, page 21

Student B
You are Geraldine Parker at Pollack Learning Alliance. You receive a call from Kamal Satinder, the IT Manager at SmileCo. You know Kamal and you've worked for his company before. In fact, they are a valuable client for you. Ask Kamal questions about the number of staff to be trained and the timescale. Arrange a meeting to talk more about your training proposal.

Unit 2, Case study, Task 2, page 21

Student B
You are Geraldine Parker. Discuss your proposal with Kamal Satinder and answer his questions.

Proposal
- Trainers to work with SmileCo's field force *before* designing the training programme.
- Will identify some sales people who will be 'power users' – to be trained separately before the system is introduced and to help with training programme development.
- Training over two days; combine face-to-face instructor-led training on Day 1 and in-store coaching and assessment on Day 2; one trainer per two sales people in real shops.
- The 'power users' can be future trouble shooters before problems are referred to the IT help desk.
- Training manual will be designed to fit in the glove-compartment of a car.

Unit 3, Business skills, Exercise E, page 26

Student B
1 You are a sales person for Taps and Pipes, a manufacturer of bathroom fittings. You are negotiating with a potential new customer, the chainstore Deco-fittings. Agree on the price per unit for some chrome taps.
- You charge €35 per unit for a minimum order of 50 units.
- Regular customers pay €30 per unit.

- Delivery time is now three months or more due to distribution problems.
2 You are a sales manager. A junior but enthusiastic member of your sales team makes a request. Be vague about whether you will agree to or decline the request unless you are asked specific questions. Your final decision depends on his/her arguments. Use expressions for being vague.

Unit 4, Business skills, Exercise E, page 38

Student B
1 You are the Human Resources Manager of a large insurance company in Europe. The staff turnover and sickness levels are significant higher in your Rotterdam branch. The branch manager reports that there is a heavy workload there. The situation is costing your company a lot of money in recruiting and training new staff. Discuss the problem with the Regional Manager and suggest what could be done to find a solution. Try to use some phrases from Exercises B and D.
2 You are the co-owner of an electrical goods shop. It is a very hot summer, and your store has already sold out of air-conditioning units. Suppliers are completely out of units and can't get any more to you until the end of the summer, by which time it'll be too late for this year. You could order more units for next summer, but you also have a storage problem (which was what prevented you from ordering more units than you did this year). Discuss the problem with your partner and suggest some solutions. Try to use some phrases from Exercises B and D.

Unit 3, Case study, Task, page 29

Student B

You represent the German construction company Laumann and the Weber-Merkel bank in the PPP negotiations. Negotiate a PPP agreement with Polish Airports and the Ministry of Infrastructure using the guidelines below. Make notes about what was finally agreed under the same headings.

Financing	• Laumann take full responsibility for designing and building new facilities at Konopnicka Airport. • Total cost: €120m. • 80% (€96m) borrowed from Weber-Merkel bank at interest rate of 4.5%. • Remaining 20% to be financed by Polish Airports.
Operation and management	Laumann would like option to manage airport services on 10-year concession.
Repayment terms	• Loan to be repaid by Polish Airports over 10 years. • Loan repayments to begin on 50% completion of the works, on a monthly basis. • Bank will collect take-off and landing charges from foreign airlines, and overflight fees (charges for planes flying through Polish airspace). • Excess charges and fees will be paid back to Polish Airports each quarter.
Building schedule	• Construction project will take 30 months. • Laumann will cooperate with Polish construction companies with a proven track record to carry out this project.
Risk allocation	• Polish Airports to assume responsibility for preliminary environmental studies and consultation of local residents. • Delays in building schedule to be transferred to Laumann. The company will not be held responsible for circumstances beyond its control, such as adverse weather conditions. • Delays in building programme which are the responsibility of Laumann incur penalty fines of €0.5m per month up to a maximum of €4m. • Risk associated with low air-traffic volumes shared on a 50-50 basis between Polish government and private contractor.

Unit 4, Case study, Task 1, page 41

Student B

You recently read this government report. Report the information to your colleagues.

Refrigeration

When warm, humid air from a store's interior meets the cold air of a refrigerated display case, condensation occurs. This can lead to ice build-up on door and to fogging and 'sweating' of the doors. To prevent this condensation and 'sweating', the refrigerated doors and frames are heated.

The only time an anti-sweat heater needs to run continuously is when a store's relative humidity is 55 per cent, which usually only happens during the warm, humid days of summer. Yet surveys have found that many stores run their anti-sweat heaters at full power 24 hours a day, 365 days a year.

Properly programmed heater controls ensure that refrigerated display case doors and frames are heated only when necessary. Thus there are two areas of energy savings: in the anti-sweat heater and in the operation of the refrigerated display case. Savings of 25–30 per cent are achievable, with a payback period of four to five years.

Unit 5, Business skills, Exercise E, page 47

Student B

You are Bohdan, a sales rep in a direct-banking organisation in the Ukraine. You work in the SME lending division, giving loans to small and medium-sized companies. There is very strong competition between teams and individual bankers. There are things that you don't like about the job, one of those is the level of competition between colleagues.

The company rule is that if you get a first visit, then the client is yours and no other banker can approach that client. But everyone is competing for clients, and it's common practice to go after clients you know your colleagues are also following up. After all, if they haven't visited the client yet, you can still phone and arrange a visit first. All's fair in love and war, as they say, and anyway, you've had colleagues steal clients from under your nose before.

You feel the company encourages this kind of competitive behaviour as nothing is ever done to stop it happening. You've come to the conclusion that the only way to survive in the company is to bend the rules a bit, too. Now your colleague Orsolya has asked to speak to you.

Talk to Orsolya. Use some of the active listening expressions.

Unit 5, Case study, Task 1, page 49

Student B

You are Tricia Monroe, a call-centre agent, and with almost three years' experience in the company, you are one of the longest-serving agents. When the work gets too stressful, you tend to get bad headaches and have trouble sleeping well at night. When you take a day off sick from time to time, it helps you to cope with a job where you have no control over your workload and you're under constant supervision and pressure to meet targets. Your Team Manager, Mira Biswas, has asked you for a one-to-one interview to discuss your sickness record for the past year – you've had eight days off in total, all on a Friday or Monday. Think about what you're going to say to Mira and hold a meeting with her.

Unit 6, Case study, Task, page 57

Student B

You are Head of Production. Look at the agenda before the meeting, take notes and add some of your own points:
• Item 2: Add 'or directly run the overseas production process'?

Unit 7, Case study, Task 2, page 69

Student B
You are one of the financial consultants at Tompkins and Kosters. Look at this bar chart showing productivity rates in Germany, Belgium, China and India. You propose the following measures:

- Cost-savings to be made by opening a new manufacturing centre, i.e. closing the Belgium factory in Antwerp and opening a new one in India with lower labour costs.
- An improved productivity plan to include an increase from a four-day to a five-day week in Germany with some kind of incentives for workers, e.g. competitions and/or holidays.
- One of your own proposals, for instance, purchasing components from low-cost countries such as China.

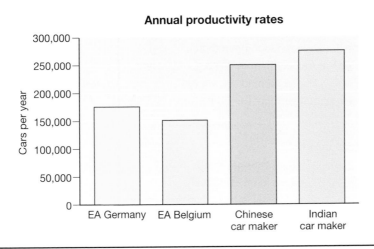

Unit 8, Business skills, Exercise D, page 75

Student B
You are a buyer for your company. You are interested in buying a fleet of nine company cars for the senior managers in the company. You are also interested in buying a car for yourself as you can get a much better price buying in the name of your company. Look at the following facts and negotiate a deal with the sales person from Fast Cars. Use some of the expressions from Exercise C on page 74.

Buyer's facts

- The latest Audi model is the car of your dreams, but you can not afford to buy one for yourself, unless you negotiate a special discount by buying it through the company.
- You have convinced the head buyer that the new Audi model will be ideal as a company car for senior managers and that you can negotiate a good deal.
- The Car Book of the Year indicates a value range of €9,000 to €13,000 for this model, depending on special features. The head buyer has agreed you can also get a car for yourself if you negotiate the company deal successfully.
- Your friend, Peter, knows the salesperson at Fast Cars, although the salesperson does not know that Peter is your friend. The salesperson told Peter that (s)he has to make a commission of at least €1,000 in the next few days so that (s)he can pay for a holiday.
- Don't disclose that you know that the salesperson's bottom line is €1,000, and that you also know that there are only a few days until his/her deadline.

Unit 8, Case study, Task 1, page 77

Student B

Unicorn Consulting: high-quality service at a fair price

Are you flexible enough to adapt to ever increasing competition in order to retain customers and improve your services?

Cartheuser, Lane and Happel are the Austrian-American partners of Unicorn Consulting, with five years of experience in the telecommunications industry. Together, we have combined the best of the old and new worlds to provide quality of service and innovative technological applications.

The impact of competitive advantage has already led to operators undertaking cross-border takeovers and strategic alliances. With specific knowledge of central and Eastern European markets, we can, furthermore, help identify and select potential partners for your telecom solutions.

Proposal and recommendations for Mobi-net

- Installation of a unified desktop that will allow Mobi-net's call-centre staff to interact with background services more effectively, using a common interface.
- An innovative, competitive pricing package designed for young subscribers (12–18-year-olds).
- A strategic alliance or partnership with a Slovenian or Croatian mobile phone company.

Unit 8, Case study, Task 2, page 77

Student B

You represent the consultancy group, Unicorn Consulting. Meet with the representative(s) of Mobi-net, answer their questions about your proposal and negotiate the best solution, fees and conditions for the project.

Contract and fees

You prefer a T&M (time and materials) contract, including an hourly consultant rate of €130 for all consultants. However, you are prepared to take a fixed-price contract if necessary, as you are a relative newcomer in the industry and don't have a wide client base at the moment. Having Mobi-net as a client would be very beneficial to your reputation.

Schedule

You are ready to start immediately. You think you could complete the project in three-and-a-half months' time, depending on staff co-operation at Mobi-net.

Competition

You suspect Mobi-net will pay you less than your competitor, Performance Consulting, a more established consultancy group. If the client questions your lack of experience, point out that you are experts in IT innovation, you have competitive prices and guarantee speedy, effective results. Request access to **company information**, especially the IT department.

Unit 10, Business skills, Exercise D, page 95

Student B

Answer your partner's questions using expressions for dealing with questions. Then ask your partner these questions, paraphrasing them using expressions for indirect questions. Add two of your own questions.

1 How might company websites encourage consumers to shop more online?
2 What can the government do to reduce online credit-card fraud?
3 Should children under five use computers for educational purposes?

Unit 11, Business skills, Exercise E, page 103

Student B

- You are Darren Bailey, the Accounts Manager at Dyson Kitchenware.
- Fenwick Plastics is one of your major suppliers. You have a good working relationship with the company; they are reliable and their products are good quality. You feel bad that sometimes you have to make them promises you can't keep.
- Today's 30 July. You've paid one of the two invoices (16987, dated 28 May) that you promised Wendy Taylor at Fenwick, but not the other one (17124, dated 8 June).
- There are also two new invoices issued which are now overdue for payment: 17289, dated 15 June, and 17356, dated 22 June.
- You're hoping Wendy will accept payment of all three invoices at the end of August. Think of a convincing reason why you've been paying your bills so late – you can't afford to let a major supplier know that you're having financial difficulties.

Unit 11, Case study, Task 1, page 105

Student B

You are José Ramón. Read the information about annual charges and final objectives of venture capital firms and summarise it for your partner. Ask questions about the ownership and control elements.

What venture capitalists want and expect

Annual charges

The investment can take several forms. The venture firm may require stock ownership which does not impose fixed charges. Alternatively, financing may also be in the form of loans with fixed rate of interest which is typically higher than bank loans. A loan may be convertible into equity shares.

Final objectives

VC firms generally intend to make capital gains on their investments in one of three ways: by arranging a stock buy-back by the company owners; by arranging a public offering of the company stock; or by providing for a merger with a larger firm that has publicly traded stock. They usually hope to do this within three to seven years of their initial investment.

As an entrepreneur, you should spend some time thinking about multiple exit strategies, e.g. who could acquire your business in the future. Be both realistic and creative regarding merger and acquisition possibilities. Clearly, venture capitalists may have different objectives than company founders. Therefore, the owner-manager of a small company seeking equity financing must consider the future impact upon his or her own stock holdings and personal ambition, since taking in a venture capitalist as a partner may be virtually a commitment to sell out or sell shares to the public.

Unit 12, Business skills, Exercise F, page 111

Student B

You are Francesca Russo, Research and Development Manager, based in Rome, Italy. You are a member of the product development team reporting to Bob Frasier, the Marketing Manager, in Sydney, Australia. You're participating in a teleconference with Bob Frasier and Gao Shan, the Production Engineer, based in Guangzhou, China.

It's now 4 p.m. in Sydney, 2 p.m. in Guangzhou and 7 a.m. in Rome. You're feeling very tired at this time in the morning. Apologise for sounding sleepy and explain why.

These are the notes you've made on your agenda:

Agenda

Status report: *The first round of product trials have been successful and the biscuit flavour has been improved.*

Next round of trials: *I'm going to Guangzhou to work with Gao Shan and his production team at the plant in a week's time. We're allowing two days for the trials.*

Product labelling: *The packaging department have had a break through with the labelling. They've found a way to adapt it to include information in both English and Chinese without the typeface being too small.*

Production capacity: *Gao Shan to report on this.*

Consumer testing: *When does Bob want to start these? It's best to wait until after the second round of trials, as there may need to be more trials.*

Unit 1, Case study, Task 3, page 13

Student C

Until recently, you have been working as a purchasing manager for a pharmaceutical company in Germany. You left the job because, after five years, you were getting bored. When you saw the ad for Logistaid on the Internet, you thought it would be the perfect opportunity to travel, to get to know people from different cultures and broaden your horizons. You have learnt a lot of things on the course, but are worried about being relocated because you don't know the area.

1 Network with the other course participants and find someone who:
- took the job for the same reason as you
- hasn't found the course very useful
- has previously done similar work in Nigeria and Mozambique
- has been to Indonesia and Thailand on holiday.
2 Think of some hobbies or interests you may have; find someone with similar hobbies/interests.
3 Agree to a further meeting before being re-located and promise to keep in touch when you are in Indonesia.

Unit 6, Case study, Task, page 57

Student C

You are Head of Purchasing. Look at the agenda before the meeting, take notes and add some of your own points:
- Item 4: suggest a partnership with the Ethical Trading Initiative (ETI) to screen suppliers against a code of practice and adopt a sustainable purchasing process.

Unit 7, Case study, Task 2, page 69

Student C
You are one of the financial consultants at Tompkins and Kosters. Look at the chart below showing hourly pay rates for assembly-line workers. You want to propose the following measures:

- Reduction of the workforce in the Belgium factory in Antwerp by 40 per cent. Suggest offering attractive redundancy packages to senior workers over 55 and asking for voluntary redundancies.
- An increase in sales discounts for car dealers in order to recapture market share and improve relations with unhappy dealers.
- One of your own proposals, for instance, cuts in salary (see bar chart).

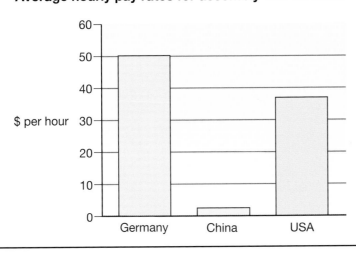

Average hourly pay rates for assembly-line workers

Unit 8, Case study, Task 2, page 77

Student C
You represent the mobile-phone company, Mobi-net. Meet separately with the representative(s) of the two consultancies, ask questions about their proposals and negotiate the best solution, fees and conditions for the project.

Contract and fees
You prefer a fixed-price contract: this will reduce risks for Mobi-net in case the project overruns. You have a budget limit of approximately €25,000 for the whole project. For any quote that is above this, you have to go to your boss for approval. Accept junior consultants only if they can start immediately and on condition you see their CVs and there is a trial period with the consultants in question.

Schedule
The consultants need to start work a.s.a.p., as the company is already losing sales to the competition. The project should be completed in three months' time.

Competition
Ask for a guarantee of a ten-per-cent increase in company sales and an improvement in your company's profile, as the market is extremely competitive.

Points to consider
- Agree to allow the consultants to interview all members of staff, although the head of customer service is resistant to the idea of consultants coming into his department.
- Training: in your opinion, customer-service staff only need training on any new system that may be adopted, such as an IT interface. Moreover, your company spent a great deal on management training last year.

Unit 12, Business skills, Exercise F, page 111

Student C

You are Gao Shan, Production Engineer, based in Guangzhou, China. You are a member of the product development team reporting to Bob Frasier, the Marketing Manager, in Sydney, Australia. You're participating in a teleconference with Bob Frasier and Francesca Russo, the R&D Manager, based in Rome, Italy.

It's now 4 p.m. in Sydney, 2 p.m. in Guangzhou and 7 a.m. in Rome.

These are the notes you've made on your agenda:

Agenda

Status report

Next round of trials: Fran is coming to Guangzhou to work with me and my production team at the plant in a week's time. We're allowing two days for the trials. Everything is set up at the factory for the trials.

Product labelling:

Production capacity: We're still working on ways to meet the production capacity required. A typhoon has caused heavy rains in Guangzhou recently, and this is slowing work down considerably. I'm hoping to get a price for some new machinery within the next few days. I need to ask Bob if we can get budget approval.

Consumer testing: When does Bob want to start these? I'd suggest it's best to wait until after the second round of trials, as there may need to be more trials.

Unit 6, Case study, Task, page 57

Student D

You are Head of Marketing and Sales. Look at the agenda before the meeting, take notes and add some of your own points:
- Item 5: Stitch Wear may need new brand name in certain countries/branches.
- Item 6: maybe a sports event in conjunction with high-profile sportspeople, etc.
- Item 8: review prices at the top/bottom end of the range to adjust to additional costs of CSR program?

Unit 3, Business skills, Exercise H, page 27

Concepts for negotiating

Executive summary
............[1] I will first define a negotiation, then outline the aims of negotiating. I will also propose various recommendations for the negotiating process, both before and after the session. Finally, in my conclusion I will highlight some useful negotiating tips.

Introduction
What is negotiation and when do you negotiate? ....[2] Negotiation is useful for resolving conflicts when the two sides share an important goal, have some differences, or, are in a position to trade things that they value with one another. If the two sides have a common goal and no differences, the appropriate activity is problem-solving. If they have only differences and no common goals, discussion will not be productive. However, in case of doubt, discussion will reveal whether they share an important goal.

............[3], e.g. in labour management relations, in marketing and so on. Some authors have defined negotiating as creative confrontation, to be used for achieving objectives.

The purpose of negotiating
The mark of a successful negotiation is to get a contract, written or verbal, which signifies that a mutually agreeable solution to conflict has been reached. If the negotiating parties must continue to work with each other and for a negotiation to be considered successful, the contract should be one that both sides 'can live with'.
............[4]

On the other hand, if the negotiation is between parties that will not interact with each other after the completion of the deal, each side may simply try to get all it can without concern for the other party. Examples would be the sale and purchase of property or a business.

Recommendations
A Preparing for a negotiation session:
  - ....[5] Identify the goals you share with your opponent.
  - Define the things you are willing to trade and their value to your opponent. Do the same for the other side: what might they offer you and how much is it worth to you?
  - Define your BATNA (Best Alternative To Negotiated Agreement). Anticipate alternative scenarios and prepare your tactics.
  - Realize that you are not weaker or stronger than your opponents. ....[6]
B During a negotiation session:
  - Start by stating the goals you share.
  - Keep notes on what is being agreed upon.
  - State your demands: usually high if you are selling; low if you are buying.
  - Listen actively: Use the silent periods to think over what the other side has said.
  - Find alternatives (see BATNA)
  - Reach for agreement, but do not insist on it. ....[7]
  - If you feel pressure to settle, be aware the other side is probably also feeling similar pressure.

Conclusion
When negotiating, avoid the following pitfalls:
- Making concessions too soon.
- Giving large concessions; make the other side earn their concessions.
- Irritating the other party or making them angry.
- Accepting a deadline for reaching agreement.

To be a successful negotiator you should:
- prepare thoroughly for the negotiation
- never enter a negotiation when you are tired, hungry or angry.
- allow for the possibility of not reaching agreement.
- ....[8] Could you have done better if you had done something differently?

Unit 6, Business skills, Exercise F, page 55

Date:

Participants: Leader/chair:

Agenda: Effective meetings
- Number of participants
- Appropriate length of meetings
- Role of leader/chairperson to rotate at each meeting.
- Functions of a good leader/chairperson:
  - makes sure everyone participates
  - controls time spent on each item
  - intervenes if necessary
  - decides on behalf of the team if the team is undecided
  - summarises each item before moving on
  - clarifies who in the meeting is responsible for each action point
- Review how you performed as a team at the end of every meeting for ten minutes.
- One of the participants to be responsible for room booking and preparing drinks/snacks.
- Minutes or action points: minutes to be written up and distributed to all participants within 24 hours, preferably by the leader/chairperson?
- AOB (Any Other Business – other important points arising on the topic of meetings)

Unit 7, Business skills, Exercise C, page 67

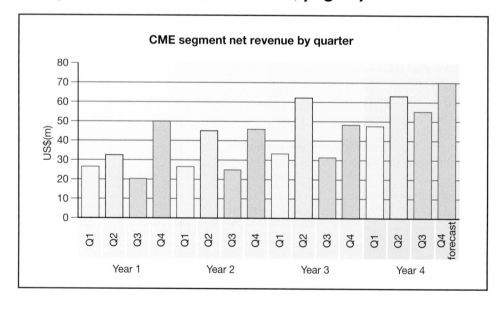

CME segment net revenue by quarter

Unit 10, Business skills, Exercise E, page 95

Choose ONE of these topics for your talk.
- How your company or organisation could improve its website
- Why companies shouldn't bother having websites
- How your favourite sports team could improve its website
- How new technologies might affect your job in the future
- Your favourite website and why you think it's effective
- A comparison between the effectiveness and usability of two websites

Unit 10, Business skills, Exercise F, page 95

Potential problems with online business

Customers expect to be able to do business with you over the Internet. It takes too long to process orders online. It should cost you less than taking an order over the phone, but it doesn't because you're still manually entering everything. You don't know who is visiting the site, who is buying, who isn't buying and why. You're taking bad credit-cards online. Someone hacked your site and stole your customer and payment information.

ISSUES
So why does that happen? Some possible reasons:

Website is just a brochure in the sky

Website isn't integrated with your back-end systems

Website doesn't have tools for tracking activity

No ties to credit-card processing to check for fraud in real-time

Site wasn't built with security in mind

You need a way to:

Check that credit cards are good in real-time

Check that you have product available as promised

Calculate accurate delivery costs so customers know the exact price

Be able to update your catalogue information online

Tie your systems together so you don't have to key in information by hand

Track who is visiting and buying

Need the ability to cross-sell and up-sell to customers on the site

SOLUTIONS
Ideas, tools and services to help:

Catalogue management

Integration with back-end systems – sales, order processing, inventory and delivery

Real-time calculation of actual delivery or shipping costs

Integration with credit card processor

User profiling, which allows cross-selling and up-selling

Strong security

Audio scripts

1 Being international

🎧 1.1

1 Last week, I was in Geneva giving a talk to executives from all over the world. And, uh, you see, you simply can't take anything for granted. There's nothing like an international audience to make me see just how much slang I use. I guess I've always felt that it gives me a casual style that I think is fun and adds a personal touch. But after seeing their faces, I realised how inappropriate and insensitive it is for those who don't get the jokes. The next time I go abroad, er, I'm gonna review my presentation and try to avoid words and expressions that might mean nothing to the listeners. I guess I'll have to remember to schedule some time to have one of my international colleagues review my talk for me.

2 I always like to do some research to find out what the local customs are when I'm giving a presentation abroad. One interesting thing I discovered recently on a trip to Bangkok is that, uh, in a meeting, it's customary to seat VIPs in the front row. Anyway, I … I normally like to have a semi-circular, theatre-style room setup whenever I can. In my Bangkok talk, when I found out approximately how many VIPs there would be, I arranged for the front row to be set with plush chairs that were sort of nicer and different than the rest of the chairs we were using. Er, I also made sure that the important people were escorted to their seats. I could tell that this small gesture was very well received and helped to pave the way for a very productive speech. It's not a major issue, I mean, after all, Thais are used to, er, 'westernised' meetings these days, but I'm sure that, you know, recognising this type of custom and, er, making some effort to adhere to it, can earn you some real points with the people that count.

3 I've found that, in my experience, people around the world respond differently to presentations. I thought I was putting them to sleep once in Japan, but then somebody told me that it's common there to show concentration by closing your eyes and nodding your head up and down slightly. Then again, maybe I really was boring them!
And while you might think applause is a universal sign of approval, there are exceptions. Um, I … I've found that in parts of Germany and Austria, listeners sitting round a table may show their approval by knocking on the table. And another thing, if you wave goodbye when you've finished your presentation in Argentina, the members of the audience might all turn round and come back to sit down. To them, the wave means, 'Hey! Come back!' Knowing what to expect with questions is another point. Nodding your head in Bulgaria actually means 'No', so think about that if someone asks you a question. Americans, and Canadian and many European audiences, will almost always ask questions, but in most Asian cultures, audiences are more likely to greet your presentation with silence.

🎧 1.2 (M = Melanie, K = Konrad, J = James)

M Excuse me, but you're Professor Slowinski, aren't you?
K That's right, but please, call me Konrad. And you are …?
M Melanie, Melanie Burns.
K Nice to meet you, Melanie.
M Pleased to meet you, too. You know, I really enjoyed your talk, Professor … I… I mean Konrad.
K Did you? That's very kind of you to say so.
M I thought what you said was fascinating, especially the importance of marketing and product adaptation for the South-East Asian market.
K Did you think so?
M Oh yes, absolutely. There are so many cultural considerations when entering new markets.
K That's right. But what about yourself? Are you giving a talk at the conference?
M Yes, just a short seminar.
K Oh really? When will you be speaking?

M Tomorrow afternoon at 5 p.m.
K Ah, that *is* a shame. I'm afraid I'm leaving tomorrow afternoon. I've promised I'd be home in time to attend our son's basketball match.
M That's a coincidence; my daughter is crazy about basketball. But it's a pity you're going to miss my talk.
K Well, you know, family commitments. What's it going to be on, by the way?
M How companies need to adapt their company culture in the light of international mergers.
K Mmm, merging companies and merging cultures, eh?
M Exactly. I've done a lot of research into how international bank mergers can go terribly wrong if cultural issues aren't taken into account.
K It sounds very interesting. I'll be sorry to miss it.
M Well, in that case, I can always e-mail you my slides from the talk.
K If it wouldn't be too much trouble. Look, um, here's my card. And do e-mail me if you have any questions about my line of investigation.
M Well, I might just take you up on that. Here's mine. Please take a look at our website, Intercultural Consulting.
J Professor Slowinksi! There you are! You're due to talk in five minutes.
K Oh, hello, James. Um, let me introduce you to Melanie … er …
M Burns, Melanie Burns.
J Ah yes. Hi.
M Hello. So, are you a colleague of Professor Slowinski?
J I'm his research assistant, actually.
K Couldn't do without him. It's been a pleasure talking to you, Melanie. You never know, we may be able to collaborate together some time. Now, if you'll excuse me …
M Yes, of course.
J I've been looking for you everywhere, Konrad. What have you been up to?
K Networking, James, just networking.

2 Training

🎧 2.1 (I = interviewer, R = Rosa Soler)

I Rosa, how do you decide what type of training or development is needed?
R First of all, I just observe and analyse a company's needs before deciding on the type of training required, you know, er, before setting up the actual courses and programmes. I use various training exercises at this stage. For example, tower-building and bridge-building work well for evaluating potential leadership skills.
I What exactly does tower-building and bridge-building involve?
R They're, um, group activities whereby the … the team has to build a tower or a bridge using just cardboard, a ruler and some glue. You have an hour and a half to do it, and, er, well, by the end, the team should have constructed a cardboard tower or bridge. The exercise is used to … is used to observe various skills such as teamwork, um, leadership skills, interpersonal communication and … and so on.
I What other training exercises might you use?
R Well, mm, there are also … case studies for evaluating people's values. These case studies, um, well, they don't have any one solution, but they're useful for seeing how people react. Sometimes the case study can be very emotive, and people, they really get carried away with the exercise. Er, then there's another activity called 'The in-tray', which is used for assessing management skills.
I 'The in-tray'? How does that work?
R You receive various e-mails and phone calls and you have to prioritise your workload. Then you get a message out of the blue that your mother has fallen sick and you have to delegate and so on. It's designed to see how managers cope under pressure.

I   And after assessing a company's needs, what kind of courses might you set up?

R   Mm, I, er, I tend to use more coaching programmes, and very occasionally there, well, there may be a mentoring programme.

🎧 **2.2** *(I = interviewer, R = Rosa Soler)*

I   Could you explain the difference between coaching and mentoring?

R   Um, basically, when you coach people, you improve on their skills so that they can do a better job. Um, people may already have the knowledge or basic skills to do something, but they don't know how to do it effectively. These skills, er, may include many business management skills, such as negotiating, time management, er, preparing meetings and presentations or organisation. But coaching isn't only for managers. Anyone in a company might do this sort of programme. The course can be intensive or over a long period of time, but the objective is to … is to improve an employee's specific skills and improve company results.

I   Isn't mentoring also about improving skills?

R   Well, the *original* idea of mentoring programmes, though, is that, er, they are long-term career programmes which are specifically designed for a select few in multinationals.

I   So, mentoring is more of an elitist training programme, then?

R   Yes, it is. It's usually for people with a lot of potential who will end up being managers in two or three years' time. The … the mentoring programme is in fact only part of a bigger picture, because the participant, or mentee, may probably be attending other training and personal development programmes. Or he or she might be studying for an MBA, as well as working on various high-profile projects. Um, really, mentoring programmes are designed to retain talented people within the organisation.

I   And how do you decide who the mentor is going to be?

R   We have to interview all the senior staff in the company, but the mentor cannot be the mentee's direct manager or boss. Usually, the mentor is someone who is high up in the company, who has a lot of experience and know-how and, er, very importantly, is someone who likes teaching and, er, sharing knowledge. Mentors have to be excellent teachers. They invest a lot of time and energy; it's very difficult to find the right person. It has to be someone who can be objective if the mentee has a problem at work or comes for advice.

I   How long does a mentoring programme last?

R   Usually about a year and a half, but the mentor and mentee may only meet once a month.

🎧 **2.3** *(M = Mel, L = Leoni)*

M   Human Resources. Mel Van Der Horst speaking.

L   Oh, hello, this is Leoni Taylor, I'm coming to the staff induction day on Thursday.

M   Hello, Ms Taylor. How can I help you?

L   Well, I'm coming to the induction course on Thursday and I don't know what time it starts or which room to go to.

M   So, you didn't receive the programme we sent to you?

L   Well, no. I don't know if it got lost somewhere …

M   Not to worry, I can give you the details now. It starts at 9 a.m. in conference room B2.

L   Uh, can I just check that? Did you say nine o'clock?

M   Yes, that's right.

L   And the room was …?

M   Conference room B2. Just ask at reception, they'll give you directions.

L   So that's B2, thanks. And it doesn't matter if I haven't got a copy of the programme?

M   No, don't worry. I'll bring some extra copies.

L   Thank you very much.

M   See you on Thursday, Ms Taylor.

🎧 **2.4** *(M = Mel, P = Pierre)*

P   Hi, Mel. It's Pierre in reception. I'm very sorry, but there's a problem with the conference room bookings for Thursday. It looks like B2 is double-booked in the morning.

M   What?

P   Well, we can't really ask the chairman to shift his meeting. But it's only occupied till 11 o'clock, you could use it afterwards.

M   What about the other meeting rooms?

P   Well, nothing is free *all* day. Uh, we could put you in B3 or C1 for the first part of the morning.

M   I think C1 is a slightly smaller room than B3, isn't it? We're going to need the space.

P   Look, I'm not sure which room would be better for you. Um, why don't you come down to reception now and get the keys to both, and you can see for yourself.

M   No, thanks. I'm sure B3 will be fine for a few hours.

P   Do you want to book it till 11 then?

M   No, er, better put us down till 12 in case the chairman's meeting runs over.

P   OK, I'll put you in B3 from nine to 12 and I'll book you into B2 from 11 for the rest of the day. Thanks for being so understanding, Mel.

M   Don't mention it. One thing though, I'll e-mail the people who are coming about the room change, but they might not all read my message in time. Could you make sure that they know where to go when they arrive on Thursday morning?

P   Sure, Mel, I'll tell the others and leave a note in reception with the attendance list.

M   Thank you, Pierre.

🎧 **2.5** *(H = Harry, G = Gabriella, K = Kamal)*

H   What's the next item? Ah, yes. As you know, there's a distinct lack of information coming from the sales force. And what information we do get is often too out-of-date to be of any use.

K   Yes, well, Harry, there's a lotta problems with the current system. I mean, staff say that they just can't afford to spend time in the office completing what they see as a complicated database.

G   Yes, and it seems that the extra training for the regional managers was inadequate, which meant that they, in turn, weren't well equipped to teach their staff. We've also now got the sales team from Reedleys, and they've only had very ad-hoc informal training with the system so far.

K   You know there are new solutions available now. We, um, we … we could use iPAQ; it's like an upmarket palm pilot.

H   How would that help?

K   Well, the sales team could record details directly in the shops. There's even a plug-in camera to take photos of product displays. The information is then uploaded via modem for analysis, and decisions can be made quickly according to the data. We could then produce reports and data in a more user-friendly format.

H   That certainly sounds interesting. I'd like to see a demo, and we need to look at the cost of implementation, of course. What do you think, Gabriella?

G   Well, I'm most concerned about what form the training will take. Given our experience with the present system, we don't want anyone left behind during implementation. And, er, we need to make sure that the regional managers buy in to this or, as we've already seen, it won't work. We probably need to train staff up as quickly as possible.

K   Yeah, I agree, but my department can't undertake training on that scale in a short period of time. I'd like to suggest we hire the training firm Pollack. They've done a very good job running other IT training courses for us in the past.

H   OK. Shall we start the ball rolling on this one, then? Kamal, would you set up a demo?

K   Sure, I'll do that.

H   And while we're on the subject of training, we have a very experienced sales team here, but we have to look at updating their skills. I mean, there are people here, doing the job for 20 years with very little if any formal training, and I'd say they really need some customer-awareness training, you know, something that will help them become a bit more, um, 'pro-active' in their approach to selling.

G   Yes, especially now that the two sales teams have merged.

H   That's another concern of mine. I know it's difficult for them to adapt to working with someone who used to work for the competition, and there's sometimes a distinct tension in the air. I don't get the feeling the teams are integrating well.

G   Mm. I suggest we find a way to, er … to accelerate the process and create a unified team more quickly. We could handle the training in our department, but I wonder if a more neutral organisation would be better under the circumstances.

3 Partnerships

3.1 *(P = presenter, G = Georgina, F = Frank)*

P On today's show we're talking about public private partnerships in the UK. My guests are the journalist Georgina Monroe and Frank Watson, a management consultant. Welcome to both of you.

G Hello, Richard.

F Good afternoon.

P So, what is the government's Private Finance Initiative? And how is it different from other forms of collaboration between the public and private sectors in the past 20 years or so?

F Well, um, before this 'initiative', public private partnerships basically meant, you know, outsourcing services. Take, for example, the case of competitive tendering for cleaning and catering services in hospitals. But now the, um, the PFI goes much further. It's become the government's main source of funds for new public-sector buildings and it, um, it basically lets the government build capital-intensive projects without increasing public spending.

P What kinds of projects are being financed by PFI? Can you give us some examples?

F Oh, literally hundreds. And they're right across the spectrum of public services: schools, hospitals, prisons, roads and waste-disposal systems.

P So, it's gone far beyond small-scale projects?

G Oh yes. We've seen the size and complexity of PFI projects grow considerably over the past decade. In the early days, it would be a single building, say a school. Now, the projects tend to be much bigger, maybe between ten to 30 schools at once or a combination of schools, libraries and community facilities at several locations as part of one contract.

3.2 *P = presenter, G = Georgina, F = Frank)*

P So what's driving this level of public-private activity?

G Well, the argument goes that the PFI allows new money to be poured into public services. Private companies put up the money, build the new hospitals or trains or whatever we need, and run them for 25 or 30 years. And, in exchange, the government pays them rent and service charges and, of course, keeps the ownership of the assets.

P And there's the added bonus that the, um, the private sector is more efficient, so it can run our public services more cheaply than the state could.

G That's certainly the theory. However, a growing number of critics claim it could end up costing the public more.

P How so?

G They claim that many PFI projects have been designed to generate as much profit as possible for these private consortiums. The Edinburgh Royal Infirmary is an example of how expensive the PFI can be. Um, the … the hospital cost 180 million pounds to build and will cost 900 million to pay for.

F What critics fail to point out in that particular example, Richard, is that the 900 million-pound fee that Georgina mentioned includes operating and maintenance costs over the 30-year contract.

P Yes, but is it still likely that the building would be cheaper to build and manage if it were traditionally funded?

F It may seem that way, but, you know, recent studies in the UK have shown that when the, um, the public sector funds such projects in a more … more traditional way, the time and cost overrun is much greater than when the private sector manages a project.

P Georgina, what's your take on this?

G Some say many of these new building projects are cheap-looking and will become run-down and dated in a few years' time when the government will still be paying for them. The truth is we won't really know the full cost of the PFI for another 30 years or so.

P Well, thank you both. Our lines are now open to callers.

3.3 *(K = Kathy, G = Giovanni)*

K I know that Olivo Benedetti has always offered us good quality and service, but couldn't you offer us a five-per-cent discount, Giovanni?

G But Kathy, the quality of our packaging and the bottle design of our olive oil is simply the best!

K Yes, you have great marketing, Giovanni, but many of our customers are now switching to Spanish olive oil. Frankly, it's good quality and much cheaper.

G As I've told you before, we can offer you exceptional delivery terms.

K Those special services would be nice, but we aren't going to order in larger quantities, as there isn't the demand for it. Could you include the special delivery conditions at no additional cost?

G I'm sorry, Kathy, that's not our company policy.

K But you're going to have to make an exception to your policy if you want to continue with our business.

G You drive a hard bargain, Kathy. I'll speak to my manager and see what I can do.

K Five per cent?

G I can't promise anything, but it'll be somewhere in the region of five per cent.

3.4 *(J = Jozef, K = Karen, S = Stefan)*

J Thank you, Dr Armstrong and Mr Znaniecki, for agreeing to this meeting. As you know, public-private partnerships are a relatively new concept for us, and we appreciate the chance to exchange ideas and discuss your experiences in the UK.

K Please, call me Karen, and I'm sure my colleague Stefan is happy to use first-name terms.

S Yes, of course. How would you like us to address you?

J Jozef is fine.

K Well, Jozef, we'll be pleased to help in any way we can.

J Thank you. Well, just to give you some background, until recently the State Treasury has always financed our infrastructure projects. But, um, we now need to consider other options.

K Well, as you know, we're now using private capital to help us develop infrastructure projects.

J Yes, that, um, that model of finance raises a number of issues, um, which concern us. For instance, if you use private-sector money to fund developments, does that mean, um, does the state risk losing control of the services?

S That all depends on your government policy and EU regulations, of course. It really hasn't happened in the UK unless the government has opted for full privatisation, for instance the telecom sector.

K And when we negotiate any public-private deal, we make sure that we negotiate ownership of the assets and that the airport authority continues to operate airport services.

J Um, I see … And about funding. As the state cannot provide funding, what are the alternatives we could consider?

S Well, public-private ventures come in many forms. You could ask commercial banks for loans, uh, or get a private company to invest in the project.

J And what about negotiating interest rates with lenders?

K We've found that banks offer lower interest rates over a longer timescale, but tend to want more guarantees from the government or will ask for an insurance policy to be taken out. Whereas private investment firms are looking for a much higher rate of return in exchange for funding more risky ventures.

S You mentioned that the option of full state finance is not possible, is the treasury going to meet some of the capital costs?

J Yes, but we don't know what percentage yet.

S And are you planning to put the contract out to competitive tender? I ask that because there are several large construction companies with international public-private experience that can take on a project of this size.

J Yes, I agree we need a company with a track record in managing this type of project.

S Might I recommend that you also ask the tenderers to propose the method of finance of the investment?

J That's a very helpful suggestion. Thank you.

K Apart from the funding, the other big advantage of these partnerships is that the risk is shared.

J In what sense?

K Well, in an agreement, the private contractor can be made responsible for the building schedule.

J So, if there are delays, then the extra cost is met by the contractor, not the state?

K In effect, yes. You need to negotiate risk allocation as part of the contract, obviously. We've found that that's really helped to keep projects on schedule.

J I can definitely see the benefits in such an arrangement. Now, shall we start the tour of the airport facilities and then we can continue our discussion over lunch.

4 Energy

🎧 **4.1** (I = interviewer, A = Anthony Fitzgerald)

I   To what extent is gas an environmentally friendly source of energy?

A   Well, er, gas is the cleanest fossil fuel, much better in terms of negative gas emissions than any other fossil fuel, such as oil and coal. But eventually it will be replaced by new environmentally friendly sources, such as solar energy or windmills. Unfortunately, any fossil fuel is limited by its existing reserves, although it's very difficult to say for how long we will have oil or gas. Um, recent studies estimate that we will have oil for oh, …, 50 or 60 years, and that we'll have natural gas perhaps for between, um, 100 and 150 years, er, but no longer than 200 years.

I   And do you consider the gas sector a prosperous one at the moment?

A   Oh, yes, it is, and it will remain so for many years, although the new regulations have made things more difficult for existing companies. That means that older companies that once had a dominant position in their national markets have now to compete with the, er, new entrants.

I   So, how is the gas sector regulated in Europe?

A   Until recently, there was a dominant company in each country supplying gas by using their *own* network. Um, in order to change this monopolistic situation, the new European regulations are allowing gas suppliers to sell gas to customers by using the existing networks in, er, in such a way that they do not need to build their own gas network to compete. This has brought about significant changes in our industry, um, one of them is that in order to avoid the monopoly of bigger companies, er, they've been forced to unbundle their activities; um, unbundling means splitting their activities between different subsidiaries in such a way that they now have a subsidiary company for transport, another for distribution and another subsidiary that deals with supply. Er, all suppliers can therefore use the same gas networks and pay the same price for them.

I   We've seen a number of joint ventures and mergers in the gas sector, why is that?

A   Er, well, er, to a large extent, this is a consequence of competition and the unbundling of activities I have mentioned. Er, this means gas companies are now looking for new activities in other sectors, activities that could be complementary to the gas business. The most obvious one is the electricity sector. Some gas companies are producing electricity, and in other cases, they simply supply electricity to their customers by using the network of existing electricity companies. In fact, electricity companies are doing the same, selling natural gas to their electricity customers.

I   And what other significant developments are we seeing in the gas sector at the moment?

A   Well, er, there is an increasing concern for security of supply. The European Union is highly dependent on external sources, mainly from, um, Russia, Algeria and the Middle East. This dependence on distant external sources implies significant risk. So the European gas sector needs to, uh, to diversify its sources of supply and to build large storage facilities to face temporary problems of external supply. In a country like Spain, for instance, they are now importing gas from 12 different countries, both as liquefied natural gas and by means of pipelines, mainly from Algeria as well as France.

🎧 **4.2**

1

A   I notice that the staff turnover in our Rotterdam branch is consistently higher than in other branches and there've been a number of transfer applications from there recently. It could be that it's just a coincidence. Have you spoken to the manager there recently?

B   No, but as I understand it, they have a lot of work there at the moment.

A   I think it's too early to jump to any conclusions, but maybe it would be a good idea to take a trip over there and talk to him.

2

A   It looks like we've sold out of air-con units already, and suppliers can't get any more to us until the end of the summer. By then it'll be too late. I've phoned around, and everywhere is completely out.

B   Yes, the hot summer has certainly been good for business.

A   It's a pity, though. We could have sold three or four times the number of units we did.

B   That's true. But who was to know it would be a record summer? You can't rely on the weather forecast, certainly not the long-term ones.

A   I know, but I think we should reconsider our order for next year.

B   Hold on, we don't know there's likely to be the same demand next summer.

A   Yes, but neither does anyone else. I think people will be keen to buy their air-con at the start of the summer rather than run the risk of going without again. The only problem I can see is the storage space …

B   Look, let's sleep on it. We don't need to make a decision right away.

🎧 **4.3** (J = Jo, B = Bill, R = Raghit)

J   OK, OK, let's move on to the next item on the agenda. Did you all get a chance to read the literature I sent you on energy efficiency?

B   Yeah, some of it. There was kind of a lot of stuff there.

J   Right, um, I suggest we start by defining the problem more clearly. I mean, we need to collect and analyse some data first. We should get a breakdown of our energy costs.

B   Sure, sure. But we can start working on reducing waste right away, can't we?

J   Yes, OK. Do you want to discuss some ideas now, then?

R   Er, yeah, why not?

B   I got a suggestion. How about turning the air-con down when personnel complain it's too cold? No, hey, I'm serious.

R   And lighting, another big expense. Maybe we leave the lights on too long, inside and outside the store.

B   That's right. Maybe we could use skylights to let in natural light.

J   Thanks, Bill. This is a really great start. Um, we need to set up an energy-management team to start working on these ideas. And we … we wanna make energy-saving a priority for everyone in the company.

R   What about when things start getting expensive, Jo? I mean, we can't afford to put in skylights or buy more energy-efficient refrigeration units overnight. A fridge that's six or seven years old is due for replacement, but what if the unit's only a few years old?

J   Good point, Raghit. We're in a chicken-and-egg situation. We … we can decide we're not going to install new equipment and technologies until the benefits are proven, but we can't be sure of the benefits if we don't invest in the new stuff.

R   Sure, yeah.

J   A related issue is the company's commitment to improving energy efficiency by monitoring CO_2 emissions. Our target is to reduce emissions by ten per cent in the next seven years.

B   How are we going to do that?

J   Good question! That's another job for our new energy project team. Um … there are … uh … for instance, we could reduce our energy consumption by using more advanced refrigeration systems, but, like, that's a big capital investment. We can also start buying some of our energy from renewable sources.

R   OK, um, if we're thinking out of the box here, why don't we just sell less frozen food and, um, cut the number of fridges? You know, promote better eating habits, um … Fresh is Best.

B   No, Raghit. Like, people won't buy that.

R   How do you know? Hey, if we promote fresh, local produce more, we can cut our transportation costs and CO_2 emissions, too.

J   OK, let's set up a project team to work on the energy audit and the other issues we've been discussing today. Any volunteers?

5 Employment trends

🎧 **5.1**

1   In our village, many women go to Spain to pick strawberries for a few months every year. This is my third year now. We save as much as we can and then come back home to Poland.

2   You see, after I had the baby, it was getting to be impossible to combine full-time work with my family commitments. So when my maternity leave was up, I negotiated a reduction in hours.

3   I always wanted to start my own business, so when the opportunity came up to take the redundancy package, the time seemed right. It's great being my own boss.

4 The company wanted to reduce the office costs, and I jumped at the chance to work from home. I don't miss travelling to the office every day, but I do miss my colleagues … sometimes.

5 There's always a group of men at the factory gates at five in the morning, and a supervisor comes out and chooses the people they want to work that day. It's all cash-in-hand, of course.

6 With the fall of communism, there was no more demand for the steel we produced, so all the industry in the region closed down virtually overnight. My wife and daughter have stayed in Bulgaria, and I've come to Italy to work in a ceramics factory. I take a bus home to see them three or four times a year.

5.2 (I = interviewer, S = Sean McGuinness)

I Sean, is the way we work really changing fundamentally? And in what ways?

S Well, the accepted wisdom, if you like, is that there is a general loosening of the relationship between staff and employers … more people on temporary contracts and more self-employment. If we look at government statistics and research evidence, though, things are changing profoundly in industrialised Western countries, but not in the ways we would expect. Like, in the UK, the Economic and Social Research Council's project on *The Future of Work* shows that the shift away from permanent and full-time jobs to temporary, short-term or part-time work is really exaggerated. In fact, permanent employment is still very much the norm – representing 90 per cent of employees in the UK. This compares with 80 per cent a decade ago. Also, only five per cent of employees have temporary contracts nowadays, and, er, self-employment is down to seven per cent. This figure, you know, it's the same as it was in 1979. And we're also seeing that people are staying in their jobs for longer. A decade ago, the average time spent in the same job was six years two months. This is now seven years four months. So this appears to give the lie to the myth about portfolio workers.

I Portfolio workers?

S Yeah, you know, when they talk about a much more flexible and mobile workforce that goes from job to job. Well, the findings seem to put the rhetoric about the new flexibility at work into a more realistic perspective. You see, we've got much greater job stability, longer employment tenure and less evidence of new forms of flexible employment contracts than many people realise.

5.3 (I = interviewer, S = Sean McGuinness)

I So, how have new technologies changed the way we work, then?

S Well, this very much depends on the professional category. The survey shows that over 80 per cent of higher professional and senior managers use the Internet and e-mail at work. However, most lower-skilled employees, while they often have PCs at home, are not using information technologies in the workplace. Um … only 29 per cent of admin staff use the Internet and e-mail in their jobs, along with 14 to 15 per cent of skilled, semi-skilled and unskilled manual staff.

I But I thought there was more demand now for workers with IT skills.

S Er, well, what we're seeing, in fact, is job enlargement rather than new jobs being created. People are required to take on additional skills and roles that in the past would have been done by other members of staff. Everyone is in fact sharing out middle-management roles, and so fewer of them are needed now. So, while higher professional jobs have risen by 3 per cent to 37 per cent in the last ten years, the middle-ranking jobs have been squeezed out. The findings could be seen as lending support to the notion of the 'hour-glass' economy, a trend first spotted in the US. It suggests there'll be large numbers of highly skilled and unskilled workers and very few people in the middle-ranking occupations. You know that also, the total number of manual workers hasn't changed in the last ten years – it still remains at 40 per cent of total employees. In fact, in terms of employment growth, it's the traditional and low-paid occupations – sales assistants, call-centre operators, security guards, care workers and generally service-sector jobs – that are growing. You know, the fastest-growing occupation in the UK is hairdressing – up by over 300 per cent from ten years ago.

I What are the possible consequences of this divide?

S Well, it's going to be very difficult to bridge that gap, with fewer opportunities for career progression and social mobility. Employees with fewer skills have less bargaining power. And I would say that there's clearly a need for employment protection measures – such as minimum wage legislation, as we've seen in the UK, and controls over working hours, as we've witnessed in the directives and regulations in the European Union.

5.4 (Y = Yolanda, T = Terry)

Y Look, Terry, your phone calls are really driving me up the wall.

T Let me see if I follow you. You're saying that you can't work because I disturb you when I'm using the phone.

Y Yes, well. It's not a big problem most of the time. Only when I've got the monthly sales reports to write or I'm … oh ... it doesn't matter.

T No, please go on.

Y Or, well, I'm trying to concentrate on something.

T I appreciate how you feel, Yolanda. The thing is, it's important for me to talk to clients and engage in some friendly small talk. It really helps to get sales.

5.5 (I = interviewer, R = Rob Giardina)

I So, Rob, why are there so many problems and misunderstandings when people write e-mails to each other?

R Primarily because you don't have the … the visual information and feedback that you have in a face-to-face conversation. You know, things like smiles or nods, or even being able to say 'I don't understand'. And … and that also makes it easier to get nasty, to … uh, to do what they call 'flaming' – sending angry or insulting e-mails to people. Another factor is that your context when you write it is different from their context when they read it. So, for example, you're in a rush, you write a quick e-mail, their context is different, they don't see it that way, they see it as brusque and direct. And … and finally, you know the truth is, some people just don't express themselves so well in writing.

I So what can we do?

R Well, first, keep those things in mind when you read and write. So when you read an e-mail, don't always believe your first impression. If something doesn't seem right or appropriate to you, think about other possible interpretations. And when you write e-mails, think about how the other person could maybe misinterpret what you're writing and then make it clear that you don't mean that. You know, those emoticons seem so silly, but sometimes they help express the tone that you want. Really, as with any conflict, the best advice is to take into account the other person's perceptions and context – what they think and where they're coming from. And to ask questions if you don't know – open, neutral questions, not the type that begin 'How could you possibly …?'

I So, when there's obviously a problem, is it best to talk about it face to face or on the phone?

R Well, for small disputes or misunderstandings, yes. But if you know how to use it, e-mail can be an effective tool to avoid and even resolve conflicts.

I And how's that?

R Well, again, it takes out the visual information; that can be particularly useful for multicultural teams because you can avoid the misunderstandings that can be caused by … by different communication styles and differences in things like body space or eye contact. Also, if a conflict already exists, well, they can't see if you're angry or frustrated, so you have more control over what you actually communicate. Secondly, you have the time to make your e-mails more rational and less emotional if you choose. You know, they say that you should count to ten when you're angry, and an e-mail forces you to do that. Uh … finally, um, you know, it's a basic but important factor, you can't interrupt and you can't be interrupted.

6 Business ethics

6.1 (I = interviewer, M = Miguel Morán)

I How would you define corporate responsibility and corporate citizenship?

M There are some distinctions between corporate responsibility and corporate citizenship, but really they're two sides of the same coin, OK? The concept of corporate citizenship is more to do with the actual action taken in relation to the environment and the local community. If I had to give a definition of corporate responsibility, it's how companies manage their production processes, or their core businesses, in order to create an overall positive impact on society. It's a sort of payback to society.

I The economics guru Milton Friedman said, 'The one and only social responsibility of business is to make profits.' Is that still true of international business nowadays?

M Actually, I think the time has come for companies to consider doing more than just making a profit. I mean, being socially responsible now has a positive impact on a company's success.

I A lot of multinationals are criticised for only paying lip service to issues such as social responsibility. To what extent do you agree 'the important thing is not to *be* ethical, but to be *seen* to be ethical'?

M Well, the most important thing is to *be* ethical, of course. But I must say, even to be *seen* to be ethical is the first step because it shows companies are becoming aware that both the market and the customers consider it important. The problem is if it's merely a cover-up, it's ultimately going to be discovered by the customers and by the market, because customers aren't stupid.

I It's said that Nokia's products would be very expensive if they were made in Finland. How difficult is it for multinationals to ensure that its workers in developing countries or transition economies are guaranteed decent working conditions and decent wages?

M I don't think it's easy. And companies have to take advantage of lower labour costs in most Asian or Latin American or North African countries. But these companies can still do something. Firstly, they obviously have to respect the labour laws in these countries. But companies need to respect human *dignity*. Companies have to carry out actions that are going to be of benefit to their workers, the local community and society at large.

🎧 6.2 *(I = interviewer, M = Miguel Morán)*

I Do multinationals still employ children?

M Well, I'll give you an example. Nestlé, the well-known Swiss food company, produces a lot of its products in Asian countries where 11- and 12-year-olds are legally allowed to work. What do they do? They hire these children part-time and they just get them to do simple tasks. The rest of the day, they send them to school. They pay for their education. The bottom line is that these children need money for their families who are living not only in poverty, but often in extreme poverty. It's very difficult.

I Don't you think it's easier for the Western world to be ethical and say to developing countries, don't employ children?

M Companies must be responsible ethically and socially, but it's not just the fault of Western companies that child labour exists; it's also the fault of the state and the government.

I Are you saying that it's the responsibility of the state and not the companies?

M I think, er, it's a mix. But our Western markets are demanding lower and lower prices and higher and higher wages. This makes it very difficult for us to produce shoes, skirts or watches to sell in our countries. The cheapest shoes manufactured in Europe would cost us about 500. But I think it's very positive that we are at this point where many companies are starting to think about whether they are acting ethically or not.
I think it's also related to the influence of new technologies and the Internet. These countries can *see* we have high standards of living. New governments in Europe are trying to repair the damage done in the past.
Let's be honest. There are an awful lot of well-known companies that have a reputation for being ethical but are producing unethically. And I'm talking about a lot of major companies, not just American companies, but Spanish, British, German or French ones. Why? Because your factory in Indonesia or Malaysia or the Philippines is not actually yours. And on the two occasions that you go there, you can say, 'I didn't see a child at the sewing machine. It's Mr Yang's factory. *He's* the one who employs all the staff. It's *his* fault.' At the end of the day, it all comes down to the difference in production costs.

🎧 6.3

1 Well, um, it depends on the hierarchy in the company. The first step would be to speak to him to confirm or reject my suspicions, because maybe his expenses were justified. The problem is, if he says 'It's none of your business'. In that case, I'd go to someone higher up in the organisation. Our internal code of conduct guarantees anonymity.

2 I'd ignore the implication. In this situation, I wouldn't respond to this kind of blackmail when I got the call. I mean, I'd accept the call and I'd wait until the decision is made. Having said that, if it were the case that the decision was made in *their* favour, and I kept on receiving presents, I'd reject them on the grounds that it's unethical. Alternatively, if this particular supplier didn't get the contract, I'd also send something in return, just, um, out of courtesy, thanking them for taking part in the bid, but only *after* the decision had been made.

3 I think it's tricky, because it really depends on your *cultural* background and your personal *values*. You know, you could argue that your job may be on the line, you might have debts, a mortgage to pay, or you might just want to get on in the company. However, in *this* case, if the two offers were *exactly* equal in merit, I'd have no problem in choosing the director's friend. If they *weren't* equal, my obligation would be to say to the director, 'Look, ultimately, it's *your* decision, but in *my* opinion, the best option is *this* one.'

🎧 6.4 *(Ali = Alison, Ala = Alan, F = Francine, I = Ian)*

Ala Hi, are we all here now?

Ali Um, I think so … oh, no, wait a minute, Francine's plane's getting in at eight thirty, so she might be a bit late.

Ala Oh great … we're missing our HR manager.

Ali Well, she gave me some notes, just in case.

Ala And do you have them there, Alison?

Ali Yes, I do, I've got photocopies for you all.

Ala Well, it might have been useful to have read them in advance.

Ali Oh, I'm sorry, I didn't realise …

Ala Right, well, let's start, because it's already nine thirty, and I need to be finished by 10.15, as I have a visitor coming. OK, so, we're here today to discuss some guidelines for taking on staff, that is, the recruitment and selection process. Are we familiar with company policy? Ian, would you like to get the ball rolling?

I Er, yeah, one sugar, please. I'm sorry, Alan. Didn't catch that.

Ala What do you think about our recruitment process?

I Well, it would be nice to have someone to, er, maybe, sort out the tea and coffee for meetings …

Ala Ian, I've called today's meeting to discuss the ethics of our recruitment policy.

I Oh, sorry. I, uh …

Ali Can I just say something here, Alan?

Ala Please, go on.

Ali Well, we often take on people that know someone in the company, when really, it's not at all politically correct. Did you know that in France, for instance, as much as 45 per cent of the workforce gets a job through contacts?

Ala Your point being?

Ali Well, I just thought that we shouldn't recruit people because of *who* they know, but *what* they know. I mean, we need to employ staff on their experience and merit.

Ala Mm. What do the others think?

I I think it's great in theory, but what if, say, I know someone, and they're interested in a position in the company. Wouldn't I mention it to them?

F Hello, everyone! Sorry I'm late. The plane from Brussels was delayed.

Ala Biscuit?

🎧 6.5 *(EC = ethics consultant, PR = Head of Public Relations)*

EC Like I was saying, you're gonna have to look very carefully at the kinda language you use in your new corporate responsibility report.

PR What do you mean?

EC You know, Stitch Wear's commitment to responsibility has to sound sincere and real. After all, you're gonna have to put those promises into action.

PR That's true. The reports I've read from competitors don't sound convincing.

EC You see! *That's* where Stitch Wear can make the difference. You need an action plan that's not just full of good intentions. It needs to be financially feasible. You might even have to do a little adjusting when it comes to your profit margins, review your pricing, that sort of thing. But you don't want to scare away your shareholders.

PR You've lost me. The way I see it, we'll have to spend a lot more on all this responsibility stuff and still keep competitive prices. Sounds like commercial suicide. What are other guys doing in the industry?

EC Er, OK, let's take a company that makes soccer balls. They're one of Pakistan's biggest exports. They used to have kids under 14 working on the special small stitches that you get on soccer balls, but now they've won *awards* for not using kids under 14!

PR Really?

EC Yeah, and you know how they did it? The local government outlawed child labour, so, here goes, the business leaders set up educational and healthcare programmes for the *former* child workers.

PR Right.

EC No less than 2,000. Imagine. That's a lot of kids.

PR Healthcare *and* education? Wow, that's a lot of dollars.

EC You bet. The thing is, they stayed in business and they've got that competitive edge over the major sports manufacturers. Now, I'm not saying these guys didn't lose any money on the way. But in the long run, you can only benefit from a more positive image.

PR I hear one of our competitors runs a 're-use a shoe' program. They get customers to hand in their old shoes or sneakers and they recycle them to create new products: basketballs, tennis courts …

EC Great, that's the kind of initiative we're looking for. And another thing: your suppliers, who are they?

PR Um, not completely sure, um, that's the purchasing department, isn't it?

EC Wrong. It's *your* department, too. You've got to trust the suppliers you're working with. Uh, I recommend you get yourself a partnership with the ETI, the Ethical Trading Initiative.

PR Ethical Trading?

EC Yup. The ETI screens all suppliers against a sourcing code of practice.

PR You mean, like, we should be making our purchasing process more ethical, too?

EC Mm, that's right. What else? You got any sponsorship ideas?

7 Finance and banking

🎧 **7.1** *(I = interviewer, J = Joan Rosás)*

I Joan, what major factors do you think have affected international banking in recent years?

J All right, I think there are four major factors which have affected international banking, uh, recently. These are: globalisation, secondly, uh, the new regulatory frameworks, thirdly, one would speak of, uh, new technology aspects and finally, direct access to capital markets by, uh, essentially, uh, small and medium-sized companies.

I And what about new technologies? What role have they had to play when it comes to international banking?

J I would say that if something is technologically feasible as well as financially viable, then, chances are, that this will become a new financial instrument. Uh, for instance, markets use nowadays very powerful technology platforms which allow banks, as well as large corporations, to transfer money at the click of a mouse, uh, so they have the ability therefore to carry out international transactions in a way which, uh, could have not been done before.

I Could you give us some examples of those international transactions?

J Yes, absolutely, there are a lot of examples. Er, new, er, banking services which have resulted from this, uh, technology, uh, developments like electronic letters of credit, electronic direct debits or even international cheque truncation where paper doesn't travel any more. Consequently, the technology, or the technological factor, is an absolutely crucial, uh, issue within the financial markets.

I And what about the final factor affecting international banking, I mean, the direct access that companies now have to capital markets?

J OK, during the 70s, only large companies had access to, uh, capital markets. Nowadays, however, we have small and medium-sized companies which also have access to the capital markets. So, uh, nowadays, companies instead of requiring, uh, the more traditional banking services, like, uh, commercial bank lending, companies are, uh, in need of more sophisticated banking services, such as, for instance, bond issues, mergers and acquisitions, corporate restructuring to name a few. So, we've seen, then, a substantial increase in investment banking services, as opposed to the traditional banking services of the past.

🎧 **7.2** *(I = interviewer, J = Joan Rosás)*

I So, how does the future look like [*sic*] from the banks' perspective?

J You basically have three different types of banks. The, uh, truly global banks, very large banks. These will continue to be the same. The second group consists of large regional banks. In this group, you *will* see, uh, a few more banks, uh, coming to play in this, uh, sphere. And third, we would include the, uh, smaller banks. These smaller banks, uh, *will* continue to do well because they have very focused business orientation and they tend to basically focus on strategic market segments.

I And where products and services are concerned, what developments are we seeing there?

J Well, uh, we'll see a lot of new things, uh, a lot of new services. Like, uh, an increase of bundled products, which consists of basically a package where you would include savings accounts, you would include the credit cards, renting, pension funds, insurance, consumer finance, all together with a single label.

I And what are going to be the new delivery channels? You mentioned Internet banking previously.

J Yes, well, we've gone from a physical branch type of banking to a new, uh, banking based on Internet. So we've gone from [what] we call a bricks-and-mortar retail banking to either a 'clicks-and-bricks' banking or a 'clicks-and-clicks' banking. The clicks-and-bricks banking is a sort of banking where you're combining both the branches, the retail branch network, with powerful Internet banking services. But then you also have banks which only operate through Internet, this is what we call the 'clicks and clicks' sort of banking activities.

I And apart from the Internet, what other new delivery channels are there?

J Well, you also have what's called WAP services, which is using cellphone, uh, cellphones to do all the banking transactions that you could be doing. Of course, the ATMs are very important. And also lately you begin to see as well the digital TV banking where you're using your TV set to do your banking needs. So, when you're sitting on your couch instead of watching TV, or during the ad time, you can do all your banking with the TV remote control.

🎧 **7.3**

Good morning. My name's Diana Holden, I'm the Finance Director for BZ Systems. I'm here today to talk to you, our shareholders, about the bright future ahead for our company. I'll start by reporting on last year's financial results. Then I'll talk about our recent performance in the past quarter. Finally, we'll look at our projections and the company's expansion plans for the future. I'm sure you'll agree that BZ is growing from strength to strength. There'll be an opportunity at the end of my presentation to ask any questions you have.

🎧 **7.4**

What we've got here is a chart showing how our markets are expected to outperform Western Europe over the medium term. The data comes from Zenith Optimedia, who do independent forecasting for TV ad markets, and what you can see from year one through to year seven is that Western Europe is expected to gradually recover in advertising terms, but that Eastern Europe, as shown here indexed to year one, by year seven will be over double the year-one market, i.e. over the next five to six years, our sales are expected to double as well.

🎧 **7.5**

We've had an impressive nine months this year. If we look at this chart, you can see our segment net revenue, which is all of our stations added together. In year one, revenue almost doubled between the third and fourth quarters to 40 million dollars. That brought our revenue for year one to 119 million dollars. In year two, our revenue rose by nearly 16 per cent to 138 million dollars. Now, as you can see here, segmented revenue for the first quarter matched the first quarter in year one. It rose to 40 million in the second quarter. Then revenue in the third quarter fell slightly to around 25 million and grew to 47 million in the fourth quarter. Last year was another successful year, with revenue reaching a new high at 176 million dollars. That's 27.5-per-cent growth. Particularly notable were the jumps in the second and fourth quarters to 48 million and 62 million dollars respectively.

This year, we're expecting another great year. Revenue for the first quarter reached 48 million. It rose again in the second quarter to match the fourth quarter of last year. In the third quarter, it dipped slightly to 46 million, and we're expecting to reach an all-time high of 70 million in the fourth quarter of this year.

7.6 *(N = newsreader, C = consultant, T = taxi driver, B = Bernd Wulf, D = Dan Foster, K = Kate Zhu)*

N   We'll have more on that in our midday bulletin. And now, turning to today's European business news …

C   Excuse me, er, could you turn up the volume, please?

T   Certainly, mate. No problem.

N   In Germany, trouble at Erstaunliche Autos continues following corporate restructuring and the resignation of former company chairman, Wolfgang Ferdinand. New head of EA, Bernd Wulf has seen the ongoing scandal as a chance to push through reform and is looking to increase productivity and boost profits by 4 billion euros over the next three years. Drastic cost cuts of up to 7 billion euros will need to be made to reach that target. Herr Wulf spoke to the press …

C   How did they hear about that?

N   … maintaining a positive front, despite the challenges faced by his company.

B   The best thing is to concentrate on producing profitable cars. We have to be competitive. The market is extremely aggressive right now.

N   More details of EA's cost-cutting plan will come after the supervisory board meets in Frankfurt to discuss the measures. Inside sources claim the new chief of EA will be closing the Belgian car plant. Our Belgian correspondent, Dan Foster, reports.

D   What you can hear in the background are the angry protests at the factory gates of Erstaunliche Autos. Today, these workers may be about to lose their jobs on the assembly line. Recently appointed company chairman, Bernd Wulf, is denying factory closure.

B   No decision has been taken on closing *any* of our factories. However, we shall certainly be studying *all* kinds of proposals to ensure steady growth in the future.

D   A decision to close the factory would be a bitter blow to Belgium and its car-making industry. But Bernd Wulf heralds the start of a new era and says the German car manufacturer has to save money in order to survive. It is said he wants to open a new factory in India, where assembly-line workers earn less than a fifth of their German counterparts. Dan Foster, Antwerp.

C   That was supposed to be confidential information!

N   Now for our Asia report. China's car makers are currently establishing themselves …

8 Consultants

8.1 *(I = interviewer, C = consultant)*

I   This morning, I'm pleased to welcome to the studio business consultant Michelle Geraghty. Michelle, how can consultants actually help a business?

C   Well, Mike, they basically provide advice or a service to make your business more successful. Consultants usually help with a specific problem or task when your company simply doesn't have the know-how. For instance, a consultant might provide training. You might take on a consultant to improve overall managerial performance and, er, they may also manage specialist projects.

I   So, once a company has identified a problem or project, how can you go about defining the exact task for the consultancy?

C   It's really important to establish your objectives and goals. I often refer to the five principles of SMART.

I   Smart?

C   Yes, it stands for: Specific, Measurable, Achievable, Relevant and Time-limited. The client then needs to set a timescale, a budget and a brief.

I   And what should your brief include?

C   A description of your organisation, what it does and its size and structure, an explanation of the problem and what you want to achieve.

I   But Michelle, there are a lot of consultants out there. How can you go about choosing a *reliable* one?

C   You should choose one that has experience of businesses of your size, that understands your industry, and that is, ideally, a member of a professional body like the Institute of Management Consultancy.

I   What's the next step?

C   You need to come up with a shortlist of, say, three consultants and ask them to submit written proposals.

I   And what should be in their proposals?

C   Their understanding of the problem, any relevant experience of the consultancy firm, a work plan and schedule, the reports and any systems that will be supplied. Not forgetting, of course, the input that is going to be required by *you*.

I   OK, imagine you're going to recruit one of these consultants. What next?

C   Well, you have to agree on a written contract, describing both the work to be done and the conditions. A written contract should include objectives, a brief, how and for how long the consultancy will be managed, fees and, of course, the deliverables.

I   Deliverables? You mean like the goods or services that are going to be delivered?

C   Yes, usually the report, the consultant's report and/or any systems required by the client.

I   You mentioned fees. How do you go about setting a fee or price?

C   Well, Mike, it's likely to fall into one or two types: T&M contracts, which are for time and materials, or fixed-price contracts. The main difference lies in the risk factor; I mean, the risk of running over in cost. With a fixed-price contract, the consultant assumes most risk, whereas in a T&M contract, the client will assume most risk, but not all.

I   I think a lot of our listeners are thinking: how can we be sure we're recruiting the right consultancy?

C   Mm. The important thing to remember is if you are not happy with any aspects of the proposal, don't take them on. It's important to make sure the chemistry is right.

I   Thanks, Michelle. And we'll be asking Michelle about managing the relationship with your consultant after the break.

8.2 *(I = interviewer, C = consultant)*

I   Welcome back. We're talking to business consultant Michelle Geraghty. We've discussed choosing the right consultant, Michelle; what about overseeing the work?

C   Well, you've got to agree on several things. What tasks have to be done by your staff? What are the short-term goals? What are the milestones, or long-term goals? What deliverables have you agreed on? Regular meetings are a good way to discuss progress. You know, what does the consultant need to know? What problems are they coming up against?

I   I see. And who talks to the consultant in these meetings? The boss?

C   I would say it's best if the consultant reports to only one person. Having said that, you should also keep your staff informed about what the consultant is doing. It's crucial they feel they're part of the process.

I   Right, so if the consultant makes several recommendations, but if your staff are resistant to change, or managers don't implement them correctly, it's going to be a waste of time, isn't it?

C   Exactly.

I   Some critics say consultants just snoop around, and only produce a report telling you something you already know!

C   You've got to understand the report is essentially the consultant's most tangible 'deliverable'. I'd ask the consultant to produce a first draft that you can discuss with colleagues before the final report is produced. The final report should contain no surprises. If there are any very confidential issues, they can always be put separately in a private letter.

I   Thank you, Michelle Geraghty. You've been listening to Business Today.

8.3 *(SM = sales manager, H = Hannah)*

SM This morning, we're going to be looking at some strategies commonly used among buyers and salespeople: your limited authority in negotiating, making concessions, the importance of a planning checklist and the power to walk away.
First of all, limited authority: if potential buyers know that you have the power to make big concessions on your own, then they may get angry if they can't get what they want. If you say, 'I'm sorry, I'm going to have to check that with my boss,' then if you

refuse the concession, some anonymous authority will be responsible, not *you*. You should maintain a good relationship, so that you can either continue to negotiate or come back to them at a later date. Right. OK, um, next we have avoiding endless negotiations, where you keep going back and forth. Amateur negotiators will usually start out with small concessions, like a one-per-cent discount, and then escalate to large ones. But this just makes the buyer feel that as the concessions get bigger, there's more to come. Even when it all ends, the customer will feel that there was more they could have got. They don't feel *good* about the negotiation. Professional negotiators, however, give their biggest concession first. As the negotiation continues, the concessions that they grant will get smaller and smaller. When it's over, the buyer feels like they've got you down to the bottom line. Keep in mind that, in win-win negotiating, you want the customer to feel as though they're a winner, too. You also want to avoid long discussions that are a waste of everybody's time. Then there's the negotiation planning checklist. What do you know about your prospect's needs, wants and problems? What is your original asking price? Is it high enough? What is your bottom line or walk-away number?

H   Sorry, what do you mean exactly by 'bottom line'?

SM   Ah, um, OK, yes, your bottom line is the minimum amount that you were anticipating. It's sometimes called BATNA, the Best Alternative To a Negotiated Agreement. BATNA represents the point at which walking away makes more sense than making a deal. So, if you have to go *below* your bottom line, it's time to walk away. The real secret of good sales negotiations is to have decided in advance what you can ask for in return for a price cut. Remember that buyers, like everyone else, tend not to value anything that they get for free or can get easily.

🎧 **8.4** *(C = Cristoph Kahnwald, A = Andrew)*

A   So, let me just recap here, Mr Kahnwald. Mobi-net wishes to maintain its position in the market by differentiation – distinguishing itself from competitors by means of product innovation and quality of service.

C   That's right. Our mobile services must remain distinctive. Then there's our reputation for customer problem-solving …

A   But you previously told me your customer-service department wasn't effective or competitive enough.

C   Yes, that's true. You know, we've spent a lot of money on customer-service training, but it's just not working out to be cost-effective. We seem to be sacrificing efficiency for a quality approach, although we've always considered it as added value for our subscribers until now.

A   But quite frankly, Mr Kahnwald, I would say you need to streamline that side of the business significantly.

C   What do you mean by 'streamline'? Dismiss staff?

A   No, no. We could implement new technologies to improve your call-centre system so that customer-service staff can handle enquiries more quickly.

C   And how do you propose to do that exactly?

A   We would strongly recommend that your call centre becomes more centralised. Mobi-net obviously still needs to retain its image of reliability, but you're going to have to do it at a more competitive price.

C   Mm, lower our prices, that's what I thought you were going to say. And what about strategic alliances? Did I mention we're looking for a potential partner?

A   That's going to take a little more time to investigate, Mr Kahnwald. It might prove a bit tricky.

C   I know, I know, that's why I'm asking your advice! It's essential we're able to carry on developing our product portfolio, and we think it makes sense to do it through acquisitions or alliances.

A   I'd agree with you there, but I'm going to have to talk things over with my boss first.

C   OK, but remember we need to have your proposal in two weeks' time.

A   Yes, of course. I promise we'll look into it. Was there anything else?

C   Just one more thing, Andrew. How much can we anticipate in fees?

A   Well, it really depends whether we're looking at a fixed-price contract or a T&M contract. If you were paying by the hour, we'd charge approximately 150 euros.

C   150 euros? But another consultancy firm I spoke to quoted me 130 euros!

A   Well, yes, but I'm sure they don't have our kind of reputation. Anyway, I'll send you the proposal in a fortnight, and we'll take it from there.

C   OK, OK; just remember, Andrew, if Mobi-net accepts this project, we'll want someone with the right expertise and know-how in IT to work with us.

A   I'm sure we won't let you down.

9 Strategy

🎧 **9.1** *(I = interviewer, J = Josep Valor-Sabatier)*

I   How important is the role of marketing when it comes to strategic management?

J   I think that marketing is important in the same way that finance is important or operational management is important. People in marketing and sales are the ones that are usually in touch with customers and are therefore often regarded as the ones that understand the market. And that brings with it both big advantages and, er, serious problems, especially when, er, your, your industry is being reinvented by some newcomer, like, for instance, Zara.
Basically, if, before Zara existed, you had asked companies like Gap or Marks and Spencer … If you had asked their marketing people what would be their best business practices, they would tell you that it would be to design new collections and outsource to some country with cheap labour costs, you know, mass-produce it, putting it all together in large quantities, so you would have, er, your spring collection or the summer collection or whatever. You'd produce it nine months in advance and have, say, the Chinese manufacture it very cheaply and then you'd put the new collection in your stores and that would be the normal method.
Zara decided not to do that, they decided to have *no* seasons and they chose to be a fast copier, a fast market follower – and to do that, by the way, you have to have your factories very close to the stores, and Zara's stores are mostly in Europe. This means you have to produce in Europe, which is not necessarily cheap. You cannot produce in large amounts in, in China and, er, ship them to Europe because that takes six months. So, you have to produce them nearby at low costs and in short runs, as cheaply as you can. And if you had told your marketing guys that, and said you would have much higher production costs, they would say, you're never going to sell that! Because you have to promote your collection, you have to make sure that you've designed in the Zara or Benetton style. The point is that Zara decided *not* to be a Benetton-like company, but to be a follower. I mean, you cannot be better than Benetton by doing what Benetton does. You have to do something else … You have to innovate and change the rules a little bit, otherwise you will never beat the more established leaders.

🎧 **9.2** *(I = interviewer, J = Josep Valor-Sabatier)*

I   So, how can a company actually *measure* how successful their strategy is? Does it just come down to the bottom line of growth, profits and sales?

J   The measures have to be consistent with what you want to do. Clearly, if you were Zara, and you decided to be the number-one fashion producer in the world, then sales and obviously profits are what are going to allow you to grow, and these are what you have to measure. If, rather than being Zara, you want to be a retailer of designer products, you're only going to sell exclusive designer clothes, then growth is not going to be your thing, it's going to be margin. And you'll probably only open up one store per year, whereas Zara opens one every month. Of course, your mission and vision are also going to be crucial. Together with where you want to go, you have to define the *measures* of how successful you're going to be.

I   But to what extent do you think companies just end up improvising when things go wrong?

J   Well, they *do* improvise for a reason that has to do with short-term goals. Many years ago, companies used to care about yearly profits, then it was quarterly profits. Now it's half-quarter forecasts, and pretty soon they'll have to care about daily sales. Once you get into these issues, long-term goals become very blurred. Because what's considered important for the stock market, which is that you make money *this* quarter. It's a lot easier to convince an 'owner' that you want to do something in the long term and that you're employing the right strategies, than to convince the stock market, which is very much focused on short-term goals and profitability, that they should bear with you for a while because you're gonna have a successful strategy in the next three years.

I Does that mean that short-term tactical goals are often in conflict with long-term strategies?

J They often are, yes, because if you invest in a company to get a return in a year, then you expect a return in a year, whereas in some companies, a return in a year is too short a time for something to happen. As individuals, it's hard to change our habits within a year. So, how can you expect a company that's made up of 25,000 individuals to behave differently in three months? So this conflict of short-term gains and long-term goals exists, and being able to resolve it successfully is crucial. Actually, good managers are the ones that can do both: they're able to maintain reasonable short-term profitability and, nevertheless, steer the company towards where they want to take it in the long term.

🎧 **9.3** *(T = trainer, S = Sarah, M = Max)*

T So, what is it that you don't like about brainstorming meetings, Sarah?

S It's just that I don't think I'm at my most creative when I'm in a large group. I prefer to work on my own.

T And what about you, Max?

M Well, I really like working in groups 'cos I think it's a really positive way of getting loads of new ideas in a short amount of time.

S Yes, but most of the ideas people come up with are usually completely impractical. I think we waste a lot of time.

T Well, it's very important that people come up with as many ideas as possible when brainstorming, but there shouldn't be more than eight or ten people per session. It's also crucial that someone writes down all the ideas, however absurd they may seem, and don't spend too long discussing any one item.

S But it's always the same people who do all the talking.

T Mmm, the role of the facilitator or chairperson should be to encourage an enthusiastic and uncritical attitude, to try to get everyone to contribute, even the quietest people. If someone's too critical, the others aren't going to feel comfortable about being creative.

S Yeah, but we don't ever seem to get anywhere or make any decisions.

T That's because you've got to clearly define the problem you want solved and keep the session focused. The idea is to generate as many ideas as possible which you can then evaluate afterwards. Um, let's try a short practical exercise. I'd like you all to think of new innovative services or promotions for Rose and Frankwright. I'm going to give you just a minute to think, and Sarah, could you write down any ideas on the flip chart?

S Sure.

M I've got one already. A … a kind of Santa train that goes around the city centre at Christmas for all the kids and parents. And Rose and Frankwright sponsor it.

S That's been done before.

T No, thank you, Max. As I was saying earlier, there are no bad ideas when brainstorming. Let me tell you about Einstein. Einstein and his associates were able to collaborate more effectively than other scientists at the time because they'd discovered some ancient Greek principles of group communication developed by Socrates. Socrates and other Greek philosophers would sit around debating various issues, but the participants were bound by seven principles that established a sense of, um, collegiality. Socrates called these principles 'Koinonia', which means 'spirit of fellowship'. These principles are: establish dialogue; exchange ideas; don't argue; don't interrupt; listen carefully; clarify your thinking; and finally, be honest. Now, has anyone else got a contribution?

🎧 **9.4** *(A = Angela Lang)*

A It's clear from the feedback that I got from our customers that we have a problem with our brand image. They see us as outdated. What's more, they say that our catalogues are unattractive and they feel just, well, overwhelmed by the number of products we offer. There could be a strong case for reducing the range of products. Let's face it, we have a lot of lines that really aren't great money spinners. We could cut down on many items, as well, by producing more global and, uh, fewer regional products. As you can also see in my report, our customers often complain about the poor quality of our products and they say that there's a lack of interesting new lines. Then we have what our sales reps have to say. I really discovered first hand the types of obstacles our reps are up against – and I'm talking about very basic things like, uh, not being able to reorder popular items and not receiving the correct items ordered. We definitely have to work on our supply-chain management and distribution systems. And our ordering procedures are as old fashioned as our image! I mean, what's with those 40-page order forms you gotta fill out by hand and mail to the office? Our own estimates show that orders aren't properly filled 30 per cent of the time! It makes it difficult for agents to increase their sales and, uh, commissions and for us to, uh, keep our reps. For me, recruiting and retaining sales reps has got to be a priority. Now, I'd appreciate your feedback on my findings …

10 Doing business online

🎧 **10.1**

1 It's so convenient. There's virtually no queuing any more, especially if I only have hand luggage. I just put my credit card in a machine when I get to the terminal, and, er, it prints out a boarding pass, and then I go straight through to the departure lounge.

2 It makes sense, I think, to download this stuff from the Internet. It's so easy to update my anti-virus scan. I've had to buy a spyware remover, too, because my computer was working so slowly. Their customer service isn't good, though. It's really frustrating sometimes, not being able to phone a real human being about a problem. You have to read the FAQs or send e-mails that never get answered.

3 I live a long way from home, and it's always been a hassle posting stuff to people. But thanks to this website, I can now choose something I think they'll like … and there are lots of recommendations on the site, plot summaries and readers' reviews. The danger is I always end up getting myself something, too, and spending more than I planned to.

🎧 **10.2** *(I = interviewer, M = Maija Pesola)*

I What caused the dot-com bubble to burst in 2000, and what have been the positive outcomes of this?

M I think the problem in 2000 was that there was just too much money coming into the market too quickly to fund companies that perhaps didn't have particularly well thought-out business plans. Um, they … they had a lot of enthusiasm and wanted to change the way that we shopped, but didn't necessarily have the back-end systems to carry out their plans. Um, also I think at that time the market probably wasn't ready, um, to … to … for Internet shopping in the way that it is today. In 2000, a much smaller population was … was using, um, the Internet and certainly not many people had broadband connections, which I think has been shown to be, uh, one of factors in getting people to spend much more time online, browsing and … and looking for things. Um, so, too much money, too quickly, that did cause the … the bubble to burst. I think the positive effect of that, though, has been that it's weeded out some of the weaker companies, and those companies that are still in existence today, um, have had to refine their business models, the way that they work and … and they are truly able to compete on a global scale.

🎧 **10.3** *(I = interviewer, M = Maija Pesola)*

I Why do you think that even popular companies like Yahoo are still struggling to make any money from the Internet?

M Well, the problem with companies like Yahoo is that they've been looking for a way to make money from advertising over the Internet, and it's taken a very long time to evolve a really working model of … of advertising on the Internet. We've tried several things. First, um, there were banner ads which were put onto websites, which were very similar to just putting an advert onto a newspaper page. And, uh, after the initial excitement, companies found that they weren't getting a lot of, er, response from those. Then other things were tried, they … they made the adverts more interactive, they made them pop up onto … to computer screens, but that just tended to annoy the, um, consumers. So, it's only really in the last few years that we've come up with … with something that's very workable, which is, um, advertising that's related to search, when … when people are looking on Yahoo or Google or one of the other, er, browsers … uh, search engines, um, for something. And this is something that companies seem happy to be … happy to pay for because they … they do see higher response rates from those kind of targeted ads.

I Which types of online business have been most successful and why?

M I think what we've seen is … is businesses that sell goods that are very easy to ship, such as books or music, have done well. Um, those are things that you don't need to physically touch. Uh, clothing tends to be difficult because people would like to feel the fabric, try on the cut of the coat or whatever it is. But with books and music, uh, and to some extent wine, you can just read a description of it and you know what you're getting. Um, the other thing … the other category that has done well is … is travel, again for similar reasons, because it's quite easy to ship … uh, to send out tickets, uh, you can … you can issue electronic tickets to people, um, there's only a small amount of paperwork that needs to physically be handed over to the customer, and online tra… booking your travel on the Internet does add something genuinely different to the experience. You get a lot more choice personally than you would if you went through a travel agent, um, whereas in other types of businesses, again coming back to the clothing retailer, it's questionable how much the experience of shopping over the Internet would have actually added.

🎧 **10.4** *(S = Sophie Rawlings, A = speaker 1, B = speaker 2, C = speaker 3)*

S I think that gives us time for a couple of questions before the break. Er, yes?

A I was, er, just wondering what you thought were the main differences between, um, er … government websites and those in the private business sector?

S Right. Well, it's really what I was talking about at the start of my talk. One of the main differences is obviously that business websites are aimed at selling, whereas a government site is offering information or free services. Er, I don't want to go into any more detail at this stage because Peter Adams will be dealing with commercial sites and credit-card security and so on in the next session.

B Excuse me.

S Yes? I'm sorry, could you speak up, please?

B Um … er, yeah, I'd, um … I'd like to know how a company can actually improve its online sales through web-page design. I mean, what is it exactly that makes it more effective?

S Well, as I've already said, Peter will be dealing with those kinds of issues later, but what I would say is, think of EasyJet and Amazon.com. What makes those sites so effective? Making the online process quick, easy and user-friendly is the key. Don't ask your user to fill in very long forms – they'll just click off the site. And build in flexibility. By this I mean, allow your user to change their mind and order two items instead of three without going all the way back to the beginning of the checkout process. When you think of successful sites, they have very user-centric design, provide enough information without overloading the user and are simple to use. I hope that answers your question.

B Yes, thanks.

C I'd be interested to know more about copy writing. I mean to say, could you tell us what kind of language you think works well in websites?

S That's an interesting question. Really, the language, or tone, as well as the look of a business site is going to be quite different. Government sites should be friendly, but authoritative and somewhat formal in tone. Commercial sites often use language that's punchy, young and trendy. I mean, copy, or the language used on websites, is designed to encourage users to spend money!

C Yes, but I was wondering whether there was any kind of language that you would avoid using?

S Well, apart from the obvious, the sort of language depends very much on the industry and the purpose of the website. Er, jargon, slang, abbreviations and acronyms should all be avoided. I often see terminology used which most people are not familiar with.

You'll find some more guidelines in the handout. Is that all? Great, let's break here for 15 minutes, then …

🎧 **10.5** *(E = Ed, L = Larry, K = Kirstie)*

E So, Larry, I take it you have there the online sales figures for the usability study on Audio Wire?

L Ah, yeah, it's not looking good, Ed. Um, really bad sales-conversion rates. Very few users are returning to purchase. High shopping-cart abandonment rates at like, um … 49 per cent.

E Yeah, well, there're obviously major pitfalls in the checkout process. If the customer wants to make changes, say ten earphones not five, it's difficult. And they get you to register before you can purchase.

K Yeah. And the navigation is really confusing. It took me forever to find the earphones I wanted.

E What about content and design, Kirstie?

K Well, they have some nice images, but that are, like, you know, just way too big. I mean this one on the homepage should be a third of the size.

E Uh-huh. Anything else?

K Their product pages have … um … again too many brochure-style photos that take up space and you get no idea of the actual product.

E You mean there isn't enough product information.

K Exactly.

E So, what's the diagnosis, folks?

L I'd say, redesign and relaunch the whole thing.

K Yup.

E OK, er, let's look at what we can come up with in four weeks. Er, deliverables? Larry?

L Oh, um, improve the online checkout process, reduce clicks. We've really gotta persuade the user to purchase.

E Yeah, I think they need a single functional web page to view all their product selections. It should include, er, pricing, delivery and payment information.

K But we need to keep some of those photos of the earphones!

E Well, OK, as long as you can make them fit.

K I'll make them tiny. What about the copy? Some of it really sucks.

E Well, we can recommend some rewrites for copy. It's gotta be short and punchy. Can you take care of that *and* design, Kirstie?

K Sure.

E Let's just go over our deliverables. I say we send them a file showing screenshots of the current site with our recommendations. We're saying we'll improve navigation and content for every page in the buying process, from the home page through checkout, right? I want both of you to work on that.

K Yep.

L Uh-huh.

E And Kirstie, you say you can do a rewrite of some of the copy? Include the exact wording of how Audio Wire should describe its earphones.

K Yeah, but what are you doing, Ed?

E Me? I gotta write the proposal. Oh, Larry, could we take a closer look at the web-traffic figures?

K Oh, great.

11 New business

🎧 **11.1** *(I = interviewer, M = Max Benson)*

I Your organisation gives advice to women on, among other things, setting up their own businesses. What advice do you give them?

M We advise women on where to get help; we encourage them to network; to learn the business skills that they are weak in and to learn from others. Um, so we signpost them to the best qual… uh, the best people qualified to help them start up. There's a lot of formal support available, but it's very time-consuming trying to find it in the first instance, so we act as a signpost. Um, we also provide networking opportunities, um, for women, so that they can get advice from others and discuss the challenges and the barriers that … that they are having to overcome in business. We do this online and, um, on the Internet, and we also do it offline. So we do have networking available on our website, and we also do offline networking events where they get to meet face to face. And we also provide workshops where they can learn business skills – skills that they don't have from a previous job or don't have at all because they haven't been in the workplace.

🎧 **11.2** (*I = interviewer, M = Max Benson*)

I Are the issues the same for men as well as women who want to start their own businesses?

M The fundamentals are the same whether you are a man starting a business or a woman. Finding support is going to be the same. Um, the facilities that are out there by various government bodies, business advisers, organisations, they're available for men and women. But there are five areas that research shows are barriers specifically for women who are starting up. That is, number one, access to finance – Where can they get money? How much can they get? Access to networks – a lot of the business networks that have been set up are, um, set up and dominated by men. Confidence, confidence is one of the huge barriers for women. A skills gap – women are not reaching the top in the corporate environment, so their range of skills is not as great as many men who then start business. And women have been slower in adopting, um, technology and how that can be used in … in small businesses to help businesses to grow, and that is also a barrier. So those, I would say, are the five key differences for men and women.

🎧 **11.3** (*I = interviewer, M = Max Benson*)

I And what kinds of new business are doing well at the moment here in the UK?

M Certainly from the areas where women are starting businesses, we're seeing a lot of women starting businesses in the health-care area, and by that I mean alternative medicines, um, alternative therapies. General well-being is an area that is attracting many women, personal care, basically. Uh, business services – there is a huge number of women also going into training and personal development, that is very big with women. A lot of coaches; a lot of trainers for various business skills – skills that they've learnt in a corporate environment, which they are now, um, using in a consultancy capacity. Those are the areas that are very big with women.

🎧 **11.4** (*I = interviewer, M = Max Benson*)

I What are the typical problems facing new businesses, in your experience?

M I think the two main problems, and this is for both men and women, although more so for women, is underestimating how much money they're going to need. Banks tell us again and again that women take their business plans to them and they have underestimated how much money they're going to need to borrow. And that causes big problems. They also, and I think this is true of everybody, when it's their first time starting a business, they always underestimate how long it's going to take until that revenue stream starts coming in. I'd say those are the two main problems.

🎧 **11.5** (*W = Wendy Taylor, D = Darren Bailey*)

W Accounts, Wendy Taylor speaking.

D Hello, Wendy, er, this is Darren Bailey; I'm calling on behalf of Dyson Kitchenware. I'd like to query a bill we received.

W I see, Mr Bailey. Er, could you give me the reference number?

D Yes, uh, it's, um, I think … er, I have it here somewhere. Um, ah yes, here it is. Um, I'm not sure which number … um …

W It's below the date.

D Ah … ah yes. Sorry about that. It's 1-6-8-7-3, dated 22nd of May.

W 1-6-8-7-3. Yes, I have it here on screen. What seems to be the problem?

D Er, well, we've been overcharged. You see, the invoice is for 16 units, but our original order, er, was for 12.

W Let me see if I've got this right. You asked for 12 units, and we've billed you for 16. Is that correct?

D Yes, that's it.

W Do you have your copy of the delivery note?

D Um, it must be somewhere around here. Let me see, um … hang on just a moment … Yeah, yeah, here it is. We definitely signed for 12 units.

W I'll need to check the original purchase order and issue a new invoice if we have made a mistake. Can I take your number and call you back, Mr Bailey?

D Please, call me Darren. The number here is 020 8658 5518. When will you call back, Wendy?

W Uh, it shouldn't take long. I'll ring you later this morning.

D OK, fine, thank you. I'll be in the office until 1 p.m.

W One p.m.? OK, Darren. I'll give you a call before then. Bye.

🎧 **11.6** (*W = Wendy Taylor, D = Darren Bailey*)

D Hello?

W Hello, Darren, this is Wendy Taylor from Fenwick Plastics. I'm phoning again about overdue payments on two of our invoices.

D Ah, right, yeah. Um … could you give me the invoice numbers?

W Yes, sure. There's 16987, dated the 28th of May, and 17124, dated the 8th of June. I also sent you a written payment reminder on the 10th of July. As you know, our credit terms are 30 days, and payment is now way overdue.

D Yeah, sure. I … I must apologise for the delay, Wendy, you know what it's like in a busy office. I'll authorise payment as soon as possible.

W I understand. Could you tell me when that will be?

D Uh … on the last banking day of the month.

W I'm sorry, but we'd expect payment sooner. We'd have to consider withdrawing credit terms if these invoices aren't settled within seven days.

D Look, I'm … I'm sure we can sort this out, Wendy. I can make an exception and settle the invoice for the 28th of May this week, but the other invoice will be paid as part of our normal monthly payment procedures. Would that be acceptable?

W Well, we would prefer payment of the outstanding invoice within 15 days.

D Fine, I … I think we can work with that.

W OK, Darren, I'll get back to you on the 30th of July if we haven't received both payments.

D Yeah, of course, Wendy. Bye.

🎧 **11.7** (*D = Doug, J = José Ramón, K = Karen*)

K Good morning. I'm Karen Fernández and in this morning's show, I'm talking to Doug Halliwell and José Ramón García about Copisistem, a Valencia-based company that duplicates and prints DVDs. Good morning to you both.

J+D Good morning. / Morning.

K So, what made you decide to set up your own company?

D Well, José and I worked for the same multinational and we often shared ideas over breakfast, and I guess we both knew we wanted to, you know, to be our own boss.

J Yes, when we started, we did nearly everything. At the time, we employed just three people on the production side, two in dispatch, two in admin, and my cousin, Pilar, did the bookkeeping for us one morning a week.

K And how many people does the company employ now?

J Ah, you see there has been an enormous boom in the sector, and we now have another eight operators, as well as a chief technician and a couple of people working on the sales side with us. Uh, Pilar works for us full-time now as company accountant, and we have three more people working on the admin and customer-service side.

K Does that mean you have more free time?

D Huh! Far from it. More orders, more staff – it's … it's good news, but it all means more work. We're still very much involved in the day-to-day running of the company.

K So, what is the volume of sales now?

J Well, to give you an idea, three years ago we had a turnover of around 6 million euros, and the company's grown organically ever since. Last year, it was almost 16 million.

K And what are some of your biggest headaches as business owners?

D Well, um, obviously, keeping, uh, our customers satisfied is a major priority. That means meeting production and delivery schedules, um, making sure the quality is maintained, goods are delivered on time and intact. We're now one of the leading companies in this sector, but there's heavy competition from start-ups and companies that have switched from VHS duplication. You gotta work hard at being the best.

K So, what are your plans for the future?

J We're looking to expand, particularly into other European markets.

D Um, yeah, we always have an eye to the future. I mean, something will come along soon and replace DVD, and we need to be ready for when that happens.

K Thank you, José and Doug, for talking to us today and all the best for the future.

J+D Thank you. / Thanks very much.

12 Project management

🎧 12.1 *(I = interviewer, M = Michael Sawyer, R = Rob Jackson)*

I   Michael, what are the qualities of a good project manager?

M   Uh ... OK I think that, uh, it's very important to have a ... to be a good leader. You need to have, um, very good interpersonal skills, to be very good at communicating, motivating people, uh, co-ordinating all their efforts, empowering people so that they, um, ... they are aware of what they are supposed to be doing and they're motivated. It's, um, ... it's very ... it's not like saying that the project leader is the, let's say, the captain of the team and he gives the orders and the others follow them, no, it's not like that. The project leader is like, um, you should be a co-ordinator, you're not the boss of the team because, um, because all of them come from different departments and they already have their own bosses, so, um, ... and the project leader is not really in charge of them, he's only co-ordinating a specific project. But, uh, he or she should discuss issues with everyone on the team and then make decisions with them, and, um, ... and so ... set and achieve the goals of the project, but without telling people what they have to do.

I   Rob, what would you say were the qualities of a good project manager?

R   Really, to be a good project manager, you need to be able to delegate, um, actions and issues to different people. You need to be able to handle multiple matters, to be able to juggle issues and handle lots of issues at the same time.

I   You mean, like, be good at multi-tasking?

R   Yes, multi-tasking, that's a good word. Be able to take an overview where needed, where you stand back and ... and take a view of it, but also be able to understand the detail and the complexities of things where required, so that you really understand what people are ... are involved in and talking about. And most importantly, you need to be able to organise a team, direct them, but also be able to motivate them so that they ... they keep the organisation and they understand the goals that everybody's aiming for.

🎧 12.2 *(I = interviewer, M = Michael Sawyer, R = Rob Jackson)*

I   Michael, is there sometimes conflict between different members in the team?

M   Er, usually the people involved in any project have their own objectives or ... or own department goals. Usually what happens is there is a conflict there between the departmental goals and the overall company aims for the project. And that's one reason we have a project sponsor, um, who is a member of the senior management team, to decide when these different departmental objectives are, let's say, working against the company strategic goal. He or she makes sure that the project leader has, um, all the help and all the resources needed for the project. The sponsor not only sets the team up but he's, uh, he or she, uh, is involved, let's say, not in the daily work of the project team but, um, in the milestones of the project. The sponsor is usually there in the, uh, in the monthly progress meetings, and he's, uh, making sure that results are being produced. If there is some obvious tension in the meeting, and the project leader isn't capable of managing it, then the sponsor has to be able to save the position of the project leader by ... uh ... by acting as ... as a moderator of all the issues that are being raised.

I   And what should a project manager do, or what should you do, if you see the project isn't actually going on track? What can be done about that?

R   The first thing to do is to understand what it is that's gone wrong by degrees, is it a major issue or a minor issue? And then you deal with it differently. And then the first thing is to understand the causes of ... of why the project isn't going on ... on track and why it is different from your plan, and then obviously you look to modify the plan to ... to get back the time. And if it's an external cause, you involve the client or the sponsor, as you ... as you may call him, get further clarification and understand why he's changed certain things, if he has done. If it's an internal issue, again you re... re... review the cause and you look at removing the obstacle, and ... and often that's about working with your team and ... and re-assessing what they're doing and redirecting them.

🎧 12.3 *(I = interviewer, M = Michael Sawyer, R = Rob Jackson)*

I   How do you know if a project's been successful, Michael?

M   Well, first, you have to spend more time than we usually do, uh, in setting the goals of the project itself at the very beginning, in the very first meeting. It's difficult, because when you start the project, you want, what people want is speed, to start working. People think, 'OK, we're going to do an efficiency project and want to get the best results we can.' But, it's very important to set specific targets and deadlines because, if not, then the tracking's going to be very subjective. If you don't do that, you aren't going to have adequate tracking measures when the project is finished. Also, if the whole team agrees from the beginning, then the relationship between the members is much easier because you have, let's say, er, constructed a common goal for that project.

I   Rob, how do you know if a project's been successful or not?

R   Um, projects can really be defined by three or four measures to see whether it's successful. There's time, and you measure the time against a programme, against different milestones, to see that you're doing it in time to pre-agreed sequences and agreements with your sponsor or client. There's obviously measuring your costs versus your budget, which is very important, er, to make sure that you make a profit. Safety, one must always take great care to ensure that all the workers on your site, um, go home each night, and have a safe site where safe systems of work are in operation. And then really long term, you need to look at whether your client, or sponsor, will return and give you repeat business. And they're probably the three or four real measures of a successful project.

🎧 12.4

1   Loss of face is not just embarrassing for us; it can often be a devastating experience. If our behaviour or appearance or what we say is judged inappropriate, this involves losing the respect of others. You know, if you lose your temper or confront someone or if you don't show them the proper respect, it can cause them to lose face. It's something to bear in mind at all times because losing face and saving face are very important in my culture.

2   We tend to be, uh, upfront, in-your-face, and we, I know other cultures like to say, we like to argue, but we call it having a frank discussion. We like to lay out our ideas on the table. No idea is bad or wrong. You can disagree with them, but at the end of the day, nothing is taken personally. It's just business, and you're, you know, you walk out the room and you, you know, I disagree with you, but let's go have a drink.

3   Things are changing and changing very fast here, so talking about business culture isn't easy. But some things are still the same, we don't have what you call in the west 'good manners', and you don't see people smiling often. Our manners aren't bad, they're just uniquely ours. It's quite a tough country, and people usually do not hesitate to say what they think in a way that doesn't leave room for any misunderstandings.

🎧 12.5

1

A   I know we weren't due to discuss this today, but I think it's important to bring the issue up. We've been trying to get these trials off the ground for weeks now, but the people at the factory in Albany aren't able to tell us when we can start. I think we should look for an alternative location. Has anyone got any suggestions?

B   I can see that's a problem for you, but we've got a lot to get through today. Could we come back to that question at the end of the meeting if we have time?

2

A   As you can see from the PowerPoint presentation, the projected sales figures are looking very good for the next ...

B   Sorry, sorry. I just couldn't get here sooner; bit of a minor emergency in the packaging department. But, it's all under control now. My apologies. Please go on.

A   As I was saying, the projected sales figures are looking very good for the next quarter.

3

A   When is the deal likely to be signed?

B   Er, well, we're at a very delicate stage in the negotiations, but we're hoping for a positive outcome.

A   I'm sure old Bill has a trick or two up his sleeve.

B   Uh, Gerry, I think you'll need to explain that for our colleagues in Hong Kong.

12.6

Well, as the client, we wanted everyone to use our Internet-based application so that all the team members could collaborate and manage their projects more efficiently. But frankly, some people aren't as familiar with this software as others. In fact, I sense there's a bit of resentment from those who aren't using the system as it was designed to be used. I mean, it's causing problems with communication; some people in Germany and China prefer to use e-mail, telephone and even paper-based systems. It makes it difficult to keep track of who's doing what. And it's frustrating, because work gets duplicated or missed, and that's causing more delays. But I'd say that our biggest obstacle isn't the technology – it's the way we work together. I think the team should be more task-driven and deadline-oriented. But our contractors and consultants in China and Germany seem to be much more focused on maintaining a very high quality, which causes more delays. I think defining 'good enough' is essential.

12.7

Um, working with a 'virtual team', if you like, that isn't located in the same place, means, um, there's obviously no face-to-face communication, and it makes it just more difficult to exchange information and solve problems. If we'd had more face-to-face meetings early on, then we, um, could have established better ground rules and, um, built some trust, you know. As it is, there's no real sense of working towards a common goal. This team really suffers from poor communication. More telecon meetings would be a start, so we can have regular progress and status reports. And another thing, there really hasn't been enough time allocated for quality design and revisions to the plans. Now they're blaming us because the revised plans were delayed.

12.8

Teleconferences aren't easy, you see – first there are the time differences. The people in Canada are 12 hours behind us, and we always have the meetings when it's first thing in the morning for them, but it's late at night here, and everyone is tired. We're too polite to ask for some adjustment, so we just put up with it. And another thing, I personally don't like speaking at telecon meetings. I feel like I'm confronting the client by discussing schedule slippage or other potential risks and problems. I can see it's creating misunderstandings and friction.

12.9

The feedback we get from the client is always so negative. I know that we are running behind schedule and the costs have run over, especially with the steel supply, but let's not forget we've achieved a lot, too, in these nine months. It's not a total disaster. My engineering team are working 60-hour weeks to get things done. I think people need to enjoy their work and have fun as a team, but there's absolutely no time for that. The work schedules are … unrealistic and, um, aggressive. I mean, we need to prevent burn-out. No one really seems to know when this phase of the project will be finished.

Pearson Education Limited
Edinburgh Gate, Harlow,
Essex, CM20 2JE, England
And Associated Companies throughout the world

www.market-leader.net

First published 2006
Second impression 2007

Set in MetaPlus 10.5/12.5pt

Designed and illustrated by Oxford Designers & Illustrators

Produced for Pearson Education by Phoenix Publishing Services

Printed in Mateu Cromo, Spain

Book
ISBN-13: 978-0-582-85461-1
ISBN-10: 0-582-85461-X

Book for Pack
ISBN-13: 978-1-4058-1277-1
ISBN-10: 1-4058-1277-X

Pack
ISBN-13: 978-1-4058-1339-6
ISBN-10: 1-4058-1339-3

Acknowledgements

Special thanks from the authors to Chris Hartley, Catriona Watson-Brown and Stephen Nicholl for their contribution to this course book. Also to Suzanne Williams for the selection of some lovely photographs.

The authors would like to thank the following for their invaluable support while we have worked on this project: Santiago Garcia Nuez, Anne Marie Hennessy, Trudy O'Keeffe, Bob O'Keeffe, Caitlin O'Keeffe, Alberto Prades and Elena Gimeno, Albert Prades and Alex Prades.

The authors would also like to thank the following for their help with the project:

Paul Byrne, Greg Cooper, Rafael García, Mª Carmen Gonzalez Díaz, Karla Köning, Bernd Colmar, María Antonia Plaxats, Gao Hu, Oxana Morugiy, Rhian Bufton Lowe, Gloria Ciria, Norman Coe, Carolyn Hardwick, Stefan Rammert, Angel Palomes, José Ramón Sainz, Toni Louki, Mike Lane, Jenny Brickman, Kimberly Nelson, Enrique Torres and the staff and students at In Company Languages and JAD Group Barcelona.

Also Chris Hartley for his great help with recording some of the interviews.

The authors and publishers are very grateful to the following people who agreed to be interviewed for the recorded material in this book: Max Benson, Antoni Flos, Rob Giardina, Rob Jackson, Sean McGuinness, Miguel Morán, Maija Pesola, Sophie Rawlings, Joan Rosàs, Miquel Serracanta, Rosa Soler, Josep Valor-Sabatier and Mark Wyllie. To ensure good sound quality, some interviews have been rerecorded under studio conditions with actors speaking from the original interview transcripts.

The authors would like to thank Kate Goldrick and the Longman team for their support.

The publishers and authors are very grateful to the following advisers and teachers who commented on earlier versions of this material: Peter Bendall, Nancy Pietragalla Dorfman, Ian Duncan and John Rogers.

We are grateful to the following for permission to reproduce copyright material:

Cheskin for an extract adapted from *Cheskin.net* by Darrel Rhea; Antion & Associates for an extract adapted from *The Advanced Public Speaking Institute* website; Executive Communications Group, A Division of ECG, Inc., for an extract adapted from its ezine, the *The Total Communicator*, Vol. II, No. 2, April 2004; The Center for Association Leadership and Tom Leech for an extract adapted from *Executive Update* by Tom Leech, August 2004 © The Centre for Association Leadership; Financial Times Limited for extracts adapted from "Nuclear energy: Come-back kid or ugly duckling" by Fiona Harvey 14th October 2004, "India and its energy needs: Demand is rising but lags rest of the world" by Kevin Morrison 17th January 2005, "Business bows to growing pressures" by Alison Maitland 29th November 2004, "Issues: Tax avoidance is rising up the ethical agenda" by Roger Crowe 29th November 2004, "Testing times for Australia's psychometric outfits" by Leora Moldofsdky 17th March 2005, "Time to break out from campus" by Sumathi Bala 26th June 2004, "HEC Montreal wins African Assignment" by Linda Anderson 26th July 2005, "India: Call centres ring the changes" by Edward Luce 27th September 2004, "Business life: Corporate responsibility without the waffle" by Alison Maitland 29th December 2004, "Business recovery" by Ross Tieman 11th October 2002, "The bruises of the bandwagon" by Paul Tyrrel 24th April 2005, "Confidence in GM hit by £1bn auto loss" by James Mackintosh, Bernard Simon and Richard Beales 21st July 2005, "Online shopping expected to grow by 35% this year" by Elizabeth Rigby 6th April 2005, and "End in sight to dotcom's five years of doubt" by Maija Pesola 7th March 2005, all © Financial Times Limited; Yale University Library for an extract adapted from "Staff Training and Organizational Development" published on their website; Sarah Murray for "Older People: Age and experience" published in the *Financial Times* 7th May 2004 and "Infrastructure: Experience of the 1990s has put people off" published in the *Financial Times* 23rd June 2004; Guardian Newspapers Limited for extracts adapted from "Red card for gas guzzling cars in pollution clampdown" by Mark Townsend published in *The Observer* 6th February 2005 © Guardian Newspapers Limited 2005, "Marconi repays £669m of debt" by Mark Tran published in *Guardian Unlimited* 2nd September 2004 © Guardian Newspapers Limited 2004, "US Airways vows to rise again" by David Teather published in *The Guardian* 14th September 2004 © Guardian Newspapers Limited 2004, "Public-private partnerships: the issue explained" by Patrick Butler published in *Guardian Unlimited* 25th June 2001 © Guardian Newspapers Limited 2001 and "Main points of the IPPR report" by David Batty published in *Guardian Unlimited* 25th June 2001 © Guardian Newspapers Limited 2001; The American Association for the Advancement of Science for an extract adapted from "Features: A Dream of a hydrogen economy" by Robert F Service published in the *Financial Times* 13th August 2005; Optimus Corporation for an extract adapted from *www.energystar.gov*; CFO Europe for an extract adapted from "Finding new ways to grow a company in today's tough climate isn't easy" by Jason Karaian published on *www.cfoeurope.com*; Sara McConnell for an extract adapted from "Could it be you when they need an expert" published in *The Guardian* 25th May 2002; Euromonitor International for an extract adapted from "Cosmetics and Toiletries: world Market Overview and Key Trends"; Mancosa for an extract adapted from *www.mancosa.co.za;* Independent News and Media Limited for an extract adapted from "Net gains on the shop front" by Gareth Chadwick published in *The Independent* 27th February 2005; The Register for an extract adapted from "Gov.uk web sites get thumbs up for usability" by Lucy Sherriff published in *The Register* 4th February 2005; Gnu World Media for an extract from "Writing for websites" published on *www.gnuworld.com*; ZweigWhite for an extract adapted from their newsletter *The Zweig Letter:* The weekly management newsletter for architecture, engineering and environmental consulting firms; ICIFM for an extract adapted from "Project management top ten - #8 Political Awareness" by Iain Maclean published on *Wikipeda.com*; Business World Magazine for an extract adapted from "Building outsourcing bridges" by Mitu Jayashankar published on *www.businessworldindia.com* and Clariant International Ltd for an extract adapted from their mission statement.

In some instances we have been unable to trace the owners of copyright material and we would appreciate any information that would enable us to do so.

Illustrations Acknowledgments

Mark Duffin p90, p111; Oxford Designers & Illustrators p41, p56, p66 Zenith Optimedia, Advertising Expenditure Forecasts, p68, p84, p96, p104, p126-127, p146, p153, p157, p160; Ray Webb p26, p54, p63, p74, p101
© 1994 United Features Syndicate, Inc. p8; © Randy Glasbergen p79 (b); Reproduced with the kind permission of King Features Syndicate and Rina Piccolo p92.

Photo Acknowledgments

Alamy/Pixoi p12 (tl) & (br), S.Holdcroft p36, P.Titmuss p38 (r), Swerve p64 (t), SuperStock p75, K.Foy p79 (t), L.Smak p80 (t), Popperfoto p82, Tetra Images p84 (b), C.Crisford p85, J.Powell p97, C.Rose p105; Arcticphoto.co.uk/p34 (t); Aviation Images/M.Wagner p65 & p80 (b); Courtesy of Max Benson p98 (b); Construction Photography/D.Partner p28 (b); Corbis/C.Savage p40; Corbis/royalty-free p12 (bc); Digital Vision/royalty-free p109; Empics/T.Melville p48 (b), STR p68; Getty Images/D.Hanson p12 (tr), B.Napthine p13, R.Estakhrian p34 (b), G.Vasan p42 (t), A.Incrocci p46, J.Cornish p48 (t), B.Erlanson p55, Microzoa p62, R.Levine p69, J.Silva p70 (t), R.Krisel p70 (b), L.Bobbe p73, D.Trood p76, T.Mareschal p78 (t), S.Watson p98 (t), R.Lockyer p104, PicturePress p108, Y.Layma p112; Courtesy of Rob Giardina p47; Impact Photos/N.Amies p28 (t), R.Conant p45; Courtesy of Rob Jackson p107; Kobal Collection/20th Century Fox p22; Courtesy of Tom Leech p9; Courtesy of Sean McGuinness p42 (b); Courtesy of Miguel Morán p50 (b); Courtesy of Maija Pesola p91; Photolibrary.com/D.Dennis p106 (t); Punchstock/S.Roberts p10, S.Mafford p20, Digital Vision p21, D.Ellis p27, M.Rakusen p29, Corbis p38 (l), S.Allen p43, Photodisc Collection p66 (t), Digital Vision p66 (b), B.Hagiwara p84 (t), T.van Pelt p90, Digital Vision p102, M.Goldman p110; Courtesy of Sophie Rawlings p95; Rex Features/Sipa p6, MAI p14 (t), N.Bailey p64 (b); Courtesy of Joan Rosàs p63; Courtesy of Michael Sawyer p106 (b); Courtesy of Rosa Soler p14 (b); Still Pictures/R.Giling p24, J.Boethling p35, B.Yoshida p50 (t), R.Giling p52, R.Giling p56; Courtesy of Josep Valor-Sabatier p78 (b); Courtesy of www.thewhitecompany.com p93

Every effort has been made to trace the copyright holders and we apologise in advance for any unintentional omissions. We would be pleased to insert the appropriate acknowledgement in any subsequent edition of this publication.

Photo Research: Suzanne Williams/Pictureresearch.co.uk

The cover photograph has been supplied by Photonica and Pearson Education/Trevor Clifford.

Project managed by Chris Hartley